THE CELTIC TRIBES

'History is the version of past events that people have decided to agree upon.'

Napoleon Bonaparte

THE CELTIC TRIBES

Origins, Ancestry and the Warrior Class

John Moss

PEN & SWORD HISTORY
AN IMPRINT OF PEN & SWORD BOOKS LTD.
YORKSHIRE – PHILADELPHIA

First published in Great Britain in 2024 by
PEN AND SWORD HISTORY
An imprint of
Pen & Sword Books Ltd
Yorkshire – Philadelphia

ISBN 978 1 39905 686 1

A CIP catalogue record for this book is available from the British Library.

Typeset in Times New Roman 10/12.5 by
SJmagic DESIGN SERVICES, India.
Printed and bound in the UK by CPI Group (UK) Ltd.

Pen & Sword Books Limited incorporates the imprints of Atlas, Archaeology, Aviation, Discovery, Family History, Fiction, History, Maritime, Military, After the Battle, Military Classics, Politics, Select, Transport, True Crime, Air World, Frontline Publishing, Leo Cooper, Remember When, Seaforth Publishing, The Praetorian Press, Wharncliffe Local History, Wharncliffe Transport, Wharncliffe True Crime and White Owl.

For a complete list of Pen & Sword titles please contact
PEN & SWORD BOOKS LIMITED
George House, Units 12 & 13, Beevor Street, Off Pontefract Road,
Barnsley, South Yorkshire, S71 1HN, England
E-mail: enquiries@pen-and-sword.co.uk
Website: www.pen-and-sword.co.uk

or

PEN AND SWORD BOOKS
1950 Lawrence Rd, Havertown, PA 19083, USA
E-mail: uspen-and-sword@casematepublishers.com
Website: www.penandswordbooks.com

MIX
Paper | Supporting responsible forestry
FSC® C013604

Contents

Introduction

Regarding the Celts, arguments abound in academic circles, where questions as to who they were and where they came from are hotly debated. Unfortunately, as they had no written language, what little we know of them comes largely from contemporary accounts by Greek and Roman commentators like Tacitus, Agricola, Polybuis, Julius Caesar and Strabo. Moreover, the reliability of these accounts tends to be coloured by the prevailing attitudes of the time – that they were warlike tribes of uncultured barbarians who practised human sacrifice and cannibalism. Certainly, their Roman invaders found them formidable in battle.

But the term 'tribes' is in some ways misleading, in that it tends to reinforce a belief that the Celts were an uncivilised people. Evidentially that is not the case, as demonstrated by the many archaeological excavations that have taken place over the past two centuries, and the wealth of sophisticated artworks, weaponry, jewels and ornate artefacts that have been unearthed.

The name 'Celts' was generally used in the sixteenth century to indicate the people of western Europe before the Roman era; by the early eighteenth century the term 'Celtic' had been applied to the languages and dialects of Scotland, Ireland, Wales, Cornwall, Brittany and the Isle of Man. In a historical sense, whether we call them Celts, Gauls, Germani, Lusitanians or Galatians, the wider collection of tribal groups that began to occupy the whole of Continental Europe share the same or very similar cultural heritage and linguistic ties which developed from a common source.

That said, the Celts were not one single group of people, and to think of them as a single homogeneous entity would be an over-simplification – they were far from unified and the concept of a Celtic nation is a flawed contemporary view. It is true that they spoke dialects of the same language, shared common or similar religious beliefs as well as the same genetic ancestry, but their sense of society seems to have operated primarily at a tribal level and they would not have thought much beyond the bounds of their village or settlement.

It was at the end of the seventeenth century that the Welsh botanist and naturalist Edward Lhuyd formulated the hypothesis of a related family of languages, which he called 'Celtic'. His conclusion was based on the discernibly similar characteristics which he identified in Welsh, Cornish, British, and Irish languages, and their similarities to the ancient Gaulish, Irish and British languages.

The twentieth century saw archaeologists reveal more details of what Celtic culture was really like. Such findings suggest that the Celts were, in fact, a highly organised, hierarchical and civilised society, and had mastered a fairly advanced ironwork technology.

Recent studies of the DNA found in skeletal remains have also significantly added to our understanding and shown how widely their racial characteristics were spread. Genetically, some twenty per cent of the resident population of Britain can trace their origins back to Western Europe and to France and Germany in particular. Another study calculated that the modern English population derived more than half of its ancestry from a combination of Celtic, Neolithic and Western European hunter-gatherers.

As to their origins and ancestry, the traditional view is that a proto-Celtic culture emerged sometime around 1200 BC in the Danube area of Central Europe. It is thought that it was here that they first developed iron smelting and forging. At a time when bronze was the hardest known metal, the wealth and prosperity that resulted from this revolutionary new technology and its introduction into early cultures gave the Celtic tribes an immediate dominance over the others that surrounded them. Their numbers increased to such a degree that these tribes were compelled to migrate eastwards as far as Turkey, westwards to the Atlantic seaboard, to the Iberian Peninsula and eventually to the furthest limits of the British Isles and Ireland. Their settlements were to dominate Europe for many centuries until their subjugation by the Romans.

The Celtic tribes of Europe faced their nemesis with the arrival of the Roman armies, led first by Julius Caesar, and then by the Emperor Claudius. They had never before encountered such an unstoppable force. Inter-tribal skirmishes and territorial disputes were common enough, and the various Celtic, Belgic and Germanic tribes had long had to live with such petty confrontations. But Rome was different – it seemed determined that its empire should span most of Europe, Asia Minor and North Africa, and it was prepared to expand vast resources and manpower in achieving that end. It was reasoned that these tribal people were little more than savages and that the imposition of Roman civilisation would ultimately be better for them. The methodology was simple: make treaties with, and Romanise the barbarian tribes if possible, but put down any resistance with brutal force.

Those tribes that capitulated without resistance were either classified as *dediticii*, (meaning 'capitulates', that is, those who had capitulated or surrendered), and those that formed ready alliances and paid taxes to their new overlords, were treated as client kingdoms or *civitates foederatae* ('allied states'), virtually self-governing communities under Roman rule. Eventually these communities would be subsumed into the greater Roman Republic, where they were granted a degree of autonomy and eventually full Roman citizenship. Some of the pacified tribes were resettled around military garrisons, known as *coloniae*, while other former tribal capital cities became *municipia*, very much as they had been before, except they were now under Roman authority.

Those that resisted the Roman advance were brutally slaughtered. In his *Commentarii de Bello Gallico* (Commentaries on the Gallic Wars), Julius Caesar recorded the numerous confrontations between Roman legions and Celtic tribal warriors. His detailed accounts form the basis of most of what we know of Iron Age Europe. It is broadly accepted that Caesar's numbers were often exaggerated and biased in favour of Rome. Time and again he recorded how tens and hundreds of thousands of opposing 'barbarian' armies were put to the sword. His accounts were often recorded with an apparent degree of relish and often included the murder of women, children, as well as the slaughter of livestock, and the burning of crops and tribal settlements. Caesar's vision was the complete subjugation of Gaulish, Belgic, Hispanic and Germanic tribes and the incorporation of their territories into the Roman republic.

For some time I debated whether I should include Germanic tribes in this book. Controversy has existed for some time as to whether certain tribes were Germanic or Celtic-Gauls. Strabo, for example, said that it was the Romans who introduced the name Germani, because he maintained that 'the Germanic tribes were the authentic Celts'. Elements of both cultures shared the same or similar origins, belonging to the greater Indo-European language group. The Celts and Germani emerged from the same Hallstatt and La Tène cultures that originated in southern Germany, Austria and Switzerland in the mid-fifth century BC.

The Germanic tribes appear to have absorbed the earlier Celtic groups of Central and Eastern Europe, so that what often emerged were mixed Germanic-Celts, to an extent that many so-called Celtic tribes contain distinct Germanic characteristics and vice-versa. Differentiation became even more complicated when Germanic tribes like the Suebi and the Batavi crossed the Rhine into Romanised Gaul, and established permanent settlements there. Clearly, the Celtic tribes of Roman Gaul entered into what has been called a 'geographical association' with the Germans and there was a gradual absorption or merging of the two through intermarriage. As an example of this phenomenon, Julius Caesar described the Eburones as a Germanic tribe that lived on the Gallic side of the Rhine, and believed that similar neighbouring tribes came from a Germanic stock.

Consequently, I have decided that I should include the tribes of Germany, in order to paint a wider inclusive picture of European tribal cultures before, during and after the Roman era.

In my earlier book, *'Celtic Place & Placenames'*, I dealt with the places in Britain and Ireland where they settled and the names they ascribed to their settlements as well as to rivers and mountains. Here I intend to look specifically at the people and their tribal groups, covering a broader canvas, to include the whole of Europe from Britain to Asia Minor, and to investigate the culture of the people of the Celtic, Gallic and Germanic tribes. This will include the effects of the first-century Roman invasion of Britain, contemporary commentaries, as well as the resistance that Celtic tribes mounted and the battles they fought, won and lost, so as to better understand the nature of their decline.

The book begins by describing where they came from, based on records left by contemporary Greek and Roman eye-witnesses, commentators and historians like Caesar, Strabo, Livy and Polybuis. It goes on to describe how, tribe by tribe, the Celts faced Roman expansion, and outlines their eventual destinations and extinction.

The Roman age effectively brought to an end the age of the Celts. What remains of this once pan-European people are the six remaining Celtic nations that are internationally recognised as the Celtic League: Cornwall, Scotland, Ireland, the Isle of Man, Wales and Brittany.

John Moss
May 2023

Chapter One

Celtic Origins, Ancestry & Migrations

The early tribal ancestors of the people who were to become known as the Celts are sometimes referred to as 'proto-Celtic'; they were a disparate group of Iron Age people who would go on to occupy an expansive territory covering most of Western and Central Europe in the Late Bronze Age and through the Iron Age (from about 700 BC to 400 AD).

Besides the many tribes that are recognised as Celtic peoples, there are a number of others who made up the wider population group, including the Gaels, Gauls, Britons and the Galatians. All of these tribes were known to the Romans as Gauls ('Galli'), a word which meant 'barbarians'.

In the first century AD, Julius Caesar wrote that the interior of Britain was inhabited by people who claimed to be Belgic immigrants. He maintained that they had come to 'plunder and make war'. In fact the Belgae, a western European Celtic people, had only arrived in Britain a century earlier. In his *Gallic Wars*, Caesar also commented that '...in their tongue they are called Celtae, and in our own language Galli'. The Greeks referred to them as 'Κελτοί' ('Keltoi'), or in Latin 'Celtae'. It is from these that we derive the word 'Celt'. In classical history the titles Celt, Gaul and Galatian were virtually interchangeable.

Although they were loose confederacies of diverse peoples, these early Europeans shared dialects of a common language, a so-called *lingua-franca*, as well as decorative art forms and religious practices. Their culture was largely overtaken and subsumed into the Roman Empire from the first century BC, though vestiges survived in the remotest parts of Ireland and the British Isles and islands, where dialects of Celtic languages can still be heard.

Eastward or Westward Migrations

Two conflicting hypotheses abound as to where the Celts came from. The traditionally long-held and dominant view is that Celtic migrations originated in central Europe around the River Danube, and gradually moved west towards the Atlantic coast, into the Iberian Peninsula and ultimately to the British Isles and Ireland.

However, in recent times a contradictory view has been expressed by some, whereby, based on the spread of languages, early Celtic peoples may have come from the west during the Bronze Age (c. 2000–750 BC), and migrated eastward along rivers and trade routes into central Europe and Asia Minor. Patrick Sims-Williams of the University of Aberystwyth was an advocate of the so-called 'Celtic from the West' hypothesis. He comments: 'As a result of archaeological digs done in the region, the "Hallstatt culture" was wrongly labelled "Celtic" and the distribution of the Hallstatt culture was misused to map the position of the Celts and their language in the sixth and fifth centuries.' Professor Sir Barry Cunliffe of Oxford University, supported by his colleague John T. Koch, writing about the spread of a Celtic language concluded: 'Celtic probably evolved in the Atlantic Zone during the Bronze Age.' As to which of the two hypotheses will be proven to be correct, it is a question that only time and more research will establish – at present the jury is out.

The Urnfield Culture

The so-called Urnfield culture had an early proto-Celtic ancestry going back to the Middle and Late Bronze Ages, and thrived around 2,000 BC in the Upper Danube and Carpathian Basin areas of central Europe. Its widespread practice of cremation rituals is thought to have originated in Hungary sometime during the second millennium BC. Their settlements were predominantly in fortified hill-forts. Little else is known about them apart from the use of a common pre-Celtic language form and their practice of storing the cremated remains and bones of their dead in clay pots or urns, usually buried in fields and sometimes inside small earthen burial mounds or tumuli. Their use of urn cemeteries (or urnfields), commonly found throughout the Middle and Late Bronze Age, accounts for the name they have been given.

The cemetery in Budapest-Bekasmegyer on the bank of the River Danube is one of the largest Urnfield sites in Hungary. More than 200 cremation burials have been found contained in urns, while a number were scattered ash burials. Many excavations at the Urnfield Cemetery at Kietrz in the Silesia region of southern Poland have also revealed more than 3000 burials, demonstrating that this kind of burial rite was most common throughout continental Europe.

In typical urn cremations, several human remains were sometimes interred together in a single urn or tumulus, and unlike the later Hallstatt and La Tène cultures, apart from personal trinkets and ornaments, few contain valuable goods buried along with them. Conversely, some burial pits, almost certainly the last resting places of local chieftains, contain vessels with traces of food offerings, as well as ceramics and weapons. In a few places across Europe the remains of four-wheeled wagons have been found as well as bronze models of wagons or chariots. In the early Urnfield period, body-shaped graves were common, sometimes stone lined to hold the cremated ashes of the deceased.

People of the Urnfield Culture are known to have undertaken migrations over several centuries, and the use of urn cemeteries over time was distributed widely across Ukraine, the Black Sea, the Baltic region, as well as Mediterranean regions including Sicily, Scandinavia, and across France to the Iberian Peninsula. The nature of such a wide distribution was almost certainly associated with tribal migrations, and represented the earliest phase of what would evolve as Celtic civilisation.

The Hallstatt Culture

A later source of Celtic ancestry is the Hallstatt people, an early Celtic culture that emerged in the village of that name in the salt-mining Salzkammergut region of Upper Austria. Their culture reached its peak sometime between the eighth and sixth century BC, and went on to spread across Austria, southern Germany, Bohemia, the Czech Republic, Slovakia, Slovenia, Hungary and Romania.

The Hallstatt people grew wealthy largely because of its prolific salt mines and the value of that product in ancient times. Through the establishment of successful trade relationships with neighbouring settlements they established a stable economy and a social order ruled by powerful chieftains.

In the late nineteenth century the archaeologist Johann Georg Ramsauer of the Vienna Academy of Sciences conducted systematic excavations of the Early Iron Age cemetery in the village of Hallstatt and some 2000 bodies were unearthed. The burial site was found to hold quantities of rich grave goods, which included finely made armour, swords and helmets as well as other ornate iron weaponry and tools, many bronze artefacts and silver or gold items. Unearthed jewellery included decorative brooches, rings and bracelets in bronze and gold, as well as imported ceramic pottery. Many graves revealed such a wealth of treasure that it is thought they may have been the burial sites of powerful leaders or monarchs. It was also discovered that some Hallstatt burials contained swords and horses' tackle, suggesting that they were the graves of warriors. In a few rare occasions, four-wheeled carts or chariots were discovered, indicating that the occupant had been of the very highest social order. Such vehicles invariably had iron-spoked wheels, demonstrating a very sophisticated technology.

The Hallstatt culture went into decline from around 500 BC as local deposits of salt and iron, on which its wealth and economy had been based, petered out.

The La Tène Culture

It is not clear whether the La Tène people were later descendants of the Hallstatt culture or if there had been some overlap of the two. Certainly, there appeared to be some historical continuity. Whichever, the La Tène people can probably be identified as the next definable ancestors of the Celtic peoples that had emerged as the dominant group by 480 BC.

La Tène is named after the village of that name, located beside Lake Neuchatel in Switzerland. Their culture saw the emergence of a thriving metal technology sometime during the mid-fifth century BC.

What we know of the La Tène tribes is that they tended to be warlike and were frequently at odds with their neighbours. Excavations by Hansli Kopp in 1885 revealed the militaristic nature of the culture, whereby the majority of the unearthed objects were weapons, including many swords, spear-heads and shield plates. There were also around 400 brooches, highly decorated in a distinctive La Tène style, with spirals, curvilinear knot work, stylised floral patterns, animal heads and the kind of interlacing patterns that have become synonymous with Celtic art. These were quite different from Hallstatt ornamentation, which tended to be more rectilinear. In the late La Tène period (400–c. 300 BC), the culture was dispersed into a series of Celtic migrations. Finally, the La Tène culture went into decline in Gaul following Julius Caesar's conquest of the region in the middle of the first century BC.

Celtic Migrations from the East

Many contemporary writers and commentators described the way the Celtic tribes migrated across Europe in the fifth and fourth centuries BC. Mass migrations came about as a result of increasing over-population and scarce resources. Greco-Roman authors describe Celtic communities travelling south on account of the luxurious items like grapes, figs, wine and olives to be found around the Mediterranean. This kind of Celtic tribal expansion and resettlement came at a price, as newly acquired territories were often bitterly fought over with indigenous populations, which substantially helped create the perception that Celtic peoples were warlike and inherently aggressive.

In the fourth century BC, Gallic Celts were known to have crossed the Apennine Mountains and overran most of central and southern Italy. The Roman historian Livy wrote that hordes of Gauls had crossed the Rhine 200 years earlier, and settled in the Hercynian Forest in western central Europe, a territory that stretched from north-eastern France to the Carpathian Mountains. Tacitus confirmed this in his *Germania*: 'The Helvetii, the furthest of the peoples of Gaul, occupy the territory between the Hercynian Forest and the Rhine and Maine rivers.'

Livy went on to record how Insubres tribesmen, descending from the north through the St Bernard Pass, went into the Po Valley where they founded the city of Milan. In this Gallic invasion of Italy, Livy described how the Senones tribe, (sometimes called 'Senonii') had defeated the Roman legions in the Battle of the Allia in 365 BC, before they went on to sack and plunder the city of Rome itself.

Other contemporary accounts describe how various Celtic tribes crossed the Alps into Italy. These included the Laevi, Libicii and the Insubres. Livy's account describes how they arrived at the Etruscan township at Clusium and demanded to be given land to form their own settlement. The negotiation went badly, a Celtic leader was killed and the Celts immediately marched on to conquer Rome. Diodorus commented: 'The Celts who had their homes in the regions beyond the Alps streamed through the passes in great strength and seized the territory that lay between the Apennine mountains and the Alps, expelling the Tyrrhenians who dwelt there.'

Marcus Terentius Varro (116–27 BC), thought by many to be Ancient Rome's greatest scholar, stated that the Celts were well integrated into the population of Massalia (modern-day Marseilles), and that its resident people spoke three languages: Greek, Latin and 'Gaulish'.

Other tribes, including the large Ananes and the Boii tribes, settled further south and east. The Greek historian Polybius in his *The Histories* wrote: 'On their first invasion they not only conquered this country, but reduced to subjection many of the neighbouring peoples, striking terror into them.'

In his *History of Rome*, Livy describes the Celtic tribes who took part in the migration over the Alps into Italy: '...a population of nations: the Bituriges, the Averni, the Senones, the Aedui, the Ambarri, the Carnutes, and the Aulerci. Starting with an enormous force of horse and foot.' His account continued, 'The country in which they had settled belonged to the Insubres, a name also borne by a district of the Aedui ...and built a city which they called Mediolanum' (modern-day Milan). At that time the territory was an Etruscan province of Rome, and the Romans demanded to know what business the Gauls had in Etruria. The Gaulish leaders replied that '...if territory is refused us we shall fight.' And so they did. The Roman ambassador, Quintis Fabius, was killed during the engagement and the Romans fled back to Rome in retreat.

Few of these migrations were done peacefully. In his *Library of History* Diodorus Siculus described one such event: 'Brennus, the king of the Gauls, invaded Macedonia with one hundred and fifty thousand infantry armed with long shields, ten thousand cavalry, a horde of camp followers, large numbers of traders, and two thousand wagons.'

By the fourth century BC Celtic tribal migrations had spread to the Adriatic coast as far as Macedonia and Dalmatia (modern-day Croatia). By the end of the third century BC, aggressive Celtic raiding parties were attacking the Aegean coast of Greece, though they would be expelled a century later by a combined Roman and Pergamene force under Manlius Vulso.

In time, descendants of the La Tène people, including the Belgic Atrebates and the Gaulish Parisi tribes, not only overran northern Italy but had also conquered much of Gaul (Western Europe). Over several migrations, they had moved west along the Loire and Marne rivers to occupy lands in modern-day France, as well as north into southern Poland, Bohemia and Lower Silesia. In 279 BC, La Tène tribes invaded Greece and fought the Romans before they were overcome by an army led by Julius Caesar in what came to be known as the Gallic War (58–51 BC).

Several La Tène tribes moved into the Iberian Peninsula and in northern France to Brittany, from where they crossed the English Channel to settle in south-eastern England and Yorkshire. In his *Agricola*, Tacitus commented: 'Who the first inhabitants of Britain were, whether natives of immigrants, is open to question: one must remember we are dealing with barbarians.'

By 300 BC, elements of La Tène art had spread to Ireland and following their decline in Europe, Ireland and the British Isles were to become their last cultural resting place.

Chapter Two

Contemporary Attitudes to the Celtic Warrior

The earliest recorded reference to the Celts was in the fifth century BC, when the Greek philosopher Herodotus of Halicarnassus described the Celts living beyond the 'Pillars of Heracles' (thought to be a reference to the Rock of Gibraltar) and border on the Cynesii (the Portuguese Algarve). He also mentioned islands to the west from which tin was imported, which is taken to be a vague reference to Britain.

According to many contemporary accounts, warfare seems to have been one common thread throughout Celtic culture, at least according to Roman sources. However, it should be said that Caesar's conquest of Gaul was a bloody affair and the Romans were ruthless in putting down all resistance. According to Caesar's own accounts, many hundreds of thousands of Celtic Gauls were slain in his expansion of the Roman Empire. Indeed, it may have amounted to millions. Certainly, most tribes stubbornly refused to give in and most fought valiantly.

Following the Senones tribe sacking of Rome in 390 BC and the plundering of Delphi, led by King Brennus, in 279 BC, their prowess in battle became known and feared throughout the ancient world. Accounts by Greek commentators described them as hard-fighting savages and their name became synonymous with terror and intimidation.

In support of the widespread contemporary belief that the Celts were intrinsically warlike and aggressive, in the twentieth book of his *Histories*, the Greek politician and astronomer Posidonius of Apameia (modern-day Rhodes) wrote that 'The Celts sometimes have single combats at their entertainments...and they even go so far as to wound one another.'

Inter-tribal warfare among Celtic peoples was rife and they often allied themselves with the Romans, Greeks and various others against each other. In Celtic culture courage was a prime virtue, and warriors seemed to enjoy a privileged status in their society, as evidenced by the many ancient Celtic gods that were associated with war and the great quantity of armour and weapons found in later tomb excavations. Their fighting prowess was so highly rated that Celtic mercenaries were employed to fight in several foreign military conflicts. For example, in the third century BC, Celtic mercenaries formed an important part of the Egyptian army's order of battle. It was recorded that King of Egypt Ptolemy II (also known as 'Philadelphus') recruited around 4000 Celtic mercenaries from the Balkans.

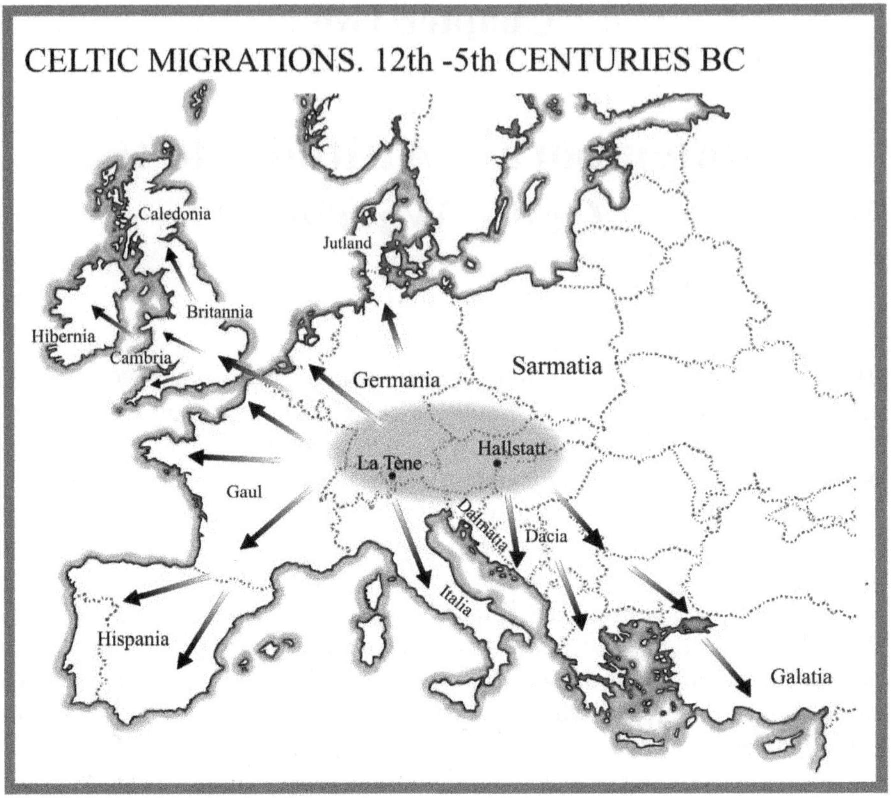

Queen Cleopatra is also known to have employed Celtic mercenaries in her army and, following her death in 30 BC, their services were no longer needed and around 400 were appointed as the personal bodyguard of the Jewish King Herod.

Antiochus II (known as 'the Great'), king of the Hellenistic Seleucid Empire, had an army that consisted of large numbers of Celtic mercenaries who under his leadership fought to put down rebellious provincial rulers at the Battle of Babylon in 221 BC.

Dionysius (known as the 'Tyrant of Syracuse', c.405 BC) employed Celtic mercenaries to aid the Macedonian army against Thebes in 367 BC, a service for which they were granted territory in Macedonia. Certain Celtic warriors also collaborated to support the Romans in later conflicts. There were many others.

Some of the best-known accounts of the Celts as warriors follow:

Julius Caesar

Caesar commented that they still fought in chariots, a strategy that the Romans had abandoned decades before, preferring tight co-ordinated infantry formations on the battlefield. Of the British tribes' fighting strategies he commented that '… in chariot fighting the Britons begin by driving all over the field hurling javelins, and generally the terror inspired by the horses and the noise of the wheels are sufficient to throw the opponents' ranks into disorder.' In his *Commentaries on the Gallic War*, he described the guerrilla-like fighting tactics of Celtic warriors: '… they never fought in close order, but in small parties and at great distances, and had detachments placed (in different parts), and then the one relieved the other, and the vigorous and fresh succeeded the wearied.' Caesar used words to describe Celtic warriors in terms that Romans might understand, frequently referring to 'equites', a word that loosely translates as 'horse-mounted warriors'.

In describing the Celtic people of Britain, Caesar said that they dyed their bodies with blue wode and that men shaved off all of their body hair except the head and that they sported long drooping moustaches. He added that it was not uncommon for men and women to go into battle alongside each other and to fight naked. Why they did this was unclear, but it was assumed that it was to demonstrate their bravery by not wearing the kind of body armour that was worn by Roman legionaries and relying on the protection offered to them by their gods. It was also a clear declaration that Celtic women were just as brave and should be equally feared as the men were.

Caesar's account of the first invasion of Britain in 55 BC seems to bear out tales of the ferocity of Celtic warriors. It was recorded that the Roman invasion fleet carried about 10,000 men of the Eighth and Tenth legions, and that as they approached the English coast at Deal in Kent, staring down on them from the clifftops were thousands of Celtic tribesmen and women, bristling with weapons. As the fleet sailed along the coast in search of a suitable landing place, the British Celts trailed them along the clifftop, walking and riding to keep pace.

A beach was found and the Roman legionaries were extremely unnerved and took some persuasion to jump into the waist-deep water, weighed down as they were by heavy weapons and body armour. Immediately the Romans stepped ashore, Celtic mounted cavalry and war chariots charged down upon them, screaming and slashing with their swords, while others pelted the invaders with rocks and javelins from the white cliffs above. Many legionnaires struggled to maintain a footing on the loose shingle and some recoiled back before order was achieved and a defensive line was assembled, at which point the Celts withdrew.

Caesar returned a year later with a Roman fleet of 800 ships carrying 50,000 soldiers. It arrived off the coast of Kent and landed unopposed on a deserted beach. The Romans had arrived and the conquest of Britain had begun. Having taken their first measure of Roman troops, henceforth, wherever possible Celtic fighters avoided open battlefield conflict and chose to employ hit-and-run guerrilla tactics.

However, the Roman army continued its advance, reached Middlesex and crossed the River Thames. Five of the British tribes, the Cenimagni, the Segontiaci, the Ancalites, the Bibroci and the Cassi, surrendered to Caesar and informed on the whereabouts of Cassivellaunus, an elite warrior and the leader of the Catuvellauni tribe. The tribe was possibly the most powerful Belgic tribe in Iron Age Britain at that time, but Cassivellaunus eventually surrendered and paid tribute to his Roman conquerors.

Writing about the Battle of Sabis (57 BC) in which his army defeated the Belgian tribe of the Nervians, Caesar commented: 'The enemy, even when their hope of safety was at an end, displayed a prodigious courage. When their front ranks had fallen, the next stood on the prostrate forms of their dead comrades and fought from them; when these were cast down, and the corpses were piled up in heaps, the survivors, standing as it were upon a mound, hurled darts on our troops, or caught and returned our javelins.' He went on to describe how extremely agile Celtic charioteers were and how they would often climb out onto the chariot yoke in the middle of battle to steer the horses better, apparently heedless of all risks.

In his memoirs Caesar described the ingenious defensive methods that the Celtic tribes used when he arrived with a substantial army to take the heavily defended and fortified city of Avaricum: 'They trapped our siege ladders with lassos, and then used winches to pull them within the walls. They caused our siege walls to collapse by undermining them.' Despite early military success, both of Julius Caesar's invasions essentially failed and he returned to Rome soon afterwards in late 47 BC.

It would not be until 43 AD that the Roman Emperor Claudius launched a successful invasion of Britain. It took the next forty-five years for the Roman army to subdue the population of present-day England, Wales and the Scottish borders to establish the Roman province of Britannia.

Tacitus

In his *Life of Agricola*, written around 98 AD, Publius Cornelius Tacitus (c.56 AD–c.120 AD), the Roman historian and politician, better known simply as Tacitus, described Celtic fighting methods as sneaky and cowardly, commenting that they chose to attack Roman soldiers while they slept. He wrote: 'Their whole force attacked the Ninth Legion by night, as being the weakest, and cutting down the sentries, who were asleep or panic-stricken, they broke into the camp.'

Despite his general derogation of Celtic warriors, even Tacitus recorded the ferocity with which they fought and the devastation they frequently caused to battle-hardened Roman legions. Of one particular engagement he described how '...the Ordovices, shortly before Agricola's arrival, had destroyed nearly the whole of a squadron of allied cavalry quartered in their territory.'

He went on to say that '...they cover their altars with the blood of captives and consult their deities through their entrails.' Elsewhere he wrote: 'Seldom is it that two or three (tribes) meet together to ward off a common danger. Thus, while they fight singly, all are conquered.' He continued by saying that their strength lay in their infantry, though some fought in chariots (as Julius Caesar had also commented), and that charioteers held the highest rank. Finally, he said that '...the swords of the Britons are not pointed, and do not allow them close contact to fight in an open battlefield'.

In his *Annals*, Tacitus describes in detail the Roman invasion of Anglesey: 'On the shore stood the opposing army with its dense array of armed warriors, while between the ranks dashed women, in black attire like the Furies, with hair dishevelled, waving firebrands. All around, the Druids, lifting up their hands to heaven, and pouring forth dreadful incantations, scared our soldiers by the unfamiliar sight.'

His description of the physique of the British tribes was quite detailed. He wrote that '...the reddish hair and large limbs of the Caledonians (lowland Scotland) proclaimed a Germanic origin, the swarthy faces and curling hair of the Silures (south-west England) could be due to invading Spaniards in ancient times'.

Plato

Plato (c.429–347 BC), the Greek philosopher, writing in *Laws*, described some of the Celtic mercenaries that he met as being prone to excessive drunkenness: 'I am not discussing the drinking of wine, nor drinking in general, but outright drunkenness.' His view echoed that of the Greek historian Diodorus Siculus of Sicily, who wrote that 'The Gauls are exceedingly addicted to the use of wine... without moderation by reason of their craving for it, (and that) when they are drunken they fall into a stupor or a state of madness.' His somewhat jaded view of the Celts may have arisen during a visit to Dionysius of Syracuse where Celtic mercenaries were employed.

Strabo

The first-century Greco-Roman geographer and historian Strabo of Amaseia (c.62 BC–24 AD), author of the seventeen-book *Geographia* ('Geography'), also gave a somewhat derogatory view concerning what these Celtic people were like. According to his account, they were 'bandy-legged', 'ungainly in build' and 'the whole race which is now called both Gallic and Galatic is war-mad, and both high-spirited and quick for battle, although otherwise simple and not ill-mannered.' Further, he commented: 'It is their custom, when they are formed for battle, to step out in front of the line and to challenge the most valiant men from among their opponents to single combat, brandishing their weapons in front of them to terrify their adversaries.'

He also described the appearance of the Celtic warrior: 'The Gallic armour is commensurate with the large size of their bodies: a long sabre, which hangs along the right side, and a long oblong shield, and spears in proportion, and a *madaris*, a special kind of javelin. But some of them also use bows and slings.'

Diodorus

Diodorus Siculus was a Greek historian, best known for writing *Bibliotheca Historica* between 60 and 30 BC. The work originally contained forty books, of which only fifteen survive intact. He wrote that '...their aspect is terrifying', and continued with a description of the Celts thus: '...around their wrists and arms they wear bracelets, around their necks heavy rings of solid gold (torcs), and huge rings they wear as well, and even corselets of gold'. His description went some way further: 'The way they dress is astonishing: they wear brightly coloured and embroidered shirts, with trousers called *bracae* and cloaks fastened at the shoulder with a brooch, heavy in winter, light in summer. These cloaks are striped or checked in various colours.' Torcs worn around the neck, often in precious metals like gold, were symbols of status and rank within the community. Diodorus distinguished the Keltoi from the other Gaulish tribes of Europe by recording that, in his opinion, '... the Gauls are taller of body, with rippling muscles, and white of skin, and their hair is blond.' He went on to say that they frequently dyed their hair in garish colours.

As to Celtic fighting strategies, he wrote that their '...manner of fighting, being in large measure that of wild beasts and frenzied, was an erratic procedure, quite lacking in military science'. Further, he commented that they frequently rode into battle in two-horse-driven chariots, hurling their javelins at opponents before stepping down and fighting in hand-to-hand combat with swords. He commented that their men and women often chose to fight naked except for a belt and sword scabbard.

We know that warriors enjoyed a high status in Celtic society and that prowess in battle was highly valued. A class of high-ranked warrior nobles, or knights, would have ridden into battle on horseback and worn helmets, breast-plates and padded armour. They would have been part of a strict hierarchy, headed by a king, a queen, or an aristocratic group, based on wealth and land ownership.

Posidonius wrote in his *Histories*: '...they sit in a circle with the most influential man in the centre whether he be the greatest in warlike skill, nobility of family or wealth... and on either side of him the others in order of distinction.' In the twenty-third book he wrote '...the Celts have in their company, even in war, (as well as in peace), companions whom they call 'parasites'. These men pronounce their praises before the whole assembly and before each of the chieftains in order as they listen. These entertainers are called Bards. These are poets who deliver eulogies in song.'

Diodorus described the Celtic warrior's practice of cutting off the heads of their enemies and displaying them above the doors of their houses. He recorded: 'When their enemies fall they cut off their heads and fasten them about the necks of their horses...all covered with blood, they carry them off as booty, singing a tribute over them and...these first-fruits of battle they fasten by nails upon their houses, just as men do, in certain kinds of hunting, with the heads of wild beasts they have mastered. The heads of their most distinguished enemies they embalm in cedar oil and carefully preserve in a chest, and these they exhibit to strangers.'

In common with many other contemporary accounts he recorded that the Celtic warrior usually carried a large oval-shaped wooden shield, which was highly ornamented and had a large metal boss at its centre. He also carried a sword and a spear or javelin. The sword was double-edged, and having little or no point it was primarily used as a slashing weapon. The javelin was usually thrown, but could be used like the spear for thrusting when in close combat.

Xenophon

The Greek chronicler Xenophon (born c.430 BC) described in his *Hellenica* how Celts had served in the Greek armies as mercenaries. The horsemanship of their cavalry was highly rated. In his account of Celtic mercenaries in the inter-city war between Sparta and Thebes, he commented: 'They charged towards the Thebans, threw their javelins, and then dashed away as the enemy moved towards them, often turning and throwing more javelins. Thus they manipulated the entire Theban army, compelling (them) to fall back at their will.'

Livy

Titus Livius (59 BC–5 AD), better known simply as Livy, in his *History of Rome* had also commented that the Celts stripped naked to the waist to fight and ran into battle singing, dancing and whooping, carrying long ornate shields that they repeatedly beat with their spears and swords to strike fear and terror into their opponents. He remarked that they were ferocious and apparently not afraid to die.

Aristotle

The Greek philosopher Aristotle (384–322 BC) stated that 'The bravery of barbarians in general is based on passion'. However, he held an otherwise dim view of the Celtic 'barbarians', commenting that they lived in a cold climate and that their children wore very few clothes and concluding that as a culture they were 'mad or insensible'. He also commented on the open acceptance that Celtic peoples had of sexual relations between men. Of their bravery, he wrote that they '...feared nothing, neither the earthquakes nor the waves'.

Polybuis

The Greek historian Polybius (264–146 BC), describing the Battle of Telemon in 225 BC, when the Roman legions came face to face with Celtic tribes, refers to the noise that the Celts made on the battlefield to frighten the enemy: '…the dreadful din (of their) innumerable horn-blowers and trumpeters and the whole army shouting their war-cries at the same time, (made) such a tumult of sound that it seemed that all the country round had got caught up the cry'.

He recorded the Battle of Clastidium in 222 BC, where he described the warriors in '…the forefront of the Celtic army, stripped naked for the fight, and the sight of these warriors, with their great stature and their fair skins, on which glittered the collars and bracelets of gold so loved as an adornment by all the Celts, filled the Roman legionaries with awe.'

Polybuis described Celtic mercenaries. He called them *Gaesatae*, a word that means 'serving for hire'. It is believed that he was writing about men of the Senones tribe; according to his own account, led by Brennus, they had attacked the Etruscan city of Clusium in the year 387 BC before going on to occupy Rome itself.

Polybuis also wrote about Celtic battle tactics during the Battle of Pedum in 338 BC: 'The Celts appeared with a great army, and the Romans did not venture to meet them in the field because of the suddenness of their attack …they were taken by surprise and did not have time to anticipate it by gathering the forces of their allies.' Eventually, the Roman army, under the leadership of the Consuls Gaius Maenius and Lucius Furius Camillus, was victorious over the Gauls, and were awarded a triumphal entry later in Rome.

In his account of the Second Punic War, Polybuis described the Celtic tribe's aggressive migration into northern Italy: 'The Celts, being close neighbours of the Etruscans and associating much with them, cast covetous eyes on their beautiful country, and on a small pretext, suddenly attacked them with a large army and, expelling them from the plain of the (River) Po, occupied it themselves.' Later, he added: 'The Celts, descending on Etruria, overran the country, devastating it without let or hindrance and, as nobody appeared to oppose them, they marched on Rome itself.'

Ammianus Marcelinus

The Roman soldier and historian Ammianus Marcelinus described the way that '…the Gallic woman, fighting beside her man, is a match for a whole troop of foreigners. Steely-eyed, she gnashes her teeth, flexes her huge biceps and rains down blows and kicks as though from the twist cords of a catapult'.

Herodotus

In the fifth century BC, Herodotus of Halicarnassus, writing about the River Istros (from 'Ister', the Greek name for the River Danube), wrote that '…from its source among Celts and the city of Pyrene, (it) flows dividing Europe in the middle.

The Keltoi are outside the pillars of Hercules, and border on the Kynesii, who dwell furthest west of the inhabitants of Europe.'

Cato the Elder

The Roman politician and orator Cato wrote about the temperament of the Gallic tribes: '…the greater part of Gaul pursues two things with great industriousness: the art of war and speaking with eloquence.'

Celtic Resistance

It must be said that Roman accounts of the Celts, though based on eye-witness accounts, tended to be extremely biased. The often repeated Roman view that Celtic peoples were barbaric and uncivilised may be more a matter of war propaganda than reliable history. In some respects the commonly held view that they were warlike frequently characterised a defensive position rather than an aggressive posture, given that they faced invasion and slaughter by the might of the Roman legions. This point is amply demonstrated by some of the Celtic tribal leaders.

Boudicca, the queen of the Iceni tribe, for example, took on the Roman legions after they overran their tribal lands in the east of England. For her rebellion, she was violently flogged and her two daughters were raped in front of her. Incensed by the barbarous crime, she headed the Iceni warriors and a confederation of neighbouring Celtic tribes against the Ninth Roman Legion. She went on to destroy Camulodunum (Colchester), the Roman capital of Britain, before going on to destroy Verulamium (St Albans) and Londinium (London). She was later defeated by the Romans under Suetonius Paulinus, the Governor of Britain, but rather than be taken prisoner, she is believed to have poisoned herself.

Another Celtic leader was Caractacus (sometimes 'Caradoc'), king of the Catuvellauni tribe, who had settlements around Hampshire and Gloucestershire. Supported by his brother, Togodumnus, he was leader of Celtic resistance against Roman invaders for almost nine years before being defeated at the Battle of Caer Caradoc by Scapula in 51 AD. He fled to south Wales where he sought refuge among the Brigantes tribe. Cartimandua, their queen, betrayed his whereabouts to the Romans, who captured him and sent him as a prisoner to Rome. The Roman historian Cassius Dio recorded that Caractacus and his family were eventually pardoned by the Emperor Claudius and spent the rest of their lives in Rome.

Vercingetorix was a celebrated chieftain of the Arverni tribe. He led a rebellion to stop the Roman subjugation of Continental Gaul. After a serious defeat in battle, he took refuge in the fortress city of Alesia before being captured, and like Caractacus, he was taken in chains as a battle trophy to Rome, where he was exhibited in Caesar's triumph.

Cassius Dio described Vercingetorix's surrender to Caesar in some detail. According to his account, Vercingetorix '...came unannounced, appearing suddenly at a tribunal where Caesar was seated in judgement. Dressed in his finest armour, Vercingetorix was an imposing figure, even in defeat.' Dio claimed that many in Caesar's camp were actually startled by his imposing stature. Without saying a word, Vercingetorix slowly removed his armour and then fell to his knees at Caesar's feet. He was executed six years later. Even to this day Vercingetorix remains a national hero of France. He courageously risked his life and the lives of his people to resist conquest and enslavement by the Roman Empire.

Many Celtic leaders fought back against Roman invasion of their tribelands, prompted not so much by aggressive warmongering as in defence of their homelands. Among them were the likes of Ambiorix (leader of the Eburones), Brennus (chieftain of the Senones), Dumnorix (leader of the Aedui) and Venutius (leader of the Brigantes).

There were many others.

Chapter Three

Celtic Tribal Leaders & Warrior Heroes

Ambiorix

Ambiorix was the leader of the Belgae tribe of Eburones, whose territory lay in lands between the Meuse and Rhine rivers in an area the Romans called Gallia Belgica (north-eastern Gaul, modern-day Belgium). When the Fourteenth Legion, commanded by Sabinus and Lucius Cotta, arrived in the Meuse Valley, despite objections from the Eburones, the Romans set up winter quarters, an act that caused the rebellion of 54 BC.

The Greek historian Cassio Dio described the insurrection: 'This war was begun by the Eburones, under Ambiorix as chief. They claimed they had been roused to action because they were annoyed at the presence of the Romans.' In fact the Eburones had been encouraged to take up arms by Indutiomarus, chief of the Treverian tribe.

In a surprise ambush attack by the Eburones, an entire Roman legion was effectively decimated, Cotta was killed and the survivors withdrew to their camp. Many legionaries committed suicide at the shame of such a defeat. It was recorded that most of the fifteen cohorts of legionaries died at the hands of the Eburones under Ambiorix. News of the great victory spread around the neighbouring tribes, and the Aduatuci and Nervii tribes were inspired to join Ambiorix in the uprising.

Julius Caesar returned with a reported 50,000 Roman soldiers, who set about slaughtering Eburones settlers and burning their fields. Caesar's brutal retribution resulted in the virtual extermination of the Eburones tribe. Many leaders of the uprising were captured and taken to Rome where they were exhibited in Caesar's triumphal procession, but it is said that Ambiorix, together with a small band of his warriors, escaped across the Rhine and was never seen again.

Ambiorix is still celebrated in Belgium as a national hero, and in 1866 a bronze statue of him was installed in the main square of Tongerens to celebrate his memorable victory over the Romans in 54 BC.

Aneroestes

Aneroestes was one of the two leaders of a group of Gaesatae mercenaries whose territory was around the River Rhône in the Alpine region of modern-day France. In 224 BC, the tribe fought the Romans at the Battle of Telamon (modern-day

Talamone in Tuscany). Aneroestes and Concolitanus were employed by the Boii and Insubres tribes to help them resist Roman occupation of their lands in Picenum, which lay between the Apennines and the Adriatic coast of northern Italy.

They were confronted by Roman legions under the command of Consul Lucius Aemilius Papus. Against overwhelming numbers, Aneroestes decided to withdraw, but his army was intercepted at Telamon by another legion led by Consul Gaius Atilius Regulus, and a pitched battle ensued. The Gaesatae warriors were outmatched by the well-trained Roman fighting machine, especially by Roman cavalry and javelin throwers, and they were forced back. During the engagement around 40,000 Celts were killed and a further 10,000 taken prisoner and were sold into slavery. Concolitanus was captured, but Aneroestes escaped with a small detachment of his men. Within the year, the Romans began to exact severe punishment on the Boii tribes of Liguria. Faced with certain capture and potential Roman retribution, Aneroestes and his men committed suicide.

Ariovistus

Ariovistus, the Germanic leader and the king of the Suebi tribe, was more of a villain than a hero. He was the chief of the Teutonic tribe that lived in a territory east of the River Rhine and near the River Elbe. He was clearly a fearsome and determined leader and conqueror, but was prompted more by a sense of power and acquisition than by justice or good government. He came to dominate much of Gaul in a brutal and tyrannical rule. He led his people, first in an alliance with Rome against other Gaulish tribes, and at the invitation of the Sequani took on and defeated the Aedui tribe at the Battle of Magetobriga in 61 BC, with an army in excess of 15,000 warriors. This was followed by a great victory over the Helvetii when his warriors supported Julius Caesar at the Battle of Bibracte in 58 BC.

Ariovistus had taken many Aedui hostages, whom he treated very badly and the Aedui complained to Caesar about his brutality. Caesar evidently saw his ally as an impediment to any hope he had of peaceful outcomes with other local tribes and attempted to calm things down. Ariovistus was intransigent; he refused to back down and his alliance with Rome promptly ended. The break-up came to a head when a decisive battle took place in 58 BC at Vosges, where a combined Roman army of six legions, accompanied by several other tribes, faced Ariovistus' Suebi army. The battle lasted for three days, but the Romans eventually gained the upper hand. Caesar claimed that most of Ariovistus' one-hundred and 20,000 men were killed. What remained of the Teutonic army retreated back across the Rhine and disappeared into the Black Forest. Ariovistus was never seen again. Traditionally, he is said to have died in obscurity in 54 BC.

Arminius

Hermann Arminius (18 BC–19 AD), was the German tribal leader, chief of the Cherusci, who led a confederation of Germanic warriors and defeated three Roman legions (the Seventeenth, Eighteenth and Nineteenth) under the command of the Senator Publius Qunictilius Varo, Governor of Germania, at the Battle of Teutoburg Forest in the year 9 AD. Arminius was cunning: he reported to the Romans that a fictitious uprising was about to happen and led them into a deadly trap, when his warriors surprised them using guerilla-type tactics. The battle that ensued lasted four days and eventually, pursued doggedly by German warriors, the Roman army withdrew back to the western side of the River Rhine. Finally admitting defeat, Varo committed suicide by falling on his sword, as defeated Roman generals were expected to do. Around 20,000 Roman legionaries had lost their lives in the conflict. Tacitus described Arminius as 'unquestionably the liberator of Germania'.

Bellovesus

Bellovesus (sometimes 'Belloves') was the nephew of King Ambigatus of the Biturges, the most powerful of the Gallic tribes, who lived around the Rhine north of the Alps. According to an account by Livy (writing six centuries later), faced with over-population, the tribe needed to expand its territory, which prompted Ambigatus to commission Bellovesus to lead a confederation of the Bituriges, Arverni, Senones, Aedui, Ambarri, Carnutes and Aulerci tribes in a migration across the Alps to find new living space in around 600 BC. His brother Segovesus went eastwards in search of new lands in the Hercynian Forest, an area stretching from north-eastern France to the Carpathian Mountains.

Meantime, Bellovesus began an invasion of northern Italy and in the Po Valley they encountered the indigenous Etruscan tribes. At the River Ticino they fought and defeated the Etruscans, settling in an area that became Insubria, which the Romans knew as Cisalpine Gaul. It was here that Bellovesus founded the settlement of *Mediolanum* (later known as Massilia, present-day Milan). In Gaulish, the name Bellovesus means 'worthy of power'. There are some who believe that the entire story of Bellovesus' migration into Italy is possibly a fiction created by Livy from older unreliable sources.

Boduognatus

Boduognatus was chief of the Belgae Nervii tribe, and their main settlement was at *Bagacum* (present-day Bavay in France). In 57 BC, intent on halting the Roman advance across Gaul, he gathered together an army of 60,000 warriors, including contingents from the Viromandui, Atrebatin and Aduatuci tribes, before leading them into battle at the River Sabis (also known as the Sambre, now the River Selle).

Even before the other supporting tribes arrived, Boduognatus had formulated a plan to take out each of the eight Roman legions as they passed down a narrow road, attacking their baggage train first. However, the plan was foiled when the Nervii were spotted by a Roman scouting party and any chance of surprise was lost. His army was defeated by a force of 40,000 under the command of Julius Caesar, who made a written record of the outcome in his *Commentaries*: 'So ended this battle by which the tribe of the Nervians, and even their name, were virtually wiped out.' According to his account, at the end of the battle fewer than 500 of the original 60,000 Nervii fighters were still alive, thanks largely to the bold attacks of the *Legio X Gemina* (the Tenth Gemini Legion) commanded by Titus Labienus. Five thousand Romans died in the engagement, but within a year of the battle, Caesar had subjugated the majority of Gaul and the Belgae tribes of northern Europe were a spent force. The Battle of Sambre had been the last stand of the Nervii. It is presumed that Boduognatus died on the battlefield with many of his men, as nothing was heard of him again. The name Boduognatus means 'he who was born of the battle crow'.

Brennus

Little is known of Brennus (sometimes spelled in Gaulish as 'Brennos'), other than his leadership of 70,000 men, mostly comprising Senones tribesmen, who crossed the Alps and sacked Rome in 390 BC. His Gaulish warriors first confronted the Roman army at the battle of the River Allia and soon overwhelmed them. When news of the rout reached Rome, its citizens fled from the city. After a six month siege, apart from the Capitoline Hill, which was strongly defended by Roman legionaries under the command of Marcus Manlius Capitolinus, the city came under Brennus's control. According to Livy, accepting their defeat, the Romans agreed to pay a ransom of 1000 pounds weight of gold.

Later, a hastily assembled army led by the ex-dictator Marcus Furius Camillus returned to Rome and after bloody street-to-street fighting, they finally drove Brennus and the Senones out of the city.

In 279 BC Brennus overran Macedonia and invaded Greece, sacking the city of Delphi in the process. Some sources maintain that his army was subsequently defeated by an Aetolian army, and that he sustained serious wounds. Seeing most of his army killed, Brennus committed suicide. According to Strabo, he did indeed die by his own hand, either through poison or by the knife,

The Senones originally lived in the Seine-et-Marne, Loiret and Yonne regions of France, but a group are known to have migrated into northern Italy sometime around 400 BC, invading Etruria and besieging the ancient city of Clusium. The name Brennus may be derived from 'Brenn', which means 'war leader'.

Calgacus

Calgacus, (sometimes 'Calgacos' or 'Galgacus'), was a renowned British leader who in 84 AD led a confederacy of Caledonian tribes against the Romans under the command of General Julius Agricola in northern Scotland at what became known as the Battle of Mons Graupius. Opinions vary as to where that place actually was, but there is a general consensus that the most likely place was at Bennachie in Aberdeenshire. Apart from being the first Caledonian leader to be known by name and famed for his heroic resistance, little else is known about Calgacus's life, other than an account of the battle by Tacitus.

In his *Agricola* Tacitus recorded that the battle cost the lives of 10,000 Caledonians and only 360 Roman legionaries. Tacitus also writes that before the battle, Calgacus gave a long rousing speech denouncing the exploitation of Britain by Rome. 'You have not tasted servitude,' he reputedly began, and continued: 'There is no land beyond us and even the sea is no safe refuge when we are threatened by the Roman fleet....We are the last people on earth, and the last to be free: our very remoteness in a land known only to rumour has protected us up till this day.'

Of the Romans, he had little good to say, describing them as 'pillagers of the world' and accusing them of 'indiscriminate plunder...robbery, butchery and rapine'. How Tacitus could have known details of Calgacus's speech is curious, as he could not have been present at the occasion, being a Roman. However, Calgacus seems to have survived the battle and disappeared. Tacitus has no more to say of him, and the heroic chieftain slipped quietly into historical obscurity thereafter. The name Calgacus means 'swordsman' or 'sword bearer'.

Camulogene

Camulogene was chief of the Parisii tribe who led a confederation of the Seine peoples in 53 BC against the advancing Roman Seventh and Twelfth legions commanded by Titus Labienus. The Gallic tribes faced the Romans as they attempted to cross the river, burning their main settlement of Lutetia (modern-day Paris) to the ground to avoid it being taken. Camulogene died in what became known as the Battle of Lutetia. The Rue Camulogène in Paris is named after him.

Caratacus

Caractacus, (also known as 'Caratacus' or 'Caradoc'), together with his brother Togodumnus, ruled the Catuvellauni tribe, whose territory was north of the Thamesis (the River Thames) in present-day county of Hertfordshire. Their father, King Cunobelinus, left his Catuvellaunian kingdom to be ruled jointly by the two brothers. Of the two, it is Caractacus who is famed for leading the revolt by a confederation of British tribes against Roman occupation of their tribelands in 43 AD. It was when Togodumnus was killed facing the Romans in Cantiaci tribal territory across the River Medway, his brother Caractacus was left to bear the responsibility of leadership.

The weight of Roman forces drove the Celtic tribes back and they withdrew across the Thames into Essex. Unlike some of the British tribes that agreed a peace with the invaders, Caractacus fought on, losing at least two more engagements in the process. Finally realising that the south was already lost, Caractacus moved his army north and westwards in support of the Silures and Ordovices tribes of Wales. It was here in 51 AD that he engaged with the legions of the newly appointed Roman Governor Publius Ostorius Scapula, in what became known as the Battle of Caer Caradoc. An alternative legend has it that his last stand actually took place in the hill-fort known as British Camp on the top of Herefordshire Beacon in the Malvern Hills.

The Romans were victorious, Caracacus's wife and children were taken prisoner, and he fled further north to seek sanctuary among the Brigantes tribe. However, their treacherous Queen Cartimandua surrendered him to the Romans and along with his family Caractacus was taken as a prisoner to Rome. It was recorded by Cassius Dio that: 'Caratacus, (was) a barbarian chieftain who was captured and brought to Rome and later pardoned by the Emperor Claudius.' Dio's account relates how the British chieftain was initially sentenced to death, but as a result of an impassioned speech that he made before his execution, Claudius was so impressed that he granted him an immediate pardon and he spent the remainder of his life in the Roman capital. Caractacus, the 'King of the Britons', died in Rome around 50 AD.

Cartimandua

The reputation of Cartimandua of the Brigantes tribe was far from heroic. As their queen, she led her tribe, the largest of all the British tribes, between the years 43 to 69 AD. They dominated northern England and held large territories that covered most of Yorkshire and eastern Cumbria at the time of the Roman invasion. Unlike the other tribes around her, together with her husband, Venutius, she allied herself to Rome with peace treaties. It was inevitable that sooner or later she would come into conflict with those other more resistant tribes that chose to fight against Roman occupation.

Her collaborative posture brought matters to a head in 51 AD, when the British King Caractacus of the Catuvellauni tribe sought sanctuary in Brigantium, and her sense of patriotism and loyalty was put to the test. She immediately placed Caractacus in chains and surrendered him to the Romans, at odds with her own people who saw it as a treacherous act. Then, when in 57 AD, she decided to divorce her husband in favour of his armour-bearer, Vellocatus, the tribe rallied into open rebellion against her.

It took the arrival of the *Legio IX Hispana*, (the Ninth Spanish Legion), led by Cassius Nasica, to secure the queen's rescue and to defeat Venutius. However, in 69 AD her scorned husband mounted another attempt on her life, and without Roman support, she was forced to flee to Deva (modern-day Chester). Thereafter, the trail peters out and nothing more is known of Cartimandua's whereabouts nor what became of her.

Venutius ruled the Brigantes for a short time until he was thrown out by the Romans in 71 AD, during the reign of the Emperor Vespasian, and Brigantian territory was annexed to the Roman Empire.

Cassivellaunus

Cassivellaunus was the chieftain and military leader of the Catuvellauni tribe, whose territory lay north of the River Thames in present-day Hertfordshire and whose capital was at *Verulamium*, (modern-day St Albans). He led a federation of native British tribes against the invading legions of Julius Caesar during his second expedition in 54 BC. Cassivellaunus' army faced the Romans across the Thames, but with heavy losses as a result of sustained cavalry charges and massed ranks of Roman legionaries, his defeated army withdrew northwards, pursued by Caesar's troops.

His whereabouts were revealed to Caesar by five defeated British tribes, (the Cenimagni, Segontiaci, Ancalites, Bibroci and the Cassi), and Cassivellaunus' northern stronghold, somewhere around Devil's Dyke near Wheathampstead, was taken. He was forced to sue for terms, agreeing to maintain the peace with his neighbouring enemy, the Trinovantes, and thereafter becoming what the Romans called a 'client kingdom', afforded a degree of self-autonomy under Roman rule.

Cassivellaunus appears in folklore and legends as Cassibelanus, one of Geoffrey of Monmouth's *Kings of Britain* and in the *Mabinogion*, as well as in the Welsh Triads as Caswallawn, son of Beli Mawr. The name, Cassivellaunus, means 'chieftain', 'leader' or 'commander'.

Cingetorix

Cingetorix was one of the four kings of Kent, who along with Segovax, Carvilius and Taximagulus, was an ally of the British leader Cassivellaunus, during Julius Caesar's second expedition to Britain in 54 BC. He received four mentions in Caesar's *Gallic Wars*.

Cingetorix was the chief of the Treveri tribe, who fought for the tribal leadership against his father-in-law, Indutiomarus. Despite his initial successes, Indutiomarus was able to have him declared a public enemy in 54 BC and to confiscate his estates. Later, when hostilities with Rome had ceased and a peace accord had been struck, Caesar reinstated Cingetorix as tribal leader of the Treveri and restored his estates as part of a 'client state' agreement. In Gaulish, the name Cingetorix means 'marching king' or 'king of warriors'.

Civilis

Gaius Julius Civilis was born into a noble family and was chieftain of the Batavi tribe in the first century AD. He became a Roman citizen and was a commanding officer in a battalion of Germanic auxiliaries of the Roman army before leading his tribe in a revolt against Roman rule in 69 AD. The Batavi had originally been subdued in 12 AD and had accepted Roman rule, with eight cohorts (battalions) of Batavi actually serving in the Roman army.

Civilis's rebellion and that of his tribe, along with several other disgruntled Germanic tribes like the Frisians, sought revenge for what was considered an unjustified and possibly illegal execution of his brother Paulus for treason, following an uprising against Nero in 68 AD. Civilis was also tried for the crime, but was acquitted by the new emperor, Servius Sulpicius Galba, after which returned to his native Germania, swearing to avenge his brother's death. His story, the only known account, was recorded in his book *Historiae* by Tacitus, who referred to him as 'Claudius' Civilis.

The rebel army fought two major battles with the Roman legions; in the first, near Nijmegen, the Romans were roundly defeated when two legions of Batavian auxiliaries, (about 6000 men), defected to join Civilis. A section of the rebel army went on to besiege the Roman camp at *Castra Vetara*, but were intercepted and defeated. However, the remaining warriors held a sustained siege and the Romans eventually surrendered, at which point the Batavians massacred every one of them. The humiliating defeat galvanised Rome into action and a large Roman force under the command of General Quintus Petillius Cerialis was sent to deal with the rebels. Castra Vetera was liberated, most of the Batavian rebels were executed, and after a long chase, Civilis surrendered and was taken prisoner at *Augusta Treverorum* (Trèves). This marked the end of the Batavian revolt. What became of Civilis is unknown – following the Batavi defeat he disappears from the pages of recorded history.

Nowadays Civilis is regarded as a Batavian resistance hero, and a memorial statue to honour his memory, sculpted by Lodewijk Van Geel in 1822, was installed in an ornamental garden that belonged to the hunting pavilion of Crown Prince Willem Frederik van Oranje in Tervuren, Belgium.

Commius

Commius (sometimes spelled 'Commios', 'Comius' and 'Comnios'), was the king of the Atrebates tribe and a leader in the resistance movement of the Gallic tribes, having pledged 15,000 warriors to fight under Chief Galba of the Suessiones, against Caesar. After a confederation of the Atrebates and Nervii were defeated at the Battle of Sambre in 57 BC, Commius and a group of followers fled to Britain where he founded a new Atrabatean dynasty and established himself as king of the British Atrebates tribe in about 30 BC, holding territories south of the River Thames that included modern-day Hampshire and Sussex. He was eventually pardoned by Julius Caesar and became a close ally of Rome in Gaul and in Britain.

Ahead of Caesar's proposed 55 BC invasion, Commius was commissioned to warn British leaders not to resist, and he managed to persuade the British King Cassivellaunus to make peace terms. However, Commius was taken prisoner, and only released at the end of the first invasion; he went on to accompany Julius Caesar in the second of his expeditions to Britain. From about 25 BC Commius ruled in collaboration with his two sons. After his father's death sometime around the year 5 BC, his son Tincommius inherited the crown.

Corocotta

According to the Roman historian Cassius Dio, Corocotta was a Cantabrian guerrilla warrior and bandit in Spain during the first century BC, whose constant raids on Roman territory caused Augustus Caesar to offer a reward, (claimed to be somewhere between 200,000 and one million sesterce), a large sum, for his capture. Corocotta could not have known that the Roman occupation of Cantabrian territory would turn him, an erstwhile bandit and highwayman, into a local hero.

Dio's account tells how Corocotta walked brazenly into the Roman encampment to claim the reward personally, in the full knowledge that he was risking his life, but by an act of self-sacrifice he intended to distribute the money among his own Cantabrian people, who had suffered many privations in their resistance to Roman domination. The account may be entirely anecdotal, and according to some a completely fictional tale, and only appears in Dio's account, but it is said that Augustus was so impressed with Corocotta's bravery that he paid him the money and granted his freedom.

Dio used the Greek word *leistes* to describe Corocotta, a word that means 'bandit' or 'robber'. According to local account, Corocotta fought with the Astures tribe against Rome in the Astur-Cantabrian wars 29 BC–19 BC. In 1985 a monumental statue to Corocotta, designed by Ramón Ruíz Lloreda, was installed in the city of Santander in Cantabria.

Ducarius

Ducarius was a Gallic warrior chieftain of the Insubres tribe who fought in the Carthaginian army of Hannibal against four legions of the Roman army, (some

25,000 men), commanded by General Gaius Flaminius at the Battle of Lake Trasimene in 217 BC, during the Second Punic War. Polybius stated that 15,000 legionaries were killed in the action and that the rest were captured, while only 1,500 Carthaginians died. The defeat was described as one of the three 'great military calamities' suffered by the Romans in the Punic Wars.

According to Livy, Ducarius personally killed Flaminius during the battle. His account was a dramatic version of what he imagined had taken place, probably based on oral tradition. A version in his *History of Rome* reads thus: 'Ducarius, who recognised the consul (Flaminus) also by his face, cried out to his countrymen, "Behold the man who massacred our legions and laid waste our fields and our city! Now will I offer him up as a sacrifice to the shades of our fellow citizens so foully slain!"' The account continues by describing how Ducarius cut down the general's armour-bearer, and '…transfixed the consul with his spear'. Various other reports say that Ducarius beheaded Flaminius after killing him. Whether or not this actually happened is uncertain, but the cult of *tête coupée* ('severed head') is known to have been common among many Celtic tribes.

Dumnacos

Dumnacos, (sometimes called 'Dumnac'), was chieftain of the Celtic tribe of the Andecaves (or 'Andegavi'), known to Julius Caesar as the Andes. The tribal territory of the Andecaves was in Anjou, in the modern Maine-et-Loire Département, which the Romans called *Andegavia*, (meaning 'the land of the Andecavi'). Under the leadership of Dumnacos, the tribe resisted Rome following the surrender of Vercingetorix at Alesia, but they were finally defeated after a long Roman siege at *Lemonum* (Poitiers) by an army under the command of Gaius Caninius Rebilus. When a large Roman relief column arrived, Dumnacos was forced to retreat from the engagement, but his army was pursued by the Romans and suffered heavy casualties in the battle that ensued. It was recorded that some 12,000 Adecaves warriors died. However, Dumnacus escaped and went into self-imposed exile.

In 1887 a commemorative statue of Dumnacos by Louis Noël was erected at Ponts-de-Cé, in the middle of a bridge spanning the River Loire.

Lucterius

Lucterius was a leader of the Cadurci, a sub-group of the Arverni tribe, who held territory around *Gallic Divona* (present-day Cahors), in the Département of Lot in the Dordogne region of France. Lucterius was despatched by the chief of the Arverni, Vercingetorix, to Ruteni territory to secure an alliance during the Gallic insurrection against Rome in 52 BC. Following Vercingetorix's capture at Alesia, Lucterius and his Cadurci warriors continued to fight, forging a new alliance with Drappes, the Senonii tribal leader of a group of Gallic rebels. The allied force attempted another invasion of Languedoc and Provence, but were halted by the Roman army commanded by Gaius Caninius Rebilus, and withdrew to set up an encampment a few miles from the fortified stronghold of *Uxellodunum*, which was under Roman siege at that time. When the stronghold surrendered, Caesar spared the lives of its inhabitants, but cut off their hands as a punishment for their resistance and supposed betrayal. Lucterius immediately fled and sought refuge from Epasnactus, a leader of the Arverni, who betrayed and handed him over to the Romans.

Maroboduus

Maroboduus, king of the Germanic Marcomanni tribe, was born in 18 BC into a noble Suebian family. As a young boy he was sent to be educated in Rome, but returned afterwards to his homeland. On reaching manhood and becoming head of a Suebi army he drove the Celtic Boians from Bavaria and Bohemia. He established a settlement and royal seat at *Boviasmum*, where he established a large confederation of foot soldiers and mounted cavalry, reportedly amounting to around 74,000 men.

His growing power soon attracted the attention of the Roman Emperor Augustus, who sent legions commanded by the future emperor Tiberius and General Sentius Saturninus to occupy Marcomanni territory. Maroboduus had long been a friend of Augustus and the other neighbouring Germanic tribes were suspicious of the association; fearing that it would compromise their sovereignty, they rose up against him. A combined force of the Cheruscans led by Arminius, but also including the Semnones and Longobards, met his army in open warfare. He was defeated, deposed from his throne and fled to Rome for refuge, where he spent the remainder of his life, some eighteen years, detained at the order of Tiberius at Ravenna.

Spartacus

Little is known of Spartacus's early years other than he was born in Thrace, (the modern-day Balkan states) and that his real name was unknown. It is thought that he served for a time in the Roman army and that he deserted to become a notorious bandit before he was captured as a slave. He was sold into a gladiatorial training school run by Quintus Lentulus Batiatus, a brutal trainer and trader of gladiators in Capri. In 73 BC, along with seventy other fellow gladiators, including Crixus, Gannicus, Castus, and Oenomaus, he escaped and set up a base near Mount Versuvius. Over time, other runaway slaves joined his group, which eventually grew to somewhere between 90 and 100,000 strong.

Initially, his rebellious slave army achieved great successes over the Roman legions, travelling as far north as Gaul (modern-day France) and in northern Italy in what became known as the Third Servile War, (73–1 BC). While at Lucania, on his way south to Sicily, about thirty-five miles south of Naples, Spartacus was defeated by eight Roman legions under the command of General Marcus Licinius Crassus.

Spartacus is believed to have died in the battle, somewhat at odds with Stanley Kubrick's 1960 film version. Six thousand captured slaves were crucified at the roadside of the Appian Way outside of Rome.

Vercingetorix

What little we know of Vercingetorix relies largely upon Julius Caesar's *Gallic Wars* memoirs. In it, Caesar recalled that in 54 AD, an alliance of Gallic tribes rebelled under the leadership of Vercingetorix, chieftain of the Arverni tribe, to offer armed resistance to the Roman legions that were wintering in Gaul. This new federation included the Senones, Parisii, Pictones, Cadurci, Turones, Anlerei and other tribes, who agreed to set aside all inter-tribal differences to fight under Vercingetorix's leadership.

By this time, Caesar had subdued almost all of Gaul, and Vercingetorix was to represent one last consolidated attempt to reverse his advance, mounting a series of guerrilla raids on Roman supply convoys. He successfully defended the Arverni hill-fort and main settlement of *Gergovia* (near present-day Clermont-Ferrand) against a siege by Caesar. The Romans were unable to scale its impressive high ramparts, and its legionaries were thrown into disarray by sustained cavalry charges. The Gallic army under Vercingetorix's command was victorious. Then, during another confrontation near the River Saone at Vingeanne in central France, Vercingetorix ambushed the Roman army while on the march with a force of some 80,000 Gallic warriors. However, the resulting battle saw his army defeated, forcing him to retreat and to take refuge in another Arverni hill-fort at Alesia. Caesar laid siege, the embattled troops in Alesia were forced to surrender and it was a decisive victory for the Roman legions. Vercingetorix was taken to Rome and displayed in chains at Caesar's triumphal procession. He remained imprisoned for seven years before he was finally executed.

In 1865, the French Emperor Napoleon III commissioned a 23-ft-high monumental statue of Vercingetorix to be erected on what is thought to be the location of Alesia. In ancient Celtic the name Vercingetorix roughly translates as 'the greatest king of warriors'.

Viridovix

Viriodix was the chief of the Gallic Unelli tribe that resisted the Roman invasion of Armorica during Julius Caesar's conquest of Gaul, between the years 58 and 51 BC. His army included warriors of the Lexovii and Aulerci Eburovices tribes, whom he had convinced to assassinate their senators and join him in the revolt. In 56 BC, the combined Breton army faced three Roman legions commanded by the Legate Quintus Titurius Sabinus, who lured them into a trap. The Romans rushed the Gauls, who, outnumbered and outmatched, fled, to be chased by Sabinus' cavalry, who cut them to pieces. Caesar's account of the battle and its outcome gives no clues as to the fate of Viridovix.

Viriathus

Viriathus, (sometimes 'Viriatus', or 'Viriato' in Portuguese and Spanish), led the Lusitanian people in their resistance to the Roman invasion of western Hispania. Not much is known of his early life, although traditionally he is said to have been a shepherd, before he served as a mercenary in the Carthaginian army during the Second Punic War.

In 206 BC, Rome seized the former Carthaginian conquered territories of southern Spain, and the Iberian tribes rose up in rebellion. As a teenager, Viriathus is thought to have joined in guerrilla raids against oppressive Roman rule. His fame soon spread and more and more tribesmen came over to join him. His bravery and leadership qualities resulted in his election as chief of the Lusitani in 146 BC, after which he spearheaded the tribal rebellion on the Iberian Peninsula.

Viriathus won a succession of victories from 147 to 142 BC, but he was finally betrayed and assassinated in 139 BC by three of his own men, who had been handsomely paid by the Roman General and Consul, Quintus Servilius Caepio. When in 150 BC, the Lusitani surrendered, all men of fighting age were put to death on the instruction of the Roman Governor, Servius Sulpicius Galba. Having re-established Roman rule and authority, Galba returned to Rome, enriched by the spoils of war. Viriathus is still regarded as a national hero in Portugal, and a life-sized bronze statue of him, sculpted by Eduardo Barra, now stands in Zamora, Spain.

Viridomarus

Viridomarus received only the briefest of historical mentions. According to writers like Livy in his *History of Rome*, and Plutarch in his *Life of Marcellus*, in 222 BC Viridomarus led the northern Italian tribe of Insubres against a Roman army commanded by the Roman Consul Marcus Claudius Marcellus, in what became known as the Battle of Clastidium. His name remains obscure – it may have been Viridomarus or Britomartus, as the name varies according to different accounts.

The Romans were victorious, and in the process, Marcellus earned the so-called 'spolia opima'. This translates roughly as 'the spoils of war', whereby the victor was awarded the armour and weapons of his defeated opponent as trophies; it was one of the highest honours awarded to any Roman commander.

The engagement at Clastidium concluded when Viridomarus challenged Marcellus to single combat. Plutarch's account is quite graphic: Viridomarus confronted Marcellus, he wrote, and '...shouting challenges and brandishing his spear... it gleamed like lightning'. He continued that Marcellus '...therefore rushed upon the man, and by a thrust of his spear which pierced his adversary's breastplate, and by the impact of his horse in full career, threw him, still living, upon the ground, where, with a second and third blow, he promptly killed him'. Livy recorded that Marcellus '...returned (to Rome) with the supreme booty'.

Chapter Four

The Druids & Celtic Religion

What little we know of Celtic religion is that its tribal people were polytheistic, worshipping and venerating many gods and goddesses, but our knowledge is otherwise sketchy. Our knowledge has been gathered from fragments of ancient folklore and the word-of-mouth stories passed down from Continental Gaul, the Iberian Peninsula, from Ireland and Britain or through contemporary Roman accounts. Almost every significant event in Celtic life seems to have been intrinsically linked to some religious or sacred phenomenon.

We know, for example, that the Irish Celts celebrated four important festivals that roughly corresponded to the change of seasons. First was 'Imbolc' (or 'Imbolg'), which marked the first day of spring; when Christianity came to the island, it was formalised to the first day of February and became a traditional Gaelic festival associated with St Brigid. Second was 'Beltaine', celebrated on the first of May to mark the end of winter and which became a traditional Gaelic May Day festival. Third was 'Lughnasa' (or 'Lughnasadh') on the first day of August, which became associated with the Celtic god Lug (or Lugh) and the beginning of the harvest season. Finally 'Samhain' was celebrated on the first day of November and marked the Celtic New Year, the end of harvest and the onset of winter.

According to Greek geographer and historian Posidonius of Apameia, (sometimes known as 'Poseidonius of Rhodes'), Gaulish religion and culture comprised three main classes in Celtic society: the Druids, the Bards, and what they called 'Vates'. According to the Roman historian Strabo, the Bards were singers and poets, the Vates (or Ovates) were diviners and soothsayers, while the Druids were probably the most important, being the intellectual and spiritual leaders as well as being arbiters of moral philosophy.

Unfortunately, the Druids are known to have practised cannibalism and to have committed ritual human sacrifice, which brought them into direct conflict with Rome. Of the Irish tribes, Strabo commented, '...the Celts consider it honourable to eat their dead fathers and to openly have intercourse, not only with unrelated women, but with their mothers and sisters as well.'

Julius Caesar described the Druids, commenting how they '...officiate at the worship of the gods, regulate public and private sacrifices, and give rulings on all religious questions'. He continued: 'Large numbers of young men flock to them for instruction and they are held in great honour by the people. They act as judges in practically all disputes whether between tribes or between individuals.' He also wrote that the Celts sacrificed animals and humans in a large wickerwork figure, known as a wicker man, and that their victims were usually convicted criminals. Also, judging by the number of human skulls found in archaeological excavations in rivers around Londinium (London), ritual beheading and head-hunting also seemed to have been practised on a large scale. Many archaeologists refer to this practice as 'the cult of the severed head', or the 'tête coupé'.

Anglesey, ('Ynys Mon' in Welsh, or 'Môna' as the Romans called the island), was the most important of the Druidic shrines and Rome set out on a mission to destroy Celtic paganism and bring to an end the Druids' perceived influence, which had long been a cohesive force among otherwise disparate Celtic tribes. The first face-to-face confrontation was in 55 BC when a force headed by Julius Caesar fought an unsuccessful engagement on Anglesey, but it was another five years before they were able to gain a foothold on the island following a ferociously fought battle that became known as the Menai Massacre. The event was recorded by the historian Tacitus in his *Annals*. He recounted the slaughter of Druids on Anglesey by a legion commanded by Suetonius Paulinus in 60 or 61 AD.

Tacitus describes how many of the seasoned Roman legionaries stood frozen with fear at the sight of the fanatical screaming Celtic women of the Ordovices tribe who ran at them, so that they had to be forcibly 'urged' to advance by their generals. His account of the Druids during the engagement was detailed: 'All around, the Druids, lifting up their hands to heaven, and pouring forth dreadful imprecations, scared our soldiers by the unfamiliar sight, so that, as if their limbs were paralysed, they stood motionless.' In the end, Roman discipline was restored and though they were victorious, it was at great cost.

Undaunted by their crushing defeat, the Ordovices continued to mount such stiff resistance that the Romans deemed it necessary to construct the Roman fort of *Segontium* (modern-day Caernarfon), across the Menai Strait, as a place to marshal troops and assemble resources in preparation for a renewed invasion attempt. However, it was not until 77 AD, that General Julius Agricola finally subjugated the tribe and their island stronghold, to bring it entirely under Roman rule.

The Druidic 'problem' was not finally laid to rest until Constantine I (c.280–337 AD) was converted to Christianity at York and that it grew to dominate the Roman Empire. Within three centuries, the Christian church had acquired three million followers, and in February 313 AD, the Roman Emperors Constantine and Licinius decreed that the Edict of Milan, which guaranteed Roman citizens freedom to follow their religious beliefs, would be enshrined in Roman law. By the end of the fourth century, Christianity had become Rome's official religion with more than thirty million followers. Consequently, Druidic customs gradually declined and the Christianisation of the Celtic tribes soon spread to the northern limits of the Empire.

Rooting out the sacred sites of Celtic peoples must have been a protracted affair as they did not set great store by temples; their ceremonies took place in forest groves, usually around oak trees. In fact, although it remains unclear what was the origin of the name 'druid', it is generally accepted as meaning 'knowing the oak tree'. It was probably related to 'doire', an Irish-Gaelic word for oak tree. We know that druids considered trees sacred, particularly the oak. They also held certain natural sites as having spiritual importance. Places like hills and mountain tops, impressive trees, forest groves and bodies of water such as springs, rivers and lakes – all were seen to have sacred or ritualistic significance. Julius Caesar concluded that '...the principal point of their doctrine is that the soul does not die and that after death it passes from one body into another.'

In his *Commentarii de Bello Gallico* ('Commentaries on the Gallic War'), dated around 52 BC, Caesar recognised five main gods of Gaul; he likened them to the Roman pantheon of gods and goddesses, and described their roles as he saw them. However, he did not refer to these deities by their Celtic names, but by their perceived Roman equivalents. In fact, rather than eradicate the Celtic deities, many were absorbed directly into the Roman pantheon.

But there were many more than Caesar's five Celtic deities; we know that they worshipped and revered scores of gods and goddesses, and assigned them to virtually every spring, river, mountain, wood and natural landscape, as well as unnatural elements and supernatural forces. Many were adopted by the Romans in the first century AD, and their names were frequently changed or conflated with existing Roman deities.

This was particularly true of Britain and Ireland, where fortunately, some vestiges of Celtic folklore were recorded in the second and third centuries by Christian monks and missionaries. Of course, how much credence we should afford to their writings is open to question; they would have regarded them as mere pagan superstitions.

Many accounts also survive in one form or another in early pre-Christian Welsh writings like the *Mabinogion*, (the fourteenth century manuscript known as 'Red book of Hergest'), and in Irish manuscripts like *The Cycle of the Kings* and *The Ulster Cycle*. In their time, the authors of these ancient chronicles intended them to be read as historical records, but with few exceptions nowadays they are generally recognised as little more than intriguing tales and fantasies with little factual basis.

The immediate problem that faced the church was the continuing pagan practices of the subjugated tribal peoples of the Roman Empire. The solution was to gradually overlay paganism with Christianity – to assimilate and absorb it. Thus, pagan temples became rededicated as Celtic churches and new churches were built on sacred pagan sites, their former shrines being renamed with Christian symbols and associations.

The Celtic High Cross is a perfect example of the church's acquisition of Celtic iconography. Many pre-Christian Celtic carvings depict the powerful sunwheel (or solar cross). It has been argued that the original circle represented the chariot wheel of the Sun God, who was widely venerated among early tribal cultures, or even the Celtic torc, which was a symbol of authority and power. When the cross was superimposed upon the wheel, the resultant Celtic cross clearly portrayed Christianity's dominance over paganism, its significance was self-evident, and its relevance was plain for everyone to see. To early Christians the circle represented a halo, and holiness, and was seen around the heads of saints in early medieval and Renaissance paintings.

As a powerful symbol of Christianity, Celtic crosses were especially prevalent in Ireland, where it is often referred to as the 'Irish Cross'. The popularity of the Celtic cross is traditionally ascribed to St Patrick, who is erroneously said to have invented it as a prop to aid his conversion of the pagan tribes of Britain and Ireland. He saw its value in enabling him to better communicate with possible pagan converts, as it was linked directly to a symbol that they already recognised and venerated.

Christmas is another example of a co-opted pagan ritual. From its earliest days the Christian church selected 25 December as an arbitrary date on which to celebrate the birth of Jesus Christ. Of course, nobody actually knows on which day Christ was born, but the pagan festival of *Sol Invictus* ('the Unconquered Sun') eminently fitted the bill. Other midwinter celebrations like *Geola* (Yule) fell around this time of year, and like many other Iron Age peoples, the Celts celebrated this mid-winter festival by bringing holly and ivy into their homes to ward off evil spirits and demons. Mistletoe was an ancient symbol of love and friendship. Even the polytheistic Romans celebrated *Saturnalia* on 17 December. It all fitted together very neatly into the new Christian calendar.

Long before the advent of Christianity, what we call Easter began as a pagan festival celebrating spring in the Northern Hemisphere. Eostre was a goddess of spring and renewal, whose symbol was a rabbit or hare, which were anciently identified with fertility and life (hence, Easter bunnies), and her feast became attached to the Vernal Equinox. Easter eggs came later. The egg, an ancient symbol of new life, was associated with pagan spring festivals. Early Christian converts considered Easter eggs as representative of Jesus's resurrection from the tomb. Likewise, the German festival of Easter, known as *Ostern*, is named after the same goddess, whom they called Ostara. It was inevitable that Easter would become associated with Jesus's conquering of death and his rebirth.

Thus, Christianity gradually overtook Druidism and the old religions, and delegated them to the realms of superstition, black magic and what became called Satanism. Christianity effectively eradicated the Celtic deities, sentencing them into the obscurity of ancient history. What follows are some of the most commonly found, more than 400 known pre-Roman Celtic deities.

THE CELTIC DEITIES

Abandinus

Abandinus was a Celtic god whose veneration was common around Grantchester in Cambridgeshire during the Roman age. He is thought to have been associated with a local freshwater spring. He is known by a single engraved stone, apparently erected and paid for by a Roman called Vatiacus. The inscription reads: 'To the God Abandinus, Vatiacus dedicates this out of his own funds'. The precise meaning of his name is still debated, but the first element ('Aba') could be a variant of the early Celtic word 'abon', meaning 'river' or 'stream', or it could be a similar derivation of the modern Welsh 'Aber', which relates to an estuary (as in Aberystwyth). Whatever, the connection to water seems likely.

Abnoba

The Celtic/Gaulish/Brittonic goddess Abnoba, (sometimes 'Arnoba', 'Avnova' or 'Arbona'), and referred to by the Romans as Dianae Abnobae (Diana Anoba), is thought to have been a forest and river deity whom the Romans identified with Diana, the goddess of the hunt and of childbirth, as well as the protector of woods, springs, rivers and wild animals. Her name means 'she of the river wetness'. Abnoba was highly venerated in the Black Forest region of Germany but her worship was wide-ranging throughout the Celtic nations. Ptolemy thought the centre of her worship was around the source of the Danube and Breg rivers, a region he called the 'Abnobaei Hills', located in the present-day district of Schwarzwald–Baar in Baden-Wurttemberg. Her name is thought to derive from the Brittonic root 'afon' or 'abon', meaning 'river', as is common in Welsh river name elements as well as in several English rivers named 'Avon'. Abonae was also the name of a Roman town at the mouth of the Avon, north-west of *Aquae Sulis* (modern-day Bath). She has variously been known as the Guardian of the Oak, Mistress of the Beasts and Lady of the Wilds.

Adsullata

Adsullata was a goddess of rivers and hot springs who came to Brittany from Celtic Gaul and her veneration ultimately spread to Britain. Her eventual connection with rivers may have been on account of her association with the river god Savus, as she was closely associated with the Sava (the River Savus) in Noricum. She was also associated with the Anglo-Celtic sun goddess, Sul, long before the Celts associated female deities with the moon and male deities with the sun. She had been thought to influence the times and effects of the sun as well as having the power of purification. Her name is derived from the proto-Celtic word 'Adsuglata', which translates as 'she who draws water'. Her name is only known to have been recorded once, in an inscription found at Saudorfel in Austria.

Agrona

The Brittonic Welsh warrior goddess Agrona derived her name from an old Celtic element 'agro', meaning 'battle', 'carnage' or 'slaughter'. Her name may be synonymous with the Irish Morrigan goddess Macha, (sometimes known as 'the Phantom Queen'), in that she is associated with rivers, especially with the River Ayr in Scotland and with the River Aeron in Cardiganshire. This goddess of war and death was sometimes depicted as a masculine figure in Welsh mythology. Ironically, there is a school of thought that maintains that her name is the root of the modern English word 'agronomy', which is related to crop and field management.

Aine

The Irish goddess Aine (pronounced 'awn-ya'), was multi-purposed, being the deity of livestock and crops as well as of love, summer and fertility. She has also been called 'the Faery Queen', 'the Love Goddess', and 'the Lady of the Lake', as well as having a role as a sun goddess and being associated with Venus, the Roman goddess of love. She was also popular with the Celtic tribes of County Limerick where the Hill of Knockainey (in Gaelic, 'Cnoc Aine') is named after her. According to tradition, Aine was the daughter of Eogabail and wife of the Celtic sea god Manannan mac Lir, as well as being one of the legendary Tuatha De Danann, the principal Gaelic deities of pre-Christian Ireland.

Alaunus

Widely worshipped across Gaul, Alaunus, (sometimes 'Alaunius' or 'Alaunos'), was a god of the sun, healing and prophecy, and was sometimes identified by the Romans with their god Mercury. His name is found on inscriptions in the Alpes-de-Haute-Provence in the south of France, as well as in Austria and western Germany. The name may be derived from the proto-Celtic word 'Alaunos', which is thought by some to mean 'shining one', and as such could be a possible reference to the sun. His name is found on inscriptions at Lurs in the Alpine region of southern France as well as in Mannheim in western Germany. Alaunus was the Roman name of the River Aulne in Brittany, and the Roman name of the River Aln in the English county of Northumberland. The river also gives its name to several towns, including Alnwick, and the villages of Alnmouth and Alnham.

Ancamna

Ancamna was a Romano-Gaulish goddess of the Celtic Treveri tribe whose territory was around the Moselle River region of Germany. Ancamna's consort was Smertrius, the Roman god Mars, and is an example of the marriage between ancient Gaulish and Roman deities. A rare statuette of Ancamna alongside Smertrius survives as part of an altar to the god at Trier in Luxembourg where the couple were regarded as integral to a protector cult. Her name is derived from a proto-Celtic Gaulish form that has been interpreted to mean 'crooked river' or 'meandering water'.

Ancasta

Ancasta was a Celtic goddess widely venerated in Britain during Roman times, and is thought to have been associated with the River Itchen near present-day Southampton in Hampshire. Her name may derive from an early proto-Celtic word 'kasto', meaning 'swift', a possible description of the Itchen. Her name is known from a single carved inscription and dedication found at Bitterne, the former Roman settlement of *Clausentum*, near Southampton.

Anu

In Irish mythology, Anu, (sometimes 'Ana', 'Anann' or 'Anand'), often confused with Danu, (though a debate is ongoing), was an ancient Celtic goddess of the earth and fertility. Medieval texts identify her as one of the Morrigan sisters and referred to Ireland as the Land of Anu, suggesting that she was the mother of all goddesses. She was also known as Earth Mother, the Goddess of Land, and Mother of Irish Gods. Anu was first mentioned around 100 AD in the Irish *Book of Invasions* (the Lebor Gabala), where she is referred to as 'queen of the fertile land'. A pair of breast-shaped hills in County Kerry, known as the Paps of Anu (Da Chich Anann) which translates as 'the breasts of Anu', are said to have been named after her. Somewhere back in ancient times, devotees built cairns on top of each hill, which are thought to have once been passage graves. As the two cairns subsequently resembled nipples, the site is sometimes referred to as 'the nipples of Anu'.

Andrasta

Andrasta was the patron Goddess of the British Iceni tribe, who venerated her as the warrior goddess of victory, battles and ravens. Her name has been variously interpreted as 'the invincible one' or 'she who has not fallen'. Her name was invoked before battles to ensure victory. Andrasta is sometimes compared to the Irish goddess Morrigan and to Andarte, who was worshipped by the Vocontii people of Continental Gaul. According to the Roman historian Tacitus, Queen Boudicca of the Iceni was known to sacrifice captured female Roman prisoners to Andrasta in sacred groves after cutting off their breasts. According to the second-century Roman historian Cassio Dio, writing in his book *The Roman History*, before setting off into battle, Boudicca '…raising her hand toward heaven, said: "I thank thee, Andraste, and call upon thee…".' Further, he describes the fate of captured women: '…they impaled the women on sharp skewers run lengthwise through the entire body. All this they did to the accompaniment of sacrifices, banquets, and wanton behaviour, not only in all their other sacred places, but particularly in the grove of Andate.'

Annwn

Annwn, (sometimes 'Annwfn' or 'Annwfyn'), is an important figure in Welsh mythology and plays a prominent role in the first and fourth branches of the *Mabinogion*, one of the four ancient manuscripts of Wales. His name derives from a Gallo-Brittonic word meaning 'very deep' or 'underworld'. In early legends, Annwn was ruled by Gwyn ap Nudd, the Welsh god of battle and the dead. He is associated in Celtic mythology with the 'Otherworld', a place described as a supernatural realm of joy, everlasting youth, beauty and abundance. He was perceived to be a great hunter and magician skilled in shapeshifting, and was demonised by later Christian writers as 'Lord of the Underworld' and as 'Lord of the Damned', and through his association with death he was often identified by early Christian missionaries as Satan.

Arduinna

Arduinna, also known as 'Arduinnae' and 'Arduinne', was a goddess of the Ardennes Forest, which was probably named after her. Worshipped by Gauls and Romans alike, she is often represented riding side-saddle on a boar. Her name is Gaulish and translates as 'height'.

Artio

Artio was a Celtic goddess of fertility and animals, especially bears, whose veneration began around 450 BC with the pre-Celtic Helvetii tribe, who lived around Berne in Switzerland and from which the name for Switzerland, 'Helvetia', is derived. Her name comes from 'artos', the Gaulish word for 'bear', and she was known to the Helvetii as the 'She-Bear'. Her association with bears is reflected in the fact that she was said to hibernate throughout winter and reawaken with plants and animals. As the goddess of wildlife, she was probably invoked during hunting rituals. The Romans compared her to the Greek goddess Artemis and to their own goddess, Diana. It is possible that with the coming of Christianity, the Latinised Saxon word 'Ursel', meaning 'she-bear', was applied to St Ursula. The religious veneration of the Celtic bear goddess survived well into the Roman age, and carved inscriptions referring to Artio have been found at Daun, Stockstadt and Heddernheim in Germany, as well as at Weilerbach in Luxembourg and at Muri, near Bern, in Switzerland.

Balor

Balor (or 'Balar') was the grandfather of Lugh and a tyrant leader of the Fomorians ('Fir Bolgs' or 'Fomoire'), a group of malevolent demonic beings who threatened the Irish. A battle took place between the Tuatha De Danann and the Fir Bolgs, until they were defeated 3000 years ago in the second great Battle of Mag Tuired (Moytura). Balor is said to have developed a large poisonous eye in the centre of his forehead during childhood, which was said to kill anyone who looked into it. He was thought to be the personification of drought, blight, and the scorching sun, and was eventually slain by his own grandson. His name is associated with the Celtic 'baleros', meaning 'deadly one', and he became known in English as 'Balor of the Evil Eye'.

Belisama

Belisama was a Gallic and Celtic goddess of lakes and rivers, venerated in Gaul and in Britain, and known to the Romans as *Minervae Belissimae*, likening her to their own goddess Minerva. Her name most probably meant 'the brightest one' or 'the most powerful'. In Roman times the River Ribble in Lancashire was known by the name Belisama, as first recorded in the second century AD by Ptolemy in his *Geographia*, where he refers to 'Belisama aest' (Belisama Estuary). She was also related to fire, and identified with the light of the sun and moon. Inscriptions to Belisama have been found in Vaison-la-Romaine in Provence and Saint-Lizier in the Pyrenees, where she is identified with Minerva.

Belatucadros

Sometimes spelled 'Belatucadrus', and also known as 'Balatucairus' or 'Baliticaurus', this Celtic god was widely worshipped in the north of Roman Britain, especially in the ancient counties of Cumberland and Westmorland. His name appears on at least twenty-eight inscriptions on Hadrian's Wall and is thought to mean 'fair (or shining) one'.

Brigantia

The Celtic goddess Brigantia rose to notoriety among the Romans, and specifically through the Emperor Septimius Severus who visited Britain and actively promoted her veneration from his headquarters in York. More than a half a dozen stone carvings and inscriptions were made to her, possibly as a gesture to placate the Brigantes, the largest of the British tribes, who dominated most of northern England and of whom she was the tribe's patron deity.

Ptolemy named the Brigantes as a people in Ireland whose territorial lands roughly corresponded to the present-day counties of Wexford, Kilkenny and Waterford. Brigantia's name comes from the proto-Celtic word 'Brigantii', which means 'the high one', and is distantly related to the Old Irish name 'Brigit'. She was universally recognised as a goddess of springs, streams, river and water. Later, Brigit was incorporated into Christianity as St Brigid. A tribal deity and protector, Brigantia was important enough for the Romans to incorporate her into their own pantheon and in 1667, following their custom, Charles I had her face placed on the coins of the realm, where she became immortalised as Britannia.

Brigid

Also sometimes spelled 'Brigit', 'Brighid' or simply 'Brig', this pre-Christian Irish Celtic goddess has a name that means 'exalted one'. She is associated with blacksmiths, with spring and poetry. Brigid was also a goddess of healing, fertility and motherhood, as well as passion and fire. She was a member of the Tuatha De Danann and a daughter of Daghda, who was regarded as the chief of the gods. The cult of Brigid extended from Ireland throughout the British Isles and islands and widely across Europe. The Christian Church appropriated her as the popular saint, St Brigid, in the mid-fifth century. She was sometimes known as St Bride or St Breed in the Hebrides where she was regarded as a female sage, a woman of wisdom, a poetess, and even today often called 'St Bride of the Isles'.

Brigid was one of Ireland's most prominent Celtic deities and has also been called the 'Goddess of the Well'. Three rivers derive their names from her: the River Brigit in Ireland, the River Braint in Anglesey, and the River Brent in London. Several altars are known to exist in devotion to the worship of Brigid in Britain: one is at the Roman fort at Castleford, one at Greetland in Yorkshire, one at Brampton near Hadrian's Wall and another at Old Carlisle in the Allerdale District of Cumbria.

Britannia

In the second century AD, the Romans identified the Celtic goddess Britannia with Minerva, their goddess of warfare and water. It was the name the Romans gave to the area of Britain that they occupied. Eventually, Britannia would be regarded by Celts and Romans alike as the personification of the British Isles. She was depicted as a warrior goddess, with a trident and shield and, ironically, wearing a Roman centurion's helmet, and became the embodied personification of Britain. Her name in popular consciousness outlived Roman rule in Britain in the fifth century and survived on British coins until relatively recent times. Although she pre-dates the event, Britannia is often associated with Queen Boudicca, the Celtic Iceni ruler who led a revolt against the Roman Empire. An image of Britannia first appeared on coinage in Britain during Roman times, and remained a dominating feature on coinage for the best part of the following 2000 years.

Cathubodua

The name of the Gallic war goddess Cathubodua translates as 'battle crow' or 'raven of battle', and it appears on a single inscription in the Haute Savoie Département of eastern France. It is possible that three other inscriptions that have been found in modern-day Austria and Slovenia, (Atebodvae, Atebodvvs and Atebodvi), from which the initial letter 'c' has been omitted, may also refer to Cathubodua. In Celtic mythology, the raven was associated with battle and death. Cathubodua is thought to be related to the Irish goddess Badb Catha, one of the triple Morrigan goddesses of war. Badb was supposed to hover over battlefields in times of war, flying over the slaughter and carnage to eat the flesh of the dead. She was sometimes represented as a bird of prey with a woman's head. It is sometimes written as 'Cath', which means 'battle' in Irish and is related to the Welsh word 'cad', the Breton 'cat' and the Gaulish 'catu', all of which have the same meaning.

Clota

Also known as Clud, Cludoita and Clutha, Clota was the patron goddess and namesake of the River Clyde (or 'Abhainn Chluaidh' in Scottish Gaelic), whose name means 'the washer' or 'the strongly flowing one'. The name of the River Clyde was first recorded as Clota in 98 AD by the Roman historian, Tacitus, in his book *Agricola*. It is thought that she is closely associated with the Gaulish water nymph, Clutoida. She was highly venerated and worshipped by the local Damnonii tribe, who held the Scottish territory that later became known as the Kingdom of

Strathclyde. The Roman historian Tacitus referred to the Forth of Clyde using its Brittonic name, 'Clota'. The name 'Strathclyde' comes from the Brythonic 'Ystrad Clud', meaning 'Valley of the Clyde', and by inference, 'the valley of Clota'. From 1884 to 1903, as Clutha, the river and its goddess gave their name to a fleet of ferries, known as the 'Cluthas', which transported passengers across the Clyde between Victoria Bridge and Whiteinch Ferry.

Coventina

Coventina was a Celtic goddess, the queen of wells and springs, and is often depicted as a water nymph or water spirit, partly clothed, resting on a leaf or a water lily, pouring water from an urn. She was acquired by the Romans in the late first century, and widely worshipped throughout Britain, the Iberian Peninsula and Gaul from about 200 BC to 400 AD. A carved stone plaque representing the goddess was found in around 130 AD at Carrawburgh near Hadrian's Wall in Northumberland. This plaque is a rare survival, as in the year 391 AD the Emperor Theodosius decreed that all shrines and temples to the old Celtic deities were to be destroyed. Fortunately, her devotees hid the carving and the shrine beneath rocks. There are many other inscriptions dedicated to her around Northumberland, often bearing inscriptions like 'sancta' (holy), and 'augusta' (revered). The veneration of Coventina was not exclusive to Britain, as archaeological evidence suggests that she was also worshipped in north-west Spain and around the Narbonne region of south-west France.

Daghda

Daghda was High King of the Tuatha De Danann, one of the most powerful deities in Irish mythology, worshipped as the god of death and rebirth, and associated with fertility and agriculture. He was usually pictured as a gigantic man wearing a brown, low-necked tunic and a hooded cape, and on his feet he wore horse-hide boots. Behind him he pulls a huge eight-pronged war club called the 'lorg mor' and has a massive cauldron known as the Cauldron of Plenty. He is said to have immense power over both the supernatural and the natural world. His name in Gaelic is 'An Dagda', which means 'the good (or great) god'. He has also been called 'Eochaid Ollathair' in Irish Gaelic, (meaning 'Eochaid the All-Father'), and as 'In Ruad Ro-fhessa' (meaning 'Mighty One of Great Wisdom'). He was able to summon the seasons with his magic harp, which played by itself. In the 'Coir Anmann', an ancient medieval manuscript, Daghda is described as '…a beautiful god of the heathens, for the Tuatha De Danann worshipped him, for he was an Earth-God to them because of the greatness of his magical power'.

Danu

Danu is an important earth mother goddess figure of the Celtic Irish gods, who was believed to have suckled many of the gods and instilled in them a sense of wisdom. She was also the ancestor of the legendary Tuatha De Danann, and as a teacher she passed many of her skills on to them. She was also known by the names Danann and Dana, and is often thought to be identical to the goddess Anu, though this is still debated. She ruled over wizards, rivers, water, wells, prosperity, abundance and wisdom and gave her name to the Tuatha De Danann, which translates as 'People of the Goddess Danu'. Her connection to water suggests that her name could mean 'the flowing one', but there is also a connection to the earth, which promoted the association of her cult to the fairies, fairy mounds, and the many standing stones and dolmens of Ireland.

Divona

Divona (also sometimes known as 'Devona') was the sacred Gallic-Roman goddess of springs and rivers, venerated by the Cardurci tribe, (sometimes 'Cadurci'), who lived beside the River Lot in the Dordogne region of France, especially around modern-day Cahors. The town was named for her by the Romans as *Divona Cardurocorum*, meaning 'Divona of the Cardurci'. Water was generally regarded as a divine entity in Celtic times, and Divona was known as 'the divine fountain' in the language of the Celts. The name Divona means 'divine', and is derived from the Gaulish word 'deuos', which translates as 'divinity'. Other places in southern France contain variants of her name, as is the case with Dionne in the Côte-d'Or, and with Dions in the Gard region. A cache of Roman coins dating from the first century BC, depicting images of Divona, were discovered in 1989 at the Fontaine des Chartreux near Cahors.

Epona

Epona was the Celtic goddess whose name contains the Celtic word element, 'epos', meaning 'horse', and the suffix 'ona', meaning 'on'. It literally translates as 'on a horse' and as the patron goddess of mares and foals, Epona was often depicted on horseback or surrounded by horses. Her name is Gaulish in origin and first appeared during the Bronze Age (c. 2000 to 700 BC) in the River Danube basin. Inscriptions to her were found in Gaul, Germany and in Rome, where she became a popular deity among Roman cavalrymen, who probably brought her cult to Britain in the first century. She is often thought to be a variation on the Welsh goddess Rhiannon and the Irish goddess Morrigan, who were also associated with horses, and like Epona were thought to be companions to the dead. Almost uniquely, she was not renamed or associated with any pre-existing Roman deity, but her Celtic name seems to have been equally embraced by Romans, Celts and Gauls alike.

Eri

The Celtic Irish deity Eri, sometimes known as Eriu, the virgin goddess of the Tuatha De Danaan, was known as 'she of the golden hair'. She appeared first in the Basque region of Spain and is often characterised as a fertility goddess, represented by the womb and by the cornucopia, the overflowing 'horn of plenty'. One of the earliest mentions of her in written literature occurred in the eleventh-century book *Lebor Gabala Erenn*, ('The Book of the Taking of Ireland'), where she and her two sisters acted as protectors of the land and its people. Thus, Ireland was named after Eriu, her name later written as 'Erin', which means something like 'abundant land' in Old Irish. As Erin she became a popular symbol for romantic folklore and songs throughout Ireland.

Fionnuala

A figure of Irish mythology, Fionnuala, (also spelled 'Fionnghuala', 'Fionnuala', 'Finola' and occasionally in English, 'Fenella'), has a name that has been interpreted as 'the fair (or white) shouldered one'. Her name derives from the Irish 'fionn', meaning 'white' or 'fair', and 'guala', meaning 'shoulder'. In Irish legend Fionnuala was one of the four children of King Lir, who was turned into a swan by her evil stepmother and set to wander the lakes and rivers of Ireland for 900 years. According to traditional Irish folklore, Fionnuala can be invoked to give the strength to aid families and to keep them together.

Lugh

Lugh, (in Irish, 'Lugus' or 'Lug'), was a mythological Irish hero, an immortal figure with supernatural powers who led the Tuatha De Danann against the Fomorians at the Battle of Mag Tuired. He was the god of justice and of kingly rulers as well as being known as a trickster and the wielder of his lightning spear, Gae Assail, which was unbeatable in battle. He was one of the most important deities in Irish mythology and literature and even Julius Caesar acknowledged his paramount position among what he described as the top deities of Celtic belief. Lugh was said to be a poet, judge, and wise ruler. The ancient tribe of Luigni, who inhabited present-day County Meath and County Sligo in the north of Ireland, considered themselves descendants of Lugh, although traditionally he was said to have had no children.

He was sometimes known as Lugh Lamhfhada ('Lugh of the Long Arm'), and in Welsh as Lleu Llaw Gyffes ('Lleu of the Skilful Hand'). The Romans associated Lugh with the Roman god Mercury, as well as the Greek gods Hermes and Apollo. There are several accounts of Lugh's death and burial: one maintains that Lugh died by drowning in Loch Lugborta and that his body was buried beneath a cairn on the shores of the loch. Another has his tomb at Brug na Boinne (Newgrange) in County Meath.

Lugh is celebrated on the first day of August every year in an event known as *Lughnasadh*, which is related to the ripening of grain crops and the coming of the harvest. Derivations of his name were found in many places around Europe, including the Roman settlement of *Lugdunum* in France (present-day Lyon), and *Luguvallium* (Carlisle) in England.

Manannan

A popular deity in Scots and Manx mythology, and known as 'Manannan mac Lir' in Irish, Manannan was a warrior king and sea god of the 'Otherworld'. He was also known as 'Lord of the Sea', 'Master of tricks and illusions', and 'Guardian of the Afterlife'. Reputedly he ruled an area under the so-called Islands of the Dead. The Isle of Man, which derives its name from Manannan, was the place he traditionally ruled and where his palace and throne were located. He was thought to protect the Isle of Man by virtue of his magical cloak, which could shroud the island in mist and fog, making it disappear from the sight of its enemies. The Romans associated him with the ancient Greek gods Poseidon and Hades. His name is spelled 'Manandan' in Old Irish, 'Manannan' in modern Irish and Scottish Gaelic, and 'Mannan' in Manx Gaelic. Many places in Ireland are named after him, including Loch Mhanainn in County Mayo, Cuan Mhanainn in County Galway and Mannin Island (Manainn) in County Cork.

Mullo

Mullo was a Celtic deity who was venerated in Brittany and Normandy and was closely related to the Redones tribe, whose main centre of his worship was around present-day Rennes. His name was associated with horses and mules, and derived from the Latin word 'mullo', which translates as 'mules'. He was often associated with the Roman god Mars, and referred to as Mars Mullo. Temples and shrines to him were established by Celts and Romans alike at Craon in the Mayenne Département of north-western France and Sarthe in the Pays de la Loire region.

Rhiannon

The Celtic horse goddess Rhiannon was also thought to be the goddess of fertility, rebirth, beauty and poetry, as well as of the moon, of dreams, of birds, of death and of the Otherworld. Her association with horses aligns her closely with Epona. Rhiannon features as a character in the first and third branches of *The Mabinogion*, the collection of tales compiled in Middle Welsh in the twelfth and thirteenth centuries from much older oral accounts. According to the tale, she appeared to her suitor, Pwyll, the Lord of Dyfed, (who became her husband), as a golden goddess upon a magnificent white horse; her hair was bathed in sunlight and magical birds flew around her head. Her name literally means 'Great Queen' and among her many powers she possessed a magic that could manifest her dreams and desires both for the good of all. According to some legends, she has been identified as the 'Lady of the Lake' in the legends of Camelot, the Celtic goddess who gave Arthur the sword Excalibur, after which he became king.

Rigana

Rigana was a celebrated Celtic war goddess. Her name derives from Old Irish, where 'rigain' means 'queen', and is related to the Welsh word 'rhiain', which can mean 'queen', 'young maiden', or simply 'virgin'. All come from the original Celtic word 'rigana', which relates to the Latin 'regina', meaning 'queen'. There is a body of opinion that Rigana was an alternative name for Epona, the horse goddess, and it has also been suggested that her name is linked to Rhiannon, the Irish goddess Moririgan.

Rosmerta

As the goddess of fertility and abundance, Rosmerta was known to the Gauls and Britons alike as 'the Great Provider'. She was also venerated around the Rhône and the Rhine rivers. Rosmerta originated among the Celts in Gaul before her veneration spread to the Rhineland, Luxembourg and eventually into Britain. The Romans inducted her into their own pantheon as the consort of Mercury. Her name is mentioned in some thirty inscriptions across Europe, especially in ancient Gaul and Germania. The name Rosmerta derives from the Celtic word elements 'ro', signifying 'very' or 'great', and 'smerta', meaning 'to distribute' or 'to give', implying bounty or abundant supply. She has been also described as 'bringer of prosperity' and 'provider of plenty'. Rosmerta was also associated with motherhood and fecundity. She is often represented in effigies bearing a cornucopia (horn of plenty) and a patera (sacrificial bowl). Several stone sculptures of Rosmerta and Mercury exist around the city of Gloucester.

Sabrina

Sabrina was the Latin name for Hafren, (or in Old Welsh, 'Habren'), who was the Welsh Goddess of the River Severn, a waterway whose name has been known since the second century BC, possibly Britain's oldest. According to legend, Hafren was drowned in the river along with her mother Gwendolen, having been defeated in battle. Subsequently, Hafren became the nymph and goddess of the river, which is still known as 'Afon Hafren' in Welsh. She was one of three sisters, who became the Wye, the Ystwyth and the Hafren, each bearing the name of a Welsh river that flows down from a plateau in the Cambrian Mountains of mid-Wales. Hafren was saved by the spirits of the water, who took her as one of their own and transformed her into a river nymph. According to Roman accounts of the second century, Sabrina drives a chariot through the river, accompanied by dolphins and salmon. The legend of Hafren was included in Geoffrey of Monmouth's *Historia Regum Britanniae* (History of the Kings of Britain), written sometime around the year 1138. Local legend has it that Hafren was drowned at Dolforwyn Castle, which overlooks the village of Abermule in Powys. The castle's name in Welsh is 'Dol-forwyn', which means 'maiden's meadow'.

Sucellus

Sucellus (or 'Succelos') was a god of poor people, popular with Gallic Celts and Romans alike, and especially venerated among peasants and slaves in southern and central Gaul, but fairly widespread in Roman Britain. Some have linked him with the Roman god of the underworld, Dyaus Pitar, and with the Irish deity, Dagda. Sucellus was thought to be a protector of woods, fields and wild places. He was usually depicted carrying a long-handled hammer or mallet and a libation saucer or wine barrel, indicative of his powers of protection. His name means 'The Good Striker', a possible reference to his hammer and blacksmithery. As he was frequently depicted carrying a barrel, he had a clear connection with wine and brewing and some think he might have been an alternative version of the Roman god Silvanus. Consequently, he is sometimes referred to as Sucellus Silvanus.

Sul

Sul was the ancient goddess of hot springs and is sometimes called by her Latin name, Sulevia or Sulis. The city of Bath was named *Aqua Sulis* in her honour by the Romans. She was worshipped throughout Gaul, Britain and Galicia, where some forty inscriptions to her are known. The Romans equated Sulis with their own goddess Minerva, and often referred to her as Sulis Minerva.

Tamesis

Tamesis, (sometimes 'Temesia' or 'Temesis'), is the Celtic goddess of fresh water and gave her name to the rivers Thames, Thame, Tame, Teme and Team. The name translates as 'dark flowing'. There is a body of thought which maintains that the name pre-dates the Celts. Tacitus called the River Thames 'Tamesa', but Julius Caesar knew it as 'Tamesis'.

Taranis

Taranis was the Celtic god of storms, bad weather and thunder, which earned him the name 'The Thunderer'. He was known in Irish mythology as 'Tuireann'. The name is derived from the pre-Celtic word 'toranos', which means 'thunder'; he was also sometimes called 'the wheel god', and his symbol was the sacred wheel, which represented mobility and the speed at which his storms raged across the heavens. His cult was popularised by the Romans and he was associated later with the Nordic god Thor. Images, dedications and inscriptions of Taranis can be found at sites around Europe, where he was extensively venerated. Statues or wheels have been found in Ireland, Britain, Gaul, Spain, and across the Rhineland and Danube areas of central and Eastern Europe. The Romans associated him with their god Jupiter and the Greeks with the Brontes cyclops, whose names both mean 'thunder'.

The Morrighan

In Celtic mythology the Morrighan, (also referred to as 'Morrigu', 'Morrighan', or 'Mor-Rioghain'), was a goddess of battle, war, and destruction. She is also known as the 'washer at the ford', after a warrior supposedly discovered her washing her blood-stained armour in a stream. In literature she has been called the 'Phantom Queen' and the 'Great Queen' and made one of her earliest written appearances in the *Ulster Cycle*, a series of tales written in Middle Irish between the eighth and twelfth centuries. She was said to be a shapeshifter and the embodiment of Death, often accompanied by crows or ravens on the battlefield. In some accounts she is depicted as a black raven feeding on the corpses of warriors slain in battle. She has been linked in Irish folklore with the banshee, or 'fairy woman'.

Tuatha De Danann

Tuatha De Danann translates as 'Tribe of the Goddess Danu' after the deities of that name, but they are also known as the 'Tuath De', or 'the Tribe of the Gods'. They were said to be skilled in art, science and poetry, and by tradition they ruled Ireland with supernatural and magical powers some 4000 years ago, despite the fact that academics and scholars doubt they ever existed beyond mythical tales. Yet, in *The Annals of the Four Masters*, compiled from earlier texts by Franciscan monks in the mid-seventeenth century, they were recorded as rulers of Ireland from 1897 BC to 1700 BC. Some maintain they were put together as a fabricated 'history' by the aforementioned monks. However, legend has it that after the arrival of the Milesians, (the ancestors of the modern Irish), they were overcome and said to have disappeared into the hills, into a place known as the Otherworld, where they are hidden from the eyes of mortals.

Chapter Five

The Tribes of Gaul

According to Julius Caesar, Continental Europe, and Gaul in particular, could be divided into three parts: one was inhabited by the Aquitani, who occupied the south-west, another by the Gauls in the central part (who, according to him, in their own language were called 'Celtae'), and in the north by the Belgae. Of course, Caesar's definition was a somewhat limited view. There were many other European tribes, among them the Germans, the Ligurians and the Galatians. Also, territorial divisions were not quite so clearly delineated at that time: borders were ill-defined and subject to change as a result of inter-tribal and territorial disputes. Although all of these peoples were of Celtic descent, they differed considerably in many ways, including the dialects of their language.

The Aquitani did indeed occupy the south-west corner of France and northern parts of the Pyrenees, an area separated from the Gauls by the River Garonne. Groups also settled in the northern part of the Iberian Peninsula, (Spain and Portugal), known to the Romans as 'Gallia Aquitania' (the Aquitanian Gauls). They spoke a form of ancient language, from which modern Basque and Gascon languages are thought to derive. According to Strabo, the Aquitani were a wealthy people. In Book IV of his *Geography*, he wrote that 'Speaking in a general way, the Aquitani differ from the Galatic race in the build of their bodies as well as in their speech; that is, they are more like the Iberians.' He stated that 'There are more than twenty tribes of the Aquitani, but they are small and lacking in repute; the majority of the tribes live along the ocean.'

The Belgae were a group of tribes living in northern Gaul, in territory that the Romans knew as 'Gallia Belgica' (the Belgian Gauls) and from these emerged the modern-day country of Belgium. Sometime in the late second or early first century BC, groups of Belgae crossed into Britain to settle in a place called *Venta Belgarum* (around modern-day Winchester). Caesar himself commented that some of the south-western British tribes were ruled by their descendants, and that Belgic tribal names like the Atrebates were found in an area that would become modern-day Sussex, Berkshire and Hampshire.

The Ligurians were an ancient Indo-European people who gave their name to Liguria, a region of north-western Italy, but their original territory extended west into Piedmont to the southern bank of the River Po, and as far as Provence and the Côte d'Azur region of France. The Greeks believed that the Ligurians were closely related to the Celts, but Strabo thought that they were of a different race from the

Celtic Gauls. Of them he wrote: 'The Alps are inhabited by numerous nations, all Keltic with the exception of the Ligurians, and these are of a different race.'

The Roman historian Livy recounted how Ligurian tribes were deported in the year 181 BC, when some 40,000 men, women and children were forcibly removed from their homeland in the Apuan Alps by the Romans and relocated to Samnium in southern Italy. This was a punishment for siding with Hannibal against Rome during the Second Punic War. Little is known of their language, but it is thought that it was closely related to Italian and Celtic, and they were often referred to as Celto-Ligurians. The Greeks called them *Κελτολίγυες*, which translates as 'Keltoligues'.

The Galatians were another group of Celtic Gauls. They occupied a region of central Anatolia around present-day Ankara in Turkey. They spoke their own Galatian language, which was closely related to that of the northern Gauls. Three migrating tribes, the Trocmi, the Tolistobogii and the Tectosages, had established settlements in Anatolia by around 278 BC.

In his *History of Rome*, of the Galatians, Livy wrote that '…so great was the terror of their name, their numbers being also enlarged…that in the end even the kings of Syria did not refuse to pay them tribute'. Galatians made an appearance in the Bible. Between the years 40 and 50 AD, the apostle St Paul was widely travelled around Galatia, and wrote his New Testament *Epistle to The Galatians*. They were among the earliest non-Jewish people in the Roman Empire to convert to Christianity and the epistle was an exhortation to them not to revert to their earlier pagan practices. In time the Galatians became Hellenised so that some Roman commentators referred to them as Greek-Gauls.

The Gauls (in Latin, 'Galli') were a major group of Iron Age Celtic peoples who emerged in mainland Europe and whose lands roughly correspond to modern-day France, parts of Belgium, western Germany, Luxemburg and northern Italy. Very little is known about the Gaulish (or Gallic) language, as in common with all other Celtic language variations it was rarely if ever written down. What survives has only been found on a few hundred inscriptions and some authorities believe it was similar to Latin.

There is a fine line of distinction between the Gauls and the Celts – both refer to invading peoples from Eastern Europe. We have to thank Emperor Julius Caesar in part for the categorisation; he linked all the peoples of the conquered European lands as Gauls, though nowadays we tend to reserve the term Gauls for those who settled in central Europe and in present-day France. Gauls remained well within the Celtic cultural group of Continental Europe, while we identify those that moved further west into Brittany, the British Isles and Ireland simply as Celts. In a nutshell, all Gauls may be regarded as Celts, but not all Celts were Gauls.

The northern expansion of the Roman Empire began with the invasion and annexation of Celtic Gaul in 121 BC, a task that was completed by Julius Caesar in the Gallic Wars of 58–51 BC. The Roman invasion, as well as repeated incursions by German tribes and regular inter-tribal disputes, meant that the Gallic Celts suffered badly; large numbers of the population were killed, starved to death or sold into slavery. However, in the year 50 BC all resistance ceased and the Gallic tribes surrendered their independence to Rome. As the gradual Romanisation of their culture took place their language was gradually replaced by Latin as the dominant tongue, which heralded the extinction of Gallic as a viable language.

In 27 BC, a complete inventory of European ethnic and territorial tribal divisions was commissioned by Augustus Caesar, to form the basis of his reorganisation of Gaul, into what became the 'Trois Gaules' (the Three Gauls): Lugdenensis, Aquitania and Belgica. In the document he dictated that '...all the (conquered) Alpine tribes which spread from the superior sea (the Adriatic) to the inferior sea (the Mediterranean) have been made subject to the empire of the Roman people'.

When Caesar turned his attention to the east, the Germanic tribes would fare no better than the Gauls or the Belgae had. Judging them to be quite different peoples, Caesar separated the tribes of Germania from the Celts. This was based on the geographical limit of the Roman Empire in the first century AD, which he identified as the River Rhine. According to him, tribes west of the river were Gauls and those to its east were 'Germani'. There are some who agree with his assessment that the Celtic and Germanic people were indeed two entirely different and unrelated cultures. However, the fact that both were Indo-European in origin and that they developed out of the Urnfield Culture of the late Bronze Age, merits their inclusion here. The word 'Teuton', (or 'Teutoni' as the Romans called them), for example, is a term used nowadays to encompass all German people, and the descriptive term 'Teutonic' is widely taken to mean 'German'. However, it was originally the name of a Celtic tribe in northern Europe.

During the third century BC, Teutonic and Cimbri tribes migrated to settle in Gaul and the interaction between these immigrant Germans and the native Gauls, resulted in a mixture of cultures, through close association, intermarriage, or both, and the creation of new tribes, like the Batavi, Cugerni, Tungri and Texuandri. We know now that the people of the region we now call Germany were formerly Celts and that sometime between the fifth and first centuries BC the Germanic and Celtic tribes started to differentiate themselves.

In his *Gallic Wars*, Caesar also describes the enforced movement of tribes like the Usipetes and Tencteri from the east as a result of constant intertribal warfare with the Germanic Suebi and their migration into the territory of the Belgic Menapii. His account was confirmed by Tacitus, who wrote that '...before their arrival the area had been an uninhabited district on the extremity of the coast of Gaul.' Those proto-Celtic tribes that lived east of the Rhine were similarly assimilated into the dominant Teutonic peoples of the eastern Rhineland. As they moved down from the north these Germanic tribes effectively displaced the Celtic tribes who had occupied much of modern-day Germany.

Further, although certain Belgic tribes, (among them the Caerosi, Condrusi, Eburones and Paemani), are thought by some to be Germanic, there is compelling evidence to suggest that they may have been Celts, or at least ruled over by a dominant Celtic authority.

Many of the smaller, less powerful tribes of continental Gaul allied themselves with larger tribes or confederations. These so-called 'client tribes' or 'client kingdoms' saw the benefit of the protection and security that larger tribes offered, especially in the face of the advancing Roman legions. To survive, a few Celtic and Gallic tribes actually allied themselves as client kingdoms of Rome and several supported the Roman army during Emperor Claudius's invasion of Britain in the first century AD.

There is a great deal of archaeological and historical evidence to suggest that when Celtic tribes came to settle alongside other 'foreign' peoples, as was the case of the Galatians in Asia Minor, many relinquished their historical La Tène culture and adopted that of the surrounding tribes, and the simple distinctions between what was Celtic, Germanic or Belgic became academic.

Therefore I have included some of the more obvious Germanic-Celtic tribes in what follows.

THE TRIBES

Aduatuci

Sometimes spelled 'Atuatuci', the Aduatuci held territory north of Namur and eastwards of Brussels near Tongeren in central Belgium in the first century BC. They were descended from the Cimbri and Teutones tribes, who had originated in present-day Denmark. Their capital was known as *Atuatuca Tungrorum* (modern-day Tongeren). Julius Caesar identified the tribe as Germanic, but said that they were descended from the Cimbri and Teutones tribes, both of whom shared elements of Celtic culture. The tribe built a hill-fort at Hastedon (present-day St Servais), a few miles north of Namur.

In 57 BC, Aduatuci warriors went to support the Nervii in the Battle of the Sabis, but learning that the battle was already lost, they retreated to the sanctuary of the Hastedon hill-fort. Caesar intended to make an example of them for assisting the Nervians, and immediately laid siege. Reportedly, about 4000 of the Nervii men were slain and the remainder were forced back into the town. The day after, the Roman army broke through, the Aduatuci laid down their weapons and surrendered en masse, at which point the legionaries proceeded to loot the place. The stronghold had fallen, and according to Caesar's account in his *Commentaries on the Gallic Wars* there had been 19,000 Aduatucan warriors who fought against seven Roman legions, (amounting to 30,000 men). Thousands of people of the Aduatuci tribe were subsequently sold into slavery. Following their subjugation, they disappear from all historical records, but some historians believe that some of the survivors were absorbed into the Tungri federation.

Aeduii

Sometimes spelled 'Aedui' or 'Haedui', this powerful Celtic Gaulish tribe exercised dominion over all the Gaulish tribes, until, together with the Arverni, they were finally defeated and subjugated by the Romans under the command of Julius Caesar.

Their early history was a matter of conquering or absorbing nearby tribes, as well as forming powerful confederacies. Aeduii territory corresponded to would become the French region of Burgundy, located between the River Saone and the Loire. Their tribal name translates loosely from a Celtic/Gaulish word meaning 'burning men'.

Initially, the Aeduii were friendly with Rome, and when they were attacked by the Sequani and Arverni tribes, supported by the Germanic Suebi tribe, they sent Diviciacus, a druid of their tribe (the only druid to be known by name), to seek the assistance of the Roman senate. At that time the Aedui were known as the 'brothers and kinsmen of Rome'. Julius Caesar arrived ahead of an army, and initially restored their lands to them. However, when the Aeduii joined in the great rebellion against the Romans, Augustus Caesar saw it as an opportunity to take over the territory, promptly incorporated it into the Empire and established *Augustodunum* (modern-day Autun), named after himself, as the new Aeduii tribal capital. In the fourth century the Aeduii were converted to Christianity.

Agnutes

According to scarce contemporary accounts by the likes of Pliny, who identified these people as Aquitani, the Agnutes tribe, (sometimes spelled 'Anagnutes' or 'Agnotes'), were settled in the forest-covered Pays de Rais (later called 'Retz'), in the Vendée region of France. They were one of a group of tribes, which included the Ambilatres and the Agnutes, that lived in the region that the Romans called Gallia Aquitania. Strabo placed them among the nations that he described as '...obscure, and which inhabited the shores of the ocean'. They were sailors, farmers and herders who may have been a sub-group of the Pictones tribe and their tribal capital is thought to have been at what is now the village of Pareds (or 'Aupareds') on the banks of the River Arcançon.

Alauni

The Alauni, (sometimes known as 'Aulauni'), were a Celtic tribe from Austria that originated as a Celtic Hallstatt people in Noricum, and who are thought to have intermingled or intermarried with the invading Scythians sometime during the sixth century BC. By the first century BC they had become known as 'Alani Scythae', and regarded as Celto-Scythians. They finally settled on the west coast of Brittany with a centre at Alauna on the Alaunus (the River Aulne), and established another territory in south-eastern Gaul at Alaunium in present-day Provence, which later became a Roman settlement. Their tribal name may have derived from the Gaulish word 'Alamnoi', which means 'wanderers' or 'nomads'. Alternatively, there is a suggestion that as the Alauni venerated the goddess Alounae, they may have been named after her.

Allobroges

The Allobroges were a Celtic tribe that lived around the Rhône and Isère rivers in south-eastern France as well as around Genua (modern-day Geneva), where they had settled sometime around 500 BC. The tribal name is sometimes spelled 'Allobrogs' or 'Allobriges', and means 'foreigner' or 'stranger'. Later, Vienne (Vienna) emerged as their tribal capital, and in 47 BC it became a Roman colony.

After crossing the Rhône on his way to Rome, Hannibal encountered the Allobroges and accounts of their meeting describe how they provisioned his army with the supplies and the warm clothes they would need to cross the Alps.

In 121 BC, a confederation of Allobroges, Arverni, and Saluvii fought the Roman army at the Battle of the River Isère, but in a decisive Roman victory they were defeated by legions under the command of Quintus Fabius Maximus, and their region was annexed to the Roman province of Gallia Narbonensis.

Ambarri

The Ambarri originally had settlements in what is now the Ain Département of the Rhône Valley in France. They were a La Tène tribe who had migrated from Germany sometime in the sixth century BC and settled between the rivers Rhône and Saône. They may have been a sept of the Aeduii tribe and at times their names have been combined as Aeduii Ambarri. Livy called them by the name 'Ambarros', and stated that they had been one of a wave of Celtic tribes that had migrated across the Alps into northern Italy in around 600 BC.

Their tribal name comprises two elements: 'ambi', meaning 'both sides', and 'arar', a reference to the River Arar (now the Saône). Their name defines the topography of their territorial tribelands. Hence, their name may be taken to mean 'those who dwell on both sides of the River Arar'. In the fourth century BC the tribe were part of a wider confederation that included the Aedui, Andes, Arverni, Biturges, Lingones and Senones tribes, led by Ambicatus of the Biturges. In the year 57 BC, the Ambarri tribe surrendered to the Romans.

Ambiani

The Ambiani (or 'Ambiens') tribal name means the 'people of the border'. Their territory was around the River Somme in northern France, and their major settlement was at *Samarobriva*, which translates as 'Somme-bridge' (the modern-day city of Amiens, whose name is derived directly from the tribe). In 57 BC, the Ambiani supplied 10,000 warriors to a confederation led by Galba, the chieftain of the Suessiones, to fight the invading Romans under Julius Caesar, and in 52 BC a further 5000 Ambiani warriors attacked the legions that were besieging Vercingetorix's rebels at Alesia. Later still, under the Bellovaci chieftain Correus they fought to regain their territory from Roman rule. The Ambiani were finally subjugated by Julius Caesar in 51 BC. They were prolific minters of gold coinage, which is found throughout the territories of the Belgic tribes, including the Belgae people of Britain.

Ambidravi

The Ambidravi were a client tribe of the Taurisci confederation. They probably settled in the territory of Noricum, located on the upper reaches of the Dravus (the River Drave) near Teurnia, on the border with Italy sometime in the fourth century BC. Noricum, a kingdom under the control of a Celtic confederacy, was ruled over by the Taurisci, and reached as far as northern Italy, central Austria and parts of Bavaria in Germany. Later, as a Roman province it was called *Regnum Noricum* (the Kingdom of Noricum). Their tribal name implies 'both sides of the River Dravus'.

Ambisontes

The Ambisontes were a Gallic Iron Age La Tène people and a client tribe of the Taurisci, whose migration under Segovesus led them into Eastern Europe where they established settlements along the River Isonzo (Isontia) in former Yugoslavia and the River Salzach in Austria. Their tribal name translates as 'the people who live around the River Isontia'. According to Pliny the Elder, they were one of the tribes subjugated by Rome in 15 BC. Their name is included on the Arch of Susa, which commemorates Augustus' victories over the Alpine tribes.

Anamares

The Anamares (also known as 'Anare' and 'Anamari') were a Ligurian tribe whose settlement was at *Clastidium* (modern-day Casteggio), south of the Padus (the River Po) in the Gallia Cispadana province of the Roman Empire. They had been led across the Alps into Italy under the leadership of Bellovesus, chieftain of the Bituriges, sometime around 600 BC, as part of a migration of tribes that established a sizeable Celtic population in northern Italy. Little else is known of them apart from a brief reference in Polybuis' *Histories*, where he recorded that in 223 BC, 'Publius Furius Philus and Caius Flaminius once more invaded the Celtic lands, marching through the territory of the Anamares, who live not far from Placentia.'

Anartes

This La Tène descended tribe was also known as the 'Anartes', 'Anarti' or 'Anartoi', and had a name that means 'free men', and tends to imply that sometime back in their history they had been enslaved. The tribe occupied an ancient region of Dacia, roughly approximating to modern-day Romania and Croatia, as well as parts of modern Slovakia and south-eastern Poland. They are regarded as Dacian-Celts, as interracial mixing took place over time. For their failure to support Emperor Marcus Aurelius in the war against the Marcomanni, in 180 AD the entire tribe was deported from its homeland and relocated by force to the Roman province of Pannonia Inferior, beside the River Danube.

Andecaves

The Celtic tribe of the Andecaves (or 'Andegavi)' were known to Julius Caesar as the Andes. Their tribal territory was in Anjou, in the modern-day Maine-et-Loire Département, which the Romans called *Andegavia* (meaning 'the land of the Andecavi'). The tribe resisted the Romans after the surrender of Vercingetorix at Alesia, under the leadership of their chieftain Dumnacos (sometimes called 'Dumnac'), but they were finally defeated following a long Roman siege at *Lemonum* (Poitiers) by the Roman army under the command of Gaius Caninius Rebilus. When a large Roman relief column arrived, Dumnacos was forced to retreat from the engagement, but his army was pursued by the Romans and suffered heavy casualties in the battle that ensued, where it was recorded that some 12,000 Adecaves warriors died. However, Dumnacus escaped and went into self-imposed exile.

In 1887 a commemorative stone statue of Dumnacos by Louis Noël was erected at Ponts-de-Cé, in the middle of a bridge spanning the River Loire.

Ardyens

According to Polybius, the Ardyens (or 'Ardyes') were a Celtae tribe whose tribal territory covered an area stretching from the Upper Rhône valley to Lake Geneva in Switzerland. It was through their territory that the army of Hannibal travelled to cross the Alps into northern Italy and entered the Po Valley. In his *Histories*, Polybuis describes the course of the River Rhône, thus: 'For much of its course it flows through a valley, the northern side of which is inhabited by a Celtic tribe called the Ardyens, while the northern Piedmont of the Alps flank its entire southern side.' Little else is known about the tribe. Some authors believe that the Ardyans were actually Aedui or Helvetii.

Arecomici

The Arecomici, (also known as the 'Volcae Arecomici'), were a Gallic tribe whose territory lay between the Rhône and the Herault rivers and their main settlement was at *Nemausus Colonia*, (modern-day Nîmes), in south-west France. There are two views as to the origin of the placename: the settlement may have been named after the patron deity of the tribe, Deus Nemausus, or possibly took its name from the Heracleid Nemausios, the son of Heracles. Little else is known about these people except that they established around twenty-four large fortified Iron Age settlements or towns, (in Latin: 'oppidum') in the region. They surrendered to the Roman legions without resistance in 121 BC.

Arverni

The Arverni, (sometimes 'Arvernes'), were a Celtic tribe whose extensive territory covered much of the Auvergne region of central France with their main settlement at Gergovia, in the modern-day Puy-de-Dôme region around Clermont-Ferrand. However, according to the Greek historian Strabo, writing in the first century AD, the name of their capital was *Nemossos*, and its whereabouts are unknown.

They were the dominant force in the region in the second century BC, before they were defeated by the Romans in 121 BC. The earliest reference to the Arverni is in the works of the Roman historian Livy, who mentions them briefly as one of the major tribes of Gaul around 400 BC. Their tribal name is Gaulish and it has been suggested that it meant 'the people of the alder' or possibly 'the dwellers of tilled land'. The tribe worshipped the god Arvernus, and might have taken their name from that deity.

The tribe's most important historical figure was Vercingetorix, (whose name means 'high warrior king'). He was a nobleman who had once served as a Gaulish cavalryman in the Roman army, but who became outraged at the Roman takeover of traditional Arverni tribelands under the governorship of Julius Caesar, and spearheaded an armed revolt. His rebel confederation included the Senones, Parisii, Pictones, Cadurci, Turoni, Aulerci, Cenomai, Diablintes, Lemovices, Andes, the Armoricans and others. Eventually, the Romans cornered Vercingetorix in the Gergovia stronghold and after a protracted siege starved the rebels into submission, numbering 35,000 men according to Caesar. Vercingetorix surrendered himself to Caesar as a sacrifice to secure the freedom of his men. He was paraded through the streets of Rome in Caesar's triumphal procession, and died by strangulation in prison in the year 44 BC. Subsequently, the Averni people were defeated by the Consul Fabius Maximus, and stripped of all power to become vassals of the Roman Empire.

Arvii

The Arvii were a tribe of Gallia Lugdunensis, briefly mentioned by Greek geographer Ptolemy. Their capital was at a place that became the Roman city of *Vagoritum*, a name that means 'ford on the River Vaige', located on the present-day River Erve in the Départements of Sarthe and Mayenne; it was destroyed at the end of the second century AD but still goes by its French name, La Cité.

Aulerci

The Aulerci (or 'Aulercs') were a confederation of Gaulish tribes that the Romans identified as the Brannovices, the Cenomani, the Diablintes and the Eburovices, all of which were frequently prefixed with the word Aulerci by Ptolemy. Julius Caesar named the Aulerci and the Veneti among other maritime states, as clients of the more powerful Aedui. It is generally thought that in the Gaulish language the prefix 'aul' translates as 'small' and where Aulerci precedes tribal names it indicates 'the lesser'. Hence, for example, 'Aulerci Brannovices' means 'the lesser Brannovices', thereby indicating a small sub-branch of the Brannovices tribe.

During the sixth century BC, warriors of the Aulerci tribe and their clans left Germany and settled in the Pays de la Loire region of western France at the headwaters of the rivers Sarthe and Huisne. The Aulerci Eburovices founded two adjacent towns in the first century BC: one known as *Mediolanum Aulercorum* (present-day Evreux), which was their most important settlement and capital, and another at the town of Gisacum. After the Roman conquest, the city of Evreux became a major garrison town as part of the Roman province of Gallia Lugdunensis.

Avatici

The Avatici lived in an area of south-east Gaul, in the Roman province of Gallia Narbonensis during the Roman period. Little is known about this tribe, except for one historical figure that stands out. A man named Flavos, (or 'Flavius'), who was an important man of the Avatici tribe, a priest of the Imperial Cult and a Roman citizen, in whose honour the yellow limestone Pont Flavien Bridge over the River Touloubre near Nîmes was constructed following his death sometime between 20 and 10 BC. It is thought that Flavos' mausoleum once stood nearby, but no trace remains. A fortified Avatici settlement was also built at St Blaise in the third century BC, but was captured by Roman forces in 125 BC.

Bastarnae

The Bastarnae are thought to have originated as a Celtic tribe that at some point in its history mixed with Germanic and Sarmatian tribes. Their actual ethnicity was widely debated. In the third century AD, Cassius Dio defined the Bastarnae as Scythians. In his *Germania*, Tacitus thought that their '…mixed marriages are giving them to some extent the vile appearance of the Sarmatians'. Strabo thought they were a Germanic tribe. Polybius referred to them as Celtic Galatians. In fact the debate remains inconclusive as to whether they were actually of Scythian, Thracian, Germanic or Celtic origin. Such associations and merging of neighbouring friendly tribes was quite common among the ancient peoples of Europe.

As early as the fourth century BC their territorial homeland was in the region between the Carpathian Mountains around the River Dnieper, to the north and east of ancient Dacia (modern-day Transylvania, Romania), and the River Vistula, which forms part of present-day Poland. The first historical reference to the tribe was by Livy, who in 179 BC identified them as allies of King Philip V of Macedonia, to whom they supplied 20,000 mercenaries to fight alongside his army in the war with Rome. They were driven back across the Danube and finally subdued by Marcus Licinius Crassus in 29 BC, and thereafter appear as subject allies of Rome. By the sixth century AD, all trace of the Bastarnae had disappeared from historical records.

Bebryces

In the first century BC, the Bebryces occupied lands around modern-day Narbonne in south-west France. They were part of the sixth-century BC migration of Celtic Hallstatt tribes that came through Germany and Bohemia, before crossing the Alps into Gaul as well as establishing settlements in northern Spain. Strabo maintained that they were a Thracian tribe that came from Asia, but the general consensus is that they were a Celtic people. Unfortunately, their history has been somewhat overshadowed by the many myths surrounding them, including their supposed defeat at the hands of Heracles.

Belaci

The Belaci were a small tribe that lived around Ad Martis (the present-day Ouix, a commune of Turin), in the Cottian Alps bordering France and the northern Piedmont region of Italy during the Iron Age. Their name was listed in 8 BC as one of fourteen tribes on the Arch at Susa, celebrating Augustus' subjugation of the Alpine tribes by the Roman Governor, Marcus Julius Cottius.

Belgae

The Belgae were a large confederation of tribes whose territory occupied most of northern Gaul. During Julius Caesar's conquest, their territory covered the lands between the Seine and the mouth of the Rhine, and included parts of present-day France, Belgium, the Netherlands and Germany. The Romans knew the region as the province of Gallia Belgica, which would eventually give its name to Belgium. Caesar thought the Belgae were separated from the rest of Gaul by language, law and custom, and that they had Germanic ancestry.

In 54 BC, Ambioriix, the leader of the Belgic Eburones tribe, led the revolt against the advance of the Roman legions under Julius Caesar and resisted his subjugation of Gaul. It came to a head when, short of supplies, the Romans seized the Eburones' harvest, plunging its people into near starvation. The Greek historian Cassius Dio says: 'This war was begun by the Eburones, under Ambioriix as chief. They claimed they had been roused to action because they were annoyed at the presence of the Romans, who were commanded by Sabinus and Lucius Cotta, lieutenants.'

For Dio to say that the Eburones were 'annoyed' was an understatement. The war that ensued was a bloody affair; there were numerous battles and many Celtic fighters were slaughtered in defence of their tribelands. However, despite setbacks, the Celts went on to destroy an entire Roman legion. Caesar's response was to engage in an even bigger assault on the Eburones with a substantially greater number of legionaries. No quarter was given and according to contemporary accounts, the outcome was little short of genocide. Thereafter, the name of the Eburones was virtually expunged from all historical record. The tragedy forced many Belgae to flee across the English Channel and form new settlements in Britain.

Bellovaci

The Bellovaci (or 'Bellovaques') were a Belgic tribe who lived in the Picardy region of northern France from the Iron Age to the Roman era, with settlements established in the River Somme, Oise and Seine regions. The 'bell' element of their tribal name is generally taken to mean 'war', an indication of their warlike reputation. Julius Caesar regarded them as the bravest, largest and most powerful tribe in the Belgic confederation. Their main capital city was at *Bratuspantium*, which was known to the Romans as *Caesaromagus Bellovacum* (present-day Beauvais). Despite the Bellovaci mounting stiff resistance to Roman encroachment, a confederated army, reportedly amounting to around 100,000 men, which included 60,000 Bellovaci warriors, led by Galba, the chieftain of the Suessiones, was defeated by Caesar in 51 BC. The leaders of the Bellovaci uprising fled across the English Channel to join other Belgic groups in Britain.

Bituriges

The Biturges were a Gallic Celtic tribal federation that originated in modern-day Germany and left their homeland to settle in southern France between the rivers Indre and Creuse sometime between the twelfth and ninth centuries BC. The federation included the Biturges Cubi, the Biturges Segalaunes and the Biturgies Vivisques, of whom twelve settlements have been discovered. Around 500 BC, described by Livy as the most powerful Celtic tribe before the Roman Conquest, the Biturges broke into two separate groups: the Cubi, whose capital was at *Avaricum* (present-day Bourges), and the Vivisci held territory in the modern Bordelais region, around the River Garonne, with their capital at the seaport of *Burdigala* (modern-day Bordeaux), which the Romans called *Noviodunum*.

According to Livy, Ambicatus, leader of the Bituriges, founded the city of *Mediolanum* (modern-day Milan). The Gaulish tribal name, Bituriges, can be translated to mean 'kings of the world' or 'perpetual kings'. In the first century BC, the Cubi joined the Aedui confederation in their fight against Caesar. In 52 BC, their capital was destroyed together with its inhabitants by Caesar at *Cenabum* (present-day Orleans). Both Cubi and Vivisci groups were later merged into the Roman province of Aquitania.

Bodiocasses

The Bodiocasses, (sometimes 'Baiocasses' or 'Uadikasioi'), were a Gallic tribe whose territory was around Bayeux in the Normandy region of France, within the ancient Roman province of Gallia Lugdunensis. Modern-day Bayeux was known to the Romans as *Civitas Baiocassium* (meaning 'City of the Baiocasses'), from which the town name is derived. After Roman occupation Bayeux was known as *Augustoduron*, (meaning the 'fortress of Augustus'), which became a civitas and their chief town according to Pliny, and was renamed after the Emperor Augustus in the first century AD. Later forms of the city were Baiex and Baieux. The tribal name roughly translates as 'blond-haired' or 'yellow-blond', thought to be a physical characteristic of Celtic colouring at that time. The tribe became celebrated for their smelting of silver and gold, of which many old coins still survive and are highly valued.

Bodiontici

Also known as the 'Brodiontii' and the 'Bodiontics', the Bodiontici were a Gallic tribe whose territory was around present-day Mallemoisson in the Bléone valley of the Alpes-Maritimes region of south-east France. Their chief settlement was at Dinia (modern-day Digne-les-Bains). The tribe was subdued by Augustus between 23 and 13 AD and their name is included on the Arch of Susa, a 50-metre-high monument to the triumphs of the Emperor Augustus over the Alpine tribes. Later, in 69 AD, the Emperor Servius Galba included their settlement at Digne, (known as *Civitas Bodiontici* at that time), in the Roman province of Gallia Narbonensis, but in the third century it was returned to the Alpes-Maritimes province.

Boii

The Boii, (sometimes 'Boiens' or 'Boies'), were a central European Celtic tribe whose original territory was to the north of the Alps and east of the River Rhine, in present-day eastern Germany and the western Czech Republic. They are thought to

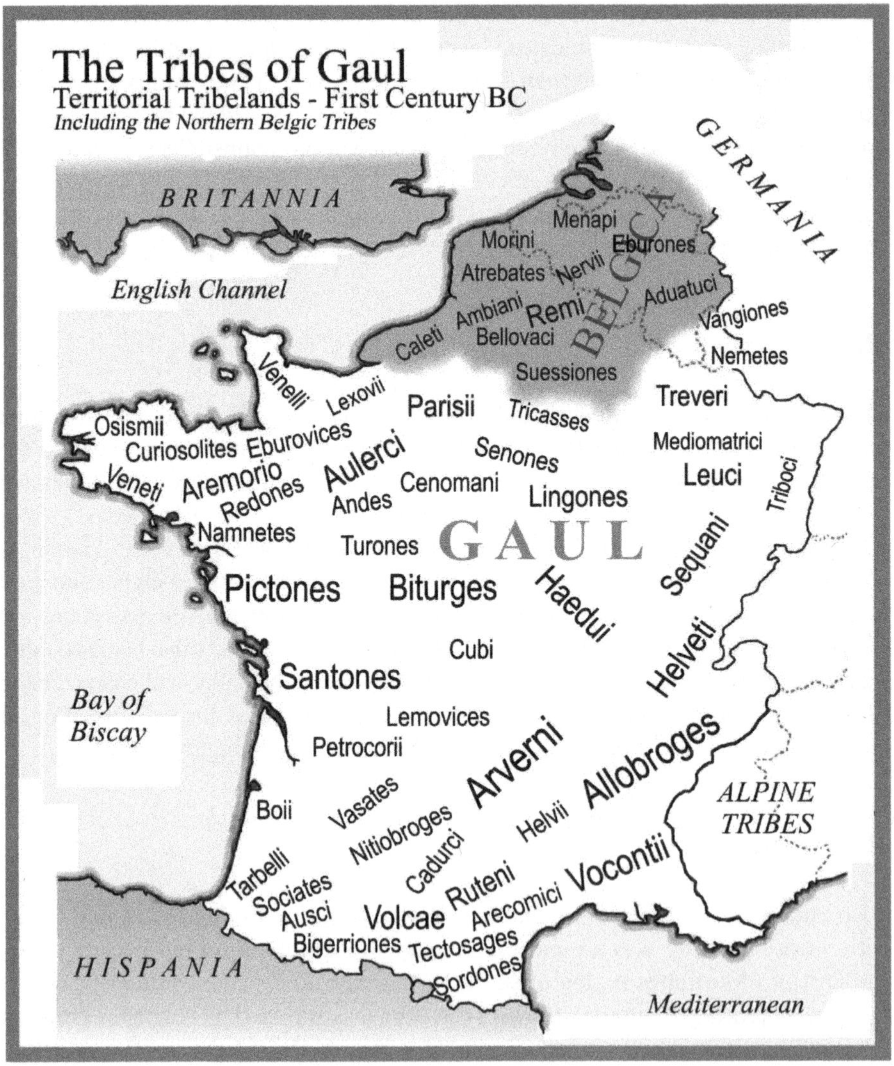

have been important migrant peoples who spread the Hallstatt and La Tène cultures widely across the continent.

At some time in their early history they split into two main groups, one of which made its way south into Italy and the other northwards into Germany. It was in 398 BC that a group of warriors of the Boii and Lingones tribes crossed the Pennine Alps, passing through the St Gotthard or Simplon Pass into the Po Valley and made fortified settlements in northern Italy.

Initially, they seem to have settled peacefully among the indigenous Etruscans and the two peoples intermarried. By the fourth century BC they had established settlements as far south as present-day Bologna and Modena, They also had settlements in Slovakia, Serbia, Hungary, Austria and Poland.

During the Second Punic War they fought against Roman invasion, and along with their Etruscan neighbours confronted a Roman army, but were defeated, many withdrawing to relocate in Bohemia, where there had been Boii settlements since at least the fifth century BC.

The tribe gave their name to Bohemia ('Boiohaemum'), meaning 'home of the Boii people'. The Boii submitted to Rome in 225 BC and by the first century had become fully integrated into the Roman republic.

Brannovices

The Brannovices, (in the Gaulish language, 'Brannouices'), were sometimes recorded as 'Aulerci Brannovices', (meaning 'the lesser Brannovices'), indicating a small sub-group of the Aulerci confederation. They were a Gallic tribe whose territory, according to some, was in the present-day Yonne Département of the Saône Valley of France around Lyon. Others place their tribeland around the district of Mâcon – the debate is ongoing. Yet others have argued that Ariolica was an important settlement of the Aulerci Brannovices tribe, which has been identified with the modern-day Commune of La Pacaudière in the Loire region of France. Their name translates as 'raven-fighters'. This derives from the Gaulish word 'branos', meaning 'raven', a commonly used clan totem and anciently used as a metaphor for a leader or fighter. The suffix '-vices' or '-uices' probably translates as 'victors'.

Brigantii

The Brigantii (or 'Brigantes') were a Gallic tribe living in an area south-east of Lake Constance, which borders Switzerland, Germany, and Austria. In Latin, the lake was known as *Lacus Brigantinus*, reflecting the name of the people who lived around it. The tribal name had the same origins as that of the Brigantes in Britain and Ireland, who probably migrated to Ireland around 500 BC. It is not clear whether the tribe was named after their patron goddess Brigantia or else the goddess was named after the tribe who venerated her. Their main settlement was at *Brigantion* (modern-day Bregenz in Austria). According to Julius Caesar, the Brigantii waged continual war against the Germanic tribes who lived on the opposite banks of the Rhine.

Buri

Ptolemy related the Buri tribe to what he called the 'Lougoi Bouroi', (which translates as 'Lugi Buri' in Latin), and reported that they lived in an area of southern Poland between the River Elbe and the upper Vistula. Their capital city was at Buridava, beside the River Aluta, (now the Olt), in a region the Romans later called Dacia Apulensis (modern-day Romania). In the fifth century BC, together with the Suebi tribe, (with whom they may have formed a confederation), they invaded the Iberian Peninsula and settled in the mountains of northern Portugal, in a region between the River Cavado and the River Homem, an area now known as Terras de Bouro, which translates as 'Lands of the Buri'.

In his *Germania*, Tacitus stated that in their language and manner of life, the Buri closely resembled the Suebi, which implied that like many other Germanic tribal settlers in Bohemia and Moravia, they had recently come from the direction of the Baltic Sea. Unlike Ptolemy, Tacitus saw no direct link between the Buri and Lugi tribes. It is thought that the Buri were probably a hybrid tribe of a mixed Celtic-Germanic peoples, and that their tribal name may have come from the proto-Celtic word 'bou-rigo', (or in Gaulish, 'bo-rix'), which taken together incorporate the words 'cow' and 'king', or in its simplest form, 'cattle kings'. It is probable that at some time in prehistory a group of German warriors took over an earlier Celtic tribe, or drove them out, as was thought to be the case with the Celtic Boii tribe.

Cadurci

The Cadurci, (sometimes 'Cadurques' or 'Carduci'), were a Gallic tribe of Aquitania whose territory was around the River Lot, in the modern-day Dordogne region of south-western France, and their main settlement was at the town of Divona. Their tribal name is derived from the proto-Celtic word 'kados', meaning 'to anger', and the name is generally taken to be translated more generally as 'angry people'. They were among the last of the Gallic tribes to offer resistance to the Romans and in 51 BC together with warriors of the Senones tribe, led by Drappes, they withdrew into their stronghold in the hill-fort at Uxellodunum, which was near the modern-day French village of Vayrac. The fort suffered a siege by forces commanded by Julius Caesar, and in his *Gallic Wars*, he describes it as the last revolt against Rome's authority in Gaul. Beaten into submission, their water supply cut off and starving, the Cadurci were eventually defeated. After they surrendered they were brutally punished, as was the Roman custom; it was reported that hundreds of Cadurci warriors had their hands cut off as punishment for their resistance. Caesar made the point of making an example of them as a warning to any other tribes who might consider defying Rome. Some sources have as many as 12,000 Gauls being killed, either in the action or in retribution afterwards. The tribe was one of the earliest to become Romanised, having submitted to Rome in 51 BC. Their tribal name was reflected in their main centre, the city of *Divona Cadurcorum* (now Cahors), named after the Celtic goddess Divona ('the Divine One').

Caerosi

The Caerosi (or 'Caeroesi') were a small Belgic-Germanic tribe of Gallia Belgica during the Roman period. Their origin is obscure, though in the first century BC, Julius Caesar saw them as part of the Germani Cisrhenani tribe, whose name may be derived from a proto-Celtic source. In his *Gallic Wars*, he wrote that they were '...called by the common name of Germani'. Their territory was in the Ardennes and Eifel region, between the River Rhône and the River Meuse. Despite Caesar's assertion that they were Germanic, they could equally have been Belgic Celts – no one is quite sure of their precise ethnicity, as inter-tribal mixtures, such as Belgae, Germans and Celts, were not unusual at that time.

In 57 BC, along with a confederation of around a dozen other Belgic and Celtic tribes including the Nervii, Viromandui and Atrebates, the Caerosi, led by Galba, chieftain of the Suessiones tribe, faced eight Roman legions amounting to between 35,000 and 40,000 men on the River Sambre, and were savagely defeated at what became known as the Battle of Sabis. The Caerosi tribal name means 'sheep (or deer) people'.

Caletes

The Caletes, (or 'Caleti', or in Gaulish, 'Caletoi'), were a Gallic tribe dwelling near the Sequana (the River Seine), in the Pays de Caux region of present-day Normandy. Their tribal name translates as 'hard or stubborn people' or simply 'hard or tough men'. They were a seafaring people, part of the Belgae confederation. They constructed three fortified villages on the right bank of the Seine estuary, at Lillebonne (*Juliobona*), Ingouville, and Harfleur (*Caracotinum*), to protect themselves against pirates and to shelter their fishing boats. In 57 BC, the Caletes sent 10,000 to a Belgae federation, commanded by Galba, chieftain of the Suessiones, to resist Julius Caesar's conquest of Belgian Gaul, and later, in 52 BC, a contingent of 20,000 Caletes warriors joined Vercingetorix at the besieged settlement at Alesia.

Calucones

The Calucones are thought to have been originally Celts, possibly Belgae, who became dominated by an influx of Germanic tribes that prompted the decline of their Celtic culture and language. They are thought to have been a Gallic or Rhaetian tribe that lived around *Curia Rhaetorum* ('Chur', or present-day Curia) in the eastern Swiss Canton of Grisons at the time of the Romans. In Book Two of his *Geographia*, the historian Ptolemy identifies a settlement of a people he called *Kaloukones*, (in Greek, Καλουκόνης), living on the bank of the River Elbe. The Calucones were one of several Alpine tribes that, according to the writings of Cassius Dio, were subjugated in 15 BC by a Roman army led by Drusus and Tiberius, stepsons of the Roman Emperor Augustus. After their defeat, many of the male population were deported or enslaved, while others were conscripted as auxiliaries into the Roman army. Along with the other Alpine tribes they eventually succumbed to Roman culture and over time became Romanised.

Carni

The Carni were an Alpine mountain tribe who lived in the Carnic Alps, known in Roman times as the *Alpes Carnicae*, in Austrian East Tyrol, bordering north-east Italy. They founded the city of Akilega in 186 BC, which was renamed Aquileia by the Romans after the subjugation of the tribe. During this first Roman conquest, Claudius Cassius ordered that thousands of Alpine tribespeople should be taken into slavery. The Carni were finally beaten into submission by the Roman legions commanded by consul Marcus Aemilius Scaurus, who defeated them in battle in 115 BC.

Carnutes

The main territories of the Carnutes (or 'Carnuti') were around *Cenabum* (present-day Orleans) and *Autricum*, (also known as *Carnutes*, which survives today as Chartres) in northern France. Their ancestral tribelands were widely regarded as the political and religious centre of the Gallic nation. In 57–56 BC, Julius Caesar sent his troops to make their winter quarters in Carnutes territory upon which civic unrest and resentment boiled over, and when a group of tribesmen slaughtered Romans that were billeted in the town of Cenabum it set in motion widespread rebellion against Roman occupation. Consequently, the Carnutes were one of the first to join Vercingetorix in his open revolt against Rome in 52 BC. During the uprising some 12,000 warriors joined his rebel army. But, after the failure of the rebellion and Vercingetorix's capture, the Carnutes were repeatedly attacked by Roman auxiliaries and eventually defeated at the Battle of Alesia in 51 BC. The settlement was burnt to the ground and its inhabitants executed or sold into slavery. Their chieftain, Gutruatos, was subsequently flogged to death and his severed head paraded before his people as a warning to others. Thereafter, some of the surviving Carnutes resettled in Aremorica (Brittany), while the remainder came under Roman control, as did much of Gaul.

Caturiges

The Caturiges (or 'Caturigae') were a small Alpine tribe whose territory was in the Durance Valley and covered much of the present-day French-Italian border and western Switzerland in the first century BC. Their main centre was at *Caturiomagus* (whose name translates as the 'market town of the Caturiges') in south-eastern France, close to the Italian border, and is nowadays known as Chorges.

In 58 BC, together with the Ceutrones and Graioceli tribes, the Caturiges faced two Roman legions sent by Julius Caesar to Bibracte where they engaged a combined Alpine tribal army in battle, following which the tribes were roundly defeated and forced to return to their homelands. In his *Gallic Wars*, Caesar recorded: 'There the Ceutrones, the Graioceli and the Caturiges, who had occupied the dominant positions, try to forbid the passage to his army.' The Caturiges were finally subdued with many other Alpine tribes in 16 BC, after which their territory was incorporated into the Roman Empire. Their name is listed as one of the vanquished Alpine tribes on the Arch of Susa.

Cavari

The Cavari (or 'Cavares') lived on the east bank of the River Rhône as far as its junction with the Isère, in the Vaucluse region around modern-day Avignon in south-eastern France. They were the dominant tribe of a confederation that included the Tricastini, Segovellauni and Memini. The Cavari established a hill-fort at Colline St Eutrope, overlooking a settlement called *Arausio*, (the modern-day town of Orange), which was taken by Julius Caesar in 52 BC. They had other settlements at Avignon and Cavaillon. Little else is known, except that Strabo said that they had become Romanised by the early first century AD.

Cenomani

In the fifth century BC, together with the Caturiges, Centrones, Medulli, Volcae Arcomici and the Volcae Tectosages tribes, the Cenomani left their homeland in Bavaria-Bohemia and migrated to France. According to Cato, they were one of the migratory Gallic tribes that at an early period crossed into Italy and formed a settlement near Massilia (Marseilles). In 390 BC, led by their chieftain,

Elitovios, and accompanied by the Andes tribe, another group of Cenomani settled between the rivers Adda and Adige, south of Lake Garda, before settling in the Po Valley of northern Italy, between present-day Verona and Cremona, an area known as Cisalpine Gaul, during the first century BC. During the third and second centuries BC, along with the Veneti, they were allied with the Romans against other Gallic tribes. The Cenomani had earlier sided with Rome when Hannibal crossed the Alps in 218 BC. Eventually, in 49 BC they became Roman citizens and Cisalpine Gaul was formally taken into the Roman Empire in 42 BC, at which time the former Cenomani territory was given over to Roman army veterans.

Centrones

The original tribal homeland of the Centrones, (sometimes spelled as 'Ceutrones'), was in present-day Bavaria and Bohemia, but during the fifth century BC they migrated to settle around the River Isère in the Tarentaise Valley of the Savoy region on the western slopes of the French Alps. They were accompanied by the Caturiges, Cenomani, Medulli, Volcae Arcomici and Volcae Tectosages tribes. Pliny terms their new territory as 'Alpes Centironicae' after the Centrones. The tribe established its capital at a place called Axima, which the Romans renamed *Forum Claudii Ceutronum* during the reign of Claudius after their subjugation; later it became the town of Alpes Graiae, before finally emerging as *Darantasia* (present-day Moutiers en Tarentaise). The tribal name 'Centrones' is thought to translate as 'the thorns', a possible reference to spear points.

According to Strabo, in 218 BC, the Centrones held a meeting with Hannibal, as he made his way through their territory during his crossing of the Alps. Under apparent protest, Centrones warriors agreed to guide the Carthaginian army for two days through the treacherous mountains, (probably via the Petit St Bernard Pass), before they finally turned against them having led them into an ambush at a place where the pass narrowed. Centrones warriors exacted such fierce attrition on the Carthaginians that by the time Hannibal's army had left Centrones territory, its numbers were significantly depleted and many of their pack animals had been slaughtered with a great loss of provisions and supplies.

Polybius described one of the Centrones assaults on the Roman army led by Julius Caesar as it passed through the Alpes Cottiae to Lake Bourget in 58 BC. From a high mountain viewpoint, they inflicted devastating losses of life on the Romans.

The Centrones were converted to Christianity in the fifth century AD.

Cimbri

The Cimbri have been variously described as a Celtic people, as a Gaulish tribe and as Germanic in origin. Such is the confusion brought about by peoples who had no written language, and about whom few contemporary sources exist. However, the prevailing opinion is that the Cimbri tribal name is Celtic, and translates as 'compatriots', a clear indication that they regarded themselves as a people with a common background and heritage. It has been proposed that the tribe may indeed have been of German stock, but were overseen by a noble Celtic elite; but this is largely supposition.

Most accounts suggest that they lived in Jutland, in present-day northern Denmark, which was earlier known as the Cimbrian Peninsula. Their numbers soon outgrew the Danish tribeland and together with the Teutoni and other tribes, they migrated south, encountering the legions as they progressed into Roman Empire lands. Their leader was a man called Boiorix, (literally meaning 'king of the Boii'), a chieftain of the Boii tribe of Celts that dominated most of central Europe at that time.

In 105 BC, following a series of victories, they managed to defeat a Roman army commanded by Gaius Marius at Arausio, (present-day Orange, in France). Finally, in 101 BC, a combined Roman force led by Quintus Lutatius Catulus confronted the Cimbri at Campi Raudii near Vercellae (present-day Vercelli in the Piedmont region), and the entire Cimbri army was virtually destroyed. Those few prisoners who survived the battle were taken back to Rome where they were sold into slavery or forced to fight in the ring as gladiators. This battle is seen as the final chapter of the Germanic threat to the Roman Republic.

Chalbici

The Chalbici were a tribe of the Narbonensis region, who were part of the Allobroges confederation and held land around Chablais, in the Savoy region, on the north coast of Lake Geneva. They were part of an army reputedly numbering 180,000 men, (probably an exaggerated number), that fought at the Battle of Vindalium on the banks of the River Isara against a Roman army led by Consul Quintus Fabius Maximus in 121 BC. Along with the Allobroges and the Gallic confederation, the Chalbici were routed in the engagement and thereafter little else is known of them.

Condrusi

The Condrusi were one of the peoples described by Julius Caesar as *Germani Cisrhenani*, although some scholars insist that they were either Belgic Celts, or possibly a Celtic people who were subject to Belgic rulers. The tribe probably lived in the Condroz region of the Ardennes as clients of the neighbouring Treveri, a more powerful tribe who acted as their protectors. Caesar listed the Condrusi among the Eburones, the Caeroesi and the Paemani, all of whom joined a confederation of Belgic and Germanic tribes against Roman occupation in 57 BC. The alliance was defeated by the Roman legions at the Battle of the Sabis. Following this event, the tribe initially became part of the *Civitas Tungrorum* in the Roman province of Gallia Belgica, but later became part of the region that the Romans called Germania Inferior.

Convenes

The Convenes (or 'Convenae') were a tribe that occupied territory on the north side of the Pyrenees in the modern-day Aquitaine, in the southern half of the Département of Haute-Garonne in the upper Garonne Valley. They were a tribal confederation that included the Bigerrions and the Consoranes. The historian Strabo identified five towns that had natural water springs in Convenae territory, including *Thermae Onesorium* (Bagnères-de-Luchon) and *Aquae Convenarum* (Capbern). He described their territory thus: '…close to the Pyrenees is the country of the Convenae, that is, of those who were a mixed people; where there is a town Lugdunum, and the warm springs of the Onesii.' The town that the Romans called *Lugdunum Convenarum*, later renamed Convenae, has been identified as Sainte Bertrand de Cominge in the district of Cominge. Lugdunum became a capital city (a 'civitas'); it was extensively developed by the Romans and formed an important administrative centre for the Romanisation of the whole region. The tribal name is derived from the Roman elements 'con', meaning 'together' or 'with', and 'ueni', signifying 'clan', 'tribe' or 'family'. Hence, taken together the name might be interpreted as 'those of the same clan or tribe'.

Cotini

According to Tacitus the Cotini were vassals of the powerful Quadi Germanic people, and part of the Suebi confederation, but spoke the Celtic language. Cassius Dio, in a reference to the Marcomannic Wars (166–180 AD), said the Cotini were identical to the Germanic tribe of Gothini, who inhabited Moravia, east of Bohemia on the borders of the modern-day Czech Republic, Poland and Slovakia.

The tribe founded a major settlement at Liptovská Mara in Slovakia in the third century BC. It was here that they became known for mining and metalworking technologies and their work in silver was much prized by the Romans. However, in the year 179 AD the Emperor Marcus Aurelius, accompanied by his son, Commodus, invaded Cotini territory, intending to annex it to the Roman Empire by applying a scorched earth policy which devastated the tribe. Those who survived were resettled in the Roman province of Pannonia, which at that time included present-day Austria, Hungary, Slovenia, Croatia and Serbia.

Cugerni

The Cugerni (or 'Cuberni') were a small obscure tribe that settled on the western bank of the River Rhine in a region that the Romans called Germania Inferior. Their culture derived from the Celtic La Tène people and is often described as Germanic. However, this is a hangover from Julius Caesar's categorisation of all inhabitants of the east bank of the Rhine as 'Germani'. Their main settlement and capital was called *Cibernodorum* near present-day Xanten, in the North Rhine-Westphalia region of Germany. The settlement name of Cibernodorum translates as 'market place of the Cugerni'.

In 69 AD, together with the Batavians, Chauci, Tencteri, Bructeri and Sinuci tribes, the Cugerni rose up in rebellion against Rome in reaction to the forced conscription imposed upon them. Order was restored a year later by General Petillius Cerialis, and the Cugerni capital was renamed *Colonia Ulpia Traiana* after the Emperor Trajan. Thereafter, numbers of Cugerni tribesmen were created a new Roman legion, as the *Cohors I Ulpia Traiana Cugernorum*, (the First Cohort Ulpian Trajan Cugernian) and posted to Britain, where they were stationed at Carrawburgh on Hadrian's Wall, then to Cramond in Scotland, before moving back to Newcastle in Northern England. The tribal name, Cugerni, is thought to mean something like 'spears together'.

Daliterni

The Daliterni tribal name was derived from the River Dala, and was an ancient name of the Veragri, one of a group of Gallic tribes living between Lake Geneva and the Pennine Alps in the Valais Canton of modern-day Switzerland. Their main settlement and capital was as *Octodurus* (modern-day Martigny). According to Livy, they were a mixed Germanic and Gallic tribe. In 56 BC, together with the Seduni tribe, the Veragri combined to fight the Roman General Servius Galba, who had billeted his Twelfth Legion and accompanying cavalry in their territory without seeking permission and demanded that the local tribes supply his army with corn and other provisions. Moreover, he looked likely to establish a permanent base there. After a series of setbacks, Galba's army finally defeated the rebellious tribes at the Battle of Octodurus. According to Julius Caesar's over-inflated account, about one-third of the 30,000 tribesmen were killed.

Dexivates

The Dexivates were a Gallic tribe mentioned by Pliny the Elder as living in what he called *Regio Dexivatium*, ('the region of the Dexivates'), which he located next to that of the Cavares, around Avignon in south-eastern France. It is thought that their tribal name derives from their veneration of the goddess Dexsiva. It was suggested by Strabo that the Dexivates may have become integrated into the Salyan confederation.

Durocasses

The Durocasses, (or 'Durocassae'), were a small Gallic tribe, possibly a sub-group of the Carnutes, whose major settlement was at *Durocassium* (present-day Dreux) in the Eure-et Loire Département of north-western France. The settlement lay along the Blaise River, north-west of Chartres where the Romans had established a fortified camp known as *Castrum Drocas*, (or 'Drocae'). Over time Drocae was shortened to Dreux. The tribal name probably derives from 'duro', meaning 'hard', and 'cass' or 'cat', meaning 'battle'. In common parlance the name may be taken to mean something like 'hard (or tough) fighters'. An alternative hypothesis argues that the '-casses' element of the tribal name, in common with others such as the Bodiocasses, Durocasses, Sucasses, Veliocasses and Viducasses, may signify 'curly hair', a possible reference to a type of hairstyle seen among certain Celtic warrior classes at that time.

Eburones

Together with the Caerosi, Condrusi and the Paemani, the Eburones were one of the four tribes that Julius Caesar designated as 'Germani'. In fact, they are nowadays regarded as Belgic Celts, whose territorial tribelands were between the River Rhine and on both sides of the River Meuse, north of the Ardennes near Limburg, in what is now part of present-day Netherlands.

In late 54 BC, the Fourteenth Roman Legion was attacked by a force of up to 40,000 Eburones warriors led by King Ambioriix in a revolt against the advance of the Roman legions under Caesar and his planned subjugation of Gaul. The Romans were soundly routed in the confrontation; its survivors reported back to Rome that the Eburones had annihilated what had once been their well-trained and heavily armed legion.

In 53 AD Caesar returned with an even larger force and retaliated by massacring the entire Eburones tribe. According to Livy, their leader Ambiorix managed to escape, but his co-leader Catuvolcus took his own life. Roman retribution was so comprehensive that, according to Caesar's own unconfirmed account, the Eburones had ceased to exist thereafter.

Edenates

The Edenates, (sometimes spelled 'Edanates' or 'Adanates'), were a small Celto-Ligurian tribe living in the Cottian Alps of the Alpes-de-Hautes-Provence

Département of France during the Iron Age. Their capital was in the border town of La Seyne (La Seyne-sur-Mer) in the Maurienne Valley. Like many other Alpine peoples, the Edanates mounted stiff resistance to the Romans and according to Pliny, the Edenates were one of the Alpine tribes conquered by Augustus' stepsons Drusus and Tiberius in 16 BC. After this time they were integrated into the Roman province of the Alpes Cottiae. Their tribal name may have meant 'those from the land (or country)'. In the township of La Turbie, near Monaco in the south of France, a twelfth-century monument dedicated to the Emperor Augustus lists the Edenates among forty-five other '…Alpine nations who live between the Adriatic and Tyrrhenian Seas, and were submitted to the Empire of the Roman people'.

Eduens

One of Gaul's most powerful tribes, the Eduens settled near the River Saône in the Bourgogne region of central France, where they built the fortified town of Bibracte at the top of Mont Beuvray as their capital in the second century BC. The site is now listed in the Registry of Historical Monuments and Sites of France. Initially, at the time of the Roman conquest, Dumnorix, the chieftain of the tribe, forged an alliance with the Roman Republic to avoid open warfare and to derive the kind of advantageous trading terms and economic benefits that such accommodations offered. However, appalled by the massacre of Avaricum and the Roman brutality under the command of Caesar, he ended the alliance. Avaricum, (present-day Bourges), was the capital city of the Biturges Cubi tribe. Following that event, the Eduens were one of the tribes that joined Vercingetorix and the Arvernii in 52 BC to fight against Caesar in his conquest of the Gauls.

Elesyces

The Elesyces, (also known as 'Helisyci', 'Elisyques' and 'Elyseens'), were a tribe of Ligurian origin who migrated from Spain and settled in the northern Roussillon region around Nîmes and Narbonne in the south of France in the fourth century BC. Their capital and main settlement was at Enserune, near the present-day city of Beziers. In his *Histories*, Herodotus mentions the Elesyces as a tribe from western Languedoc who fought alongside Ligurians against Carthaginian troops in the Battle of Himera in Sicily in 480 BC.

In his poem *Ora Maritima*, the fourth-century poet Avienius wrote that '…the tribe of the Elesyces inhabited …the city of Narbo (present-day Narbonne) which was the great capital of a warlike kingdom'. His poem is regarded as important in a historical sense in that it records references to more than fifty ancient places and peoples of Gaul and Iberia.

Elusates

The Elusates were a small tribe of the Aquitainian people, (sometimes referred to as proto-Basque), who settled in what today is south-western France, around the city (oppidum) of Elusa, (present-day Eauze), on the banks of River Gelise in the French Département of Gers. Little is known of this tribe, but by the end of the third century the Sotiates tribe had been incorporated into their number, and following a period of stiff resistance they were subdued in 56 BC by a Roman army under the command of Legatus Publius Crassus. Elusa became a civitas capital and later a colonia of Roman Gaul. The city of Eauze takes its name from the tribe.

Epomandui

The Epomandui were a small tribe living round Montbeliard, a town in the Doubs Département in the Bourgogne-Franche-Comte region in eastern France. Together with the Aulerci Brannovices and the Mandubians, they were probably a client or sub-group of the powerful Aedui tribe. Their name means 'warriors of the horse', a reference no doubt to their equine skills, so-named on account of their veneration of the Celtic goddess Epona, who was always represented on horseback and later became a popular deity among Roman cavalrymen.

Esuvii

The Esuvii, (in Gaulish, 'Esuuii', or in Latin, 'Esubii', and sometimes known as 'Sesuvii'), were a small Gallic people who held territory in the Orne Département of north-western France, between the lower Seine and the Loire rivers in Normandy. Their main settlement and capital was at Exmes, a few miles from Argentan. They may have been a sub-group of the Aulerci tribe and a group of the Esuvii were probably some of the earliest migrants to inhabit the Channel Island of Jersey. The Baiocasses, the Viducasses, and the Saii tribes formed part of an enlarged Esuvii Confederation. According to an account in Julius Caesar's *De Bello Gallico* (on the Gallic Wars) the Esuvii were one of the tribes from whom Crassus requisitioned corn on his campaign to conquer Normandy and Brittany. Their tribal name is thought to relate to their worship of the Gaulish god Esus (or Hesus), who the Romans identified with Mercury and Mars, the god of war.

Germani Cisrhenani

During the Gallic Wars of the first century BC, the Romans under Julius Caesar used the Latin expression *cis-rhenanus*, (which translates as 'this side of the

Rhine'), in reference to the western side of the river, which lay within the bounds of the Roman Empire. The Romans considered the River Rhine as the eastern limit of their empire in Gaul and a natural border beyond which lay the rest of the world. The territory on the left bank, the eastern side, outside of the Empire, they called *Germania Transrhenana*, (that side of the Rhine), and its tribal people they called 'Germani'; according to Caesar they included the Eburones, the Condrusi, the Caeraesi, the Segni and the Paemani.

Graioceli

The Graioceli, (sometimes known as the 'Garocelli'), were a small Alpine tribe living in western Switzerland and the Maurienne Valley of France. They are difficult to classify in that their original Celtic ancestry would almost certainly have become mixed with the Ligurian tribes in the area where they had settled. Consequently, they are sometimes referred to as 'Celtic-Ligurians'. The Graioceli were one of the tribes who supported the Helvetii in their attempt to stop six Roman legions, amounting to between 24,000 and 30,000 troops, commanded by Julius Caesar, from advancing through the Alps in 58 BC. Unfortunately the tribal alliance was defeated at the decisive Battle of Bibracte and was pushed back into their homeland. Caesar claimed that of the 368,000 barbarians, only 110,000 returned home. Strabo revised Caesar's figure, claiming that only about 8000 Alpine warriors survived the battle. How many of these were of the Graiceli tribe we shall never know.

Helvetii

The Helvetii (also known as 'Helvetians') were the largest of about eleven Celtic tribes that migrated from the south of modern-day Germany and settled in what would become Switzerland sometime between 500 BC and 400 AD. Their territory was known as Helvetia, a name that has survived as the Latin name of Switzerland. The Greek writer Poseidonios described them as 'a peaceful people, rich in gold'.

The Helvetian tribes, of which only the Tulingi and Latobrigi were named by Caesar, began a mass migration southwards to the south of France in 58 BC, having burned their Swiss settlements to the ground, which according to Caesar amounted to about 12 strongholds and 100 villages. Their intended route would take them through the Roman province of Gallia Narbonensis. It was reported that en route they badly treated the resident tribes of the province, among them the Aedui, the Ambarri and the Allobroges. When Caesar heard this he despatched an army to intercept them; a bloody battle ensued and they were halted at the Arar (the

River Saône). The Helvetii were routed in the engagement and the remainder fled, followed close at heel by the Romans, who put all they could find to the sword.

The Helvetii fought one last engagement against six Roman legions at the Battle of Bibracte later that same year, but were soundly defeated; captured Helvetii were sold into slavery and the surviving tribal leaders sued for peace. The remnant of this once large and powerful people was allowed to return to their territories and to rebuild their homes. Like most of Gaul, the Helvetians came under the yoke of Roman domination and by the second century AD they had become completely Romanised.

Histri

The Histri, (sometimes spelled 'Istri'), have been variously described as Venetic, Illyrian and Thracian. Their territory was on the Istrian Peninsula, the largest on the Adriatic, and spanned parts of modern-day Croatia, Italy and Slovenia. They were described by the Romans as fierce pirates. It took two bitter campaigns before they were finally subdued and their capital city of Nesactim, the royal seat of King Epulon, was destroyed in 177 BC by the *Legio X Venetia et Histria*, (the Tenth Venetia & Histria Legion), commanded by Gaius Sempronius Tuditanus. The city was rebuilt and remained a Roman town until 46 BC. The area was abandoned in the sixth century. Pliny the Elder described Tudutanius as 'the conqueror of the Istrians'.

Insubres

The Insubres were a powerful Celtic people who occupied a territory between the Alps and the Apennine Mountains north of the River Po in northern Italy around Mediolanum, (Milan), a region known by the Romans as Gallia Cisalpina. According to Livy they were a sub-branch of the Aedui tribe, who crossed the Alps, fought a victorious battle with the resident Etruscans and established settlements there. In 225 BC, the Insubres, joined by the Boii, Senones and Lingones tribes, rebelled against Rome. The Romans mounted an attack against the tribe in 223 BC, and though the Insubres sued for peace, their offer was rejected and they eventually surrendered. There were several other clashes, but in 194 BC the Insubres finally made an alliance with Rome and by 49 BC they had become Roman citizens and were granted a degree of autonomous rule.

Laevi

The Laevi were a tribe of Cisalpine Gauls, who co-occupied territory with the Insubres. Polybuis maintained that they were one of half a dozen Gaulish tribes who had crossed the Alps and settled about the Ticinus (the River Ticino), a tributary of the Po, in Northern Italy, an area known to the Romans as Gallia Transpadana. Livy and Pliny both regarded them as Ligurians, but nowadays they are regarded as Celto-Ligurian, an admixture of both. Along with the Marici tribe, the Laevi founded the city of *Ticinum* (modern-day Pavia), but it was later taken over by the Insubres. The geographer Ptolemy actually listed it among the cities of the Insubres, and for some time it was regarded as such, even though it was not Insubrian in origin.

Lemovices

The Lemovices were a Gallic tribe that settled in the present-day Limousin region of the Haute-Vienne Département and included Creuse, Corrèze, and part of Charente sometime between 700 and 400 BC. The tribe gave their name to the city of Limoges. The tribal name translates as 'conquerors with the elm', a probable reference to the elm branches used as hafts to their spears. Their main oppidum (city) was called *Durotincum* (modern-day Villejoubert), but after their subjugation it was renamed *Augustoritum Lemovicum* by the Romans. In 52 BC, 10,000 Lemovices warriors, led by their chief Sedullos, joined in Vercingetorix's rebellion against Caesar during the Gallic Wars. In the engagement at the Battle of Alesia, Sedullos was killed, the tribe was routed and following their subjugation, Lemovices territory was subsumed into the Roman province of Aquitania.

Lepontii

In the first century AD, the Lepontii, (or 'Leponzi'), were a Celtic Alpine tribe who occupied the Roman province of Rhaetia, which corresponded to modern-day Switzerland and northern Italy. They lived on the Southern Alps, (known to the Romans as 'Alpes Lepontiae'), overlooking Lake Como and Lake Maggiore. A debate continues as to Lepontii origins – some say they were Celtic, others Raetian and yet others that they were Germanic. The chief town was *Oscela*, (present-day Domodossola), in Italy. They spoke a language called Lepontic, which is closely related to the Celtic branch of the Indo-European language family.

Leuci

The Leuci were a Belgic tribe who occupied a territory in the Roman province of Gallia Belgica, in the upper reaches of the Mosella (the River Moselle) and the Mosa (the River Meuse), in the southern part of the present-day Lorraine region of France. Julius Caesar identified them as one of the tribes, along with the Lingones and Sequani, who supplied grain to feed his army in the campaign against Ariovistus, the king of the Germans in 58 BC. Their tribal name is derived from Celtic 'leucos', meaning 'white', 'shining', 'bright' or 'clear', earning them the title of 'the Whites'. They were called 'Leucos' by Julius Caesar, 'Leukoi' by Strabo and 'Leuci' by Pliny. Their main settlement and capital was at *Tullum* (present-day Toul), and they held a substantially fortified hill-fort at Boviolles in the Ornan Valley and smaller ones in the Vosges Mountains near the German border.

Lingones

The Lingones originally occupied territory around the River Seine and the River Marne, but sometime around 400 BC, groups of Celtic tribes, including the Lingones, the Boii and the Senoni, migrated across the Alps and settled in the Po River Valley of northern Italy. Their occupation came at the expense of the Etruscans, whose land it had formerly been. Archaeological studies have established that the Lingones were part of the La Tène culture, which defines them as a tribe with very ancient Celtic roots.

According to Polybuis, the Lingones may have taken part in the sack of Rome in 390 BC. However, in 52 BC the Lingones refused to support Vercingetorix and supplied Caesar with mounted warriors in his campaign against the Bellovaci. In tribute to their skilled horsemanship, Lingones featured in significant numbers of Roman cavalry cohorts. They were granted full Roman citizenship in 69 AD.

The Lingones leader, Julius Sabinus, led a revolt and proclaimed himself emperor that same year, before being defeated. The new Emperor Vespasian decided that the Lingonian auxiliary units should be sent to Britain. The First and Second Cohorts of the Roman legions were largely made up of Lingones tribesmen and the Fourth Cohort helped build Hadrian's Wall in northern England.

Ligauni

In the first century AD, Pliny the Elder referred to Ligauni territory as *Ligaunorumque*, which translates as 'region of the Ligauni'; it was probably on the right bank of the River Siagne, which flows through the Départements of Var and Alpes-Maritimes in south-east France, which became the Roman province of Gallia Narbonensis. Apart from the fact that it is believed that they were a Celto-Ligurian people, practically nothing else is known about this tribe.

Mandubii

The Mandubii are thought to have been a sub-group of the Aedui tribe. Their territory included part of the western foothills of the Jura and the Morvan, as well as a portion of the Saône valley, in a region that the Romans called Gallia Lugdunensis. Their tribal name means 'those who trample underfoot' and their chief settlement was at a hill-fort called Alesia. The fort was besieged by a massive army amounting to thirteen cavalry cohorts (about 60,000 men) and an army of a further 60,000 infantry under the command of Julius Caesar in 52 BC. Fatigue and starvation forced the tribe and their leader, Vercingetorix, to surrender. Thousands of Gaulish warriors were slaughtered or executed and Vercingetorix was taken in chains to Rome. The outcome of the siege marked the last big battle of the Gallic Wars.

Maracomanii

The Maracomanii, (sometimes 'Marcomanni'), may have been a sept or sub-tribe of the Suebi. In 9 BC, fleeing from Roman aggression, the Maracomanii migrated eastwards into Bohemia, where through alliances with all the neighbouring tribes, they established a powerful tribal confederation. The Marcomanni's destruction of the Boii tribal capital at Boiohaemum was an attempt to extend their territory by expelling the Celtic Boii from Bohemia. They continued to advance and gradually extended their domination of territories up to the River Danube, where they came into conflict with the Roman legions.

Between the years 166 and 180 AD, they fought Rome in what became known as the Marcomannic Wars. To accomplish this they entered an alliance with a number of other tribes, including the Quadi, Sarmatians, Goths and Vandals, to overthrow the Roman Empire under Marcus Aurelius, and end its dominance of Europe. The Marcomanni and the Quadi attacked Roman legions stationed at the town and legionary fortress of *Carnuntum* and captured it. The conflict saw the next twelve years occupied by war on the banks of the River Danube. Marcus Aurelius died in 180 AD before the war was over, and it took his son Commodus to sign a peace treaty and bring the fighting to an end.

The debate continues regarding Maracomanii lineage, with arguments as to whether they were Germanic or Gallic-Celtic people. Their name may have originated from the proto-Germanic term for 'marko', meaning 'border' or 'boundary', by which they may have delineated the frontier of their tribal territory to others. Alternatively, it may better translate as 'borderers'. During the fourth century, under the influence of their queen, Fritigil, the Maracomanii were converted to Christianity, and by the end of the fifth century they had completely disappeared from historical records.

Mediomatrici

The Belgic Mediomatrici tribe lived around modern-day Luxembourg from the mid-fifth century BC until Roman times. According to Ptolemy, their territory was south of Treviri lands, and *Divodurum* (Metz) was their capital. Caesar said they occupied the regions of Lorraine and the Upper Moselle region. Their name is a Latinised form of the Gallic 'medio-matres', which literally translates as 'middle mothers'. This is taken to signify their location between the Matrona (the River Marne) and the Maas (the River Meuse), which were possibly regarded as 'mother rivers'.

In 52 AD, the Mediomatrici supplied 5000 men to support Vercingetorix in the siege of Alesia. Following their defeat and the seizure of Vercingetorix, Mediomatrici territory was ceded to the Vosges, Tribocci and other tribes. Later, in 69 AD, the city of Divodurum was sacked by the Roman army under Vitellius (who later became Emperor), and 4000 of its inhabitants were slaughtered.

By 400 AD, Divodurum had been created a Roman civitas and renamed *Mediomatricorum*, (meaning the 'city of the Mediomatrici'). By this time they were fully Romanised and Mediomatrici warriors served in the Roman army. Following the collapse of the Western Roman Empire in the early fifth century AD, their territory came under the rule of King Clovis of the Franks.

Medulli

The Medulli (or 'Medulles') were a small Gallic mountain tribe whose territory was among the Alpine valleys, in present-day Maurienne in the French province of Savoie (Savoy). The tribe had territory in the upper reaches of the River Arc, a tributary of the River Isère, around the town of Modane. The Medulli tribal name reflects their beekeeping culture – the word 'Medu' means 'mead', an alcoholic drink made from honey; therefore the name might be interpreted as 'mead drinkers'. They were one of many Gaulish tribes whose mountain residences were well off the beaten track and apart from the fact that they controlled some of the Alpine paths, little is really known about them.

In his *Geographia*, Strabo wrote that they were a tribe that held the loftiest peaks of the Alps, and according to Pliny the Elder they were one of the Alpine tribes that were conquered by Rome in 15 BC. Their name appears on two carved monuments that commemorate Roman victories over the barbarian tribes: one on the Tropaeum Alpium in La Turbie in France, and the other on the Arch of Susa near Turin in the Piedmont region of northern Italy.

Menapii

The Menapii was one of the Belgic tribes whose culture was decidedly Celtic. Their main settlement and capital was at a place that the Romans called *Castellum*

Menapiorum, and may have been the present-day town of Cassel, near Dunkerque in the Nord Département of France on its border with Belgium. It is thought that, along with other tribes, a branch of the Menapii may have migrated to the Atlantic coast and invaded Ireland, given that the Menapii share the same name as the ancient Irish tribe Manapi, whose territory was in County Fermanagh. However, their original territory lay between the rivers Rhine and the Schelde, in northern Belgium and the southern Netherlands.

In 57 BC, 9000 warriors of the Menapii tribe had been part of a Belgic confederacy that was defeated by Julius Caesar in 57 BC. Despite this early setback, the tribe continued its opposition to Roman advances and the following year they sided with the Veneti against Caesar. In a final push in 53 BC to end what Rome regarded as Menapii 'rebels', Caesar entered Menapii territory ahead of five legions, burning villages and slaughtering men, women and animals as he went. This campaign of wanton devastation finally forced the Menapii to submit, and Caesar returned to Rome, leaving Commius, an ally and leader of the Atrebates, headed by mounted soldiers to oversee the tribe and to maintain the peace.

Warriors of the Menapii tribe later served as auxiliaries in the Roman army and carved inscriptions reading *Cohors Primae Menapiorum*, (the First Menapii Cohort) are recorded in several places around Britain. One of their number, Marcus Aurelius Mausaeus Valerius Carausius, was the Menapian commander of the Roman fleet that was based in the English Channel in the third century; he declared himself Emperor of Britain and served as such for seven years, before he was assassinated. A Menapii legion was also listed in the *Notitia Dignitatum*, a fifth-century register of Roman government positions and military commands.

Morini

The Morini were one of the tribes of the Belgae confederation, whose territory was around modern-day Calais and ancient *Bononia* (Boulogne-sur-Mer), bordering the River Canache and the River Scheldt. Their capital city and main settlement was at Tarvenna (present-day Thérouanne in the Pas-de-Calais Département). Julius Caesar was particularly keen to capture Morini territory, because of its English Channel coastline and the feasibility of using it as a launching point for his proposed invasion of Britain. During the Roman invasion of Belgica in 57 BC, the Morini tribe contributed 25,000 warriors to fight against the Roman advance under Galba, the chieftain of the Suessiones tribe. However, Gallic resistance ultimately failed and along with warriors of the Osismi, Lexovii, Namnetes, Ambiliati, Diablintes, and Menapii tribes, supported by Celtic auxiliaries from Britain, they faced mass slaughter. The Romans laid waste to all of their fields and crops, and burned their villages and farm-buildings. Despite the force and scope of the Roman assault, Caesar was only successful in conquering a relatively small part of Morini territory around Calais. The remainder was later annexed to the Roman Empire by the Emperor Augustus between the years 33 and 23 BC.

Nantuates

The Nantuates (or 'Nantuatae') are one of the four Celtic tribes living in present-day Valais Chablais. Their main settlement and capital was at Massongex (present-day Tarnaiae), in the modern Canton of Valais in the Swiss Alps, around Lake Geneva and adjacent regions of France. Caesar also mentioned a tribe of the Nantuates dwelling on the Upper Rhine, but whether they are branches of the same people or completely unrelated is uncertain. The name of Nantuates is said by some to be derived from the Celtic 'nantu', a similar word to the Welsh 'nant', meaning 'watercourse' or 'stream', and taken in its widest sense to mean 'men of the rivers'. Others prefer a translation of 'those of the valley'.

During the Gallic Wars the tribe openly resisted Caesar's military push to protect the Poeninus Pass and to establish free passage for trade. Together with the Veragri and Seduni tribes, the Nantuates constantly attacked Roman merchants and forced them to pay heavy tolls for passage through the Alps. Caesar sent the Twelfth Legion, commanded by Servius Galba, with a contingent of cavalry, initially to agree a treaty of free passage, but found it necessary to impose Roman authority on the mountain tribes. The Romans finally subdued the region following the Battle of Octodurus in 56 AD.

Nearchi

The obscure Nearchi tribe were part of the Salubian confederation that lived in Provence, near the River Silyes and the Rhône in the south of France. Their chief settlement was at a place called *Bergine*, (modern-day Emaginum, near Tarascon). It was one of the towns that were destroyed by the Romans when the tribes of the confederation were subjugated in 121 BC.

Nemetes

The Nemetes, (sometimes 'Nemeti'), were a Germano-Celtic tribe with a Celtic name, though according to Tacitus, the Nemetes were 'unquestionably Germanic'. In fact, they were a sub-group or sept of the Suebi confederation and along with the Triboci and Vangiones, led by Ariovistus, they migrated across the Rhine to settle on its eastern banks in modern-day Rhenish Bavaria sometime around the year 70 BC.

The tribe venerated Nemetona, the goddess of healing, which is the probable origin of their tribal name. Their capital, Speyer, later renamed by the Romans as *Noviomagus Nemeton*, became a Roman military base under Drusus, stepson of the Emperor Augustus. In 58 BC, the entire Suebi federation submitted to Roman authority and gradually assumed a Celtic culture. Noviomagus Nemeton became a Roman municipality (a so-called 'Colonia Nemetum'), but it was destroyed by Germanic warriors led by Attila the Hun in 451 AD.

Nervii

The Nervii were a reputedly fierce tribe of Gallia Belgica, thought to have been the most powerful in northern Gaul. Julius Caesar regarded them as the most warlike of all the Belgic tribes. Their main settlement and capital was at *Bagacum*, (modern-day Bavai), near Maubeuge, on the upper Sambre River, which flows through northern France and Wallonia, Belgium. They are thought to have spoken a language dialect that was a transitional stage between Celtic and a Germanic language. Both Strabo and Tacitus claimed that the tribe were of Germanic origin. Along with other tribes of the region, in 57 BC the Nervii were defeated and virtually exterminated by Caesar at the Battle of the River Sambre. Caesar described the fallen Nervii warriors as heroes. Ironically, their tribal name might have come from a proto-Celtic source meaning 'heroes'. Despite suffering losses during the siege of Alesia in 52 BC, the Nervii supplied 5000 warriors to fight the Romans. The tribe was the main subject of the comic book *Asterix the Gaul.*

Nitiobroges

The Nitiobroges, (sometimes, 'Nitiobriges'), were a Gallic people who settled in the Dėpartement of Lot and Garonne, on the right bank of the River Garonne, between the valleys of the Tarn and the Dordogne, early in the fourth century BC. Their name translates from the original Gaulish as 'the indigenous people', and their capital was *Aginnon* (present-day Agen). The tribe were one of the first to cooperate with the Romans, and initially prospered under their rule, being declared 'friends' of the Republic. This favourable alliance ended when in 52 BC, as part of the Gallic coalition of tribes, they rallied in support of Vercingetorix, the Arverni leader, against Rome, and sent some 5000 warriors under the leadership of King Teutomatos to his aid. They engaged in a major battle at Gergovia, the chief fortified town of the Arverni. The engagement was disastrous for Caesar's army, and many thousand were slain before the Romans turned heel and withdrew. Caesar made serious attempts to downplay the disaster in his account of the battle in his *Commentaries*, stating that his legions faced an opposing army of 250,000 Gauls, which was a self-evident exaggeration.

Orobii

The Orobii, (also known as 'Orobi', 'Oromobi' or 'Orumbovii'), were a Celto-Ligurian tribe dwelling around the present-day Como, Bergamo and Lecco valleys of Italy, a region called 'Gallia Cisalpina', during the first millennium BC and into the Roman age. According to Pliny, they established the main capital, which the Romans called Bergomum, (the modern-day city of Bergamo), about thirty miles north-east of present-day Milan. Julius Caesar created it as a Roman city in 49 BC, and after the fall of the Western Roman Empire in the early fifth century AD, it was overrun by several barbarian tribes, including the Visigoths in 402 AD, by Attila the Hun in the mid-fifth century, followed by later conquests of the Rugii, the Ostrogoths, Byzantines and the Lombards, who made it their capital. Little is known about this tribe, other than the gold coin hoards they left behind, as evidenced by the several hundred Orobii gold coins dating from 474 AD that were discovered in 2018 in the basement of the former Cressoni Theatre in Bergamo.

Osi

The Osi, (sometimes 'Osii', and occasionally 'Onsi'), were a small tribe whose territory was originally in the region of present-day Moravia. They were part of the larger Suebi confederation and migrated north and east from their Celtic homeland in Germany around the sixth century BC, finally settling in the Silesia area of Poland and the borderlands of Ukraine, an area once known as Galicia. It is thought that the Osi were forced to migrate due to Marcus Aurelius' campaign in the Marcomanni Wars, after which their territory was probably taken into the possession of the Quadi people.

A small group of the Osi migrated into Pannonia, an ancient area that covered much of western Hungary and eastern Austria. Debates continue concerning their exact ethnicity; some claim they were Germanic, others Celtic, and yet others maintain that they were Dacian. In fact they may well have been a racial admixture of several or all of these, as such inter-tribal associations through marriage was not uncommon in central Europe at that time. Tacitus identified the tribe as German, but they were more likely to have been one of the Celtic tribes taken over by more dominant Germanic rulers at the end of the first century BC. Despite their physical separation from the Celtic world, the Osi became a flourishing lowland farming community and succeeded in retaining their language.

Paemani

The precise ethnicity of the small Paemani tribe, (sometimes 'Poemani' or 'Caemani'), remains an open question; most authorities regard them as a Celtic people, though they are sometimes identified as a Belgic-Germanic tribe. Together with the Condrusi, Eburones and Caeroesi, in his *Gallic Wars* Caesar cited them as one of the four rebellious tribes of the Germani who were said to have contributed 40,000 warriors to fight under Galba, chieftain of the Suessiones. It is known that they had been assimilated into Celtic culture by the time of the Roman invasion in 57 BC. The Paemani name might be translated as 'the herdsmen'. Their tribal lands were in the Ardennes Forest and Eiffel regions and in the valley of the Lesse River in northern Gaul (present-day Belgium).

Parisii

From the middle of the third century BC the Parisii territorial lands were on the banks of the Sequana (the River Seine) in France, an area that may have been granted to them by the Senones, to whom they may have been related. Their capital and main settlement was on an island in the River Seine, (nowadays the Ile de la Cité), known at that time as *Lutetia Parisiorum*, a city in the Roman province of Gallia Lugdunensis. This became modern-day Paris, whose name derives directly from the Parisii tribe.

In his *Commentaries*, Julius Caesar wrote that the inhabitants of this island razed their own settlement to the ground rather than surrender it to his forces. The Parisii joined Vercingetorix in his rebellion against Caesar in 52 BC and a great final battle took place between Rome and the Parisii on the banks of the Seine, known as the Battle of Lutetia. Roman legions decimated the Gallic warriors, and as a result, the city came under Roman rule. The Parisii had been beaten into submission, just as were the rest of Gaul; under Roman domination, they eventually became Romanised, and Paris emerged as an important Roman 'civitas' (city).

Recent archaeological investigations have revealed that between 400 BC and 500 BC, at least three groups of Parisii migrated to resettle in present-day Yorkshire, where their name is frequently spelled with a single 'i', as Parisi.

Petrocorii

The Petrocorii, were a Gallic tribe whose territory was in the present-day Départment of the Dordogne, in the Perigord region of France, and their main settlement was originally at La Boissiereat. However, following their subjugation, (to which they appeared to offer little resistance), they moved to the Roman city of *Vesunna*, (now Perigueux) on the Garunna (the River Garonne). Perigueux has been an important Petrocorii settlement since the second century BC and the former province of Perigord takes its name from the tribe. In 52 BC, the Petrocorii fought under the Arverni commander, Vercassivellaunus, during the Battle of Alesia. In Gallic, the tribal name Petrocorii means 'four armies'. The tribe was known for its fine ironwork.

Pictones

In common with the Picts of northern Scotland, the first element of the Pictones tribal name means 'painted', a reflection of the custom that both tribes had of painting their bodies with blue wode. The name was given to them by Julius Caesar, and means 'those who paint their faces'. The Pictones', (sometimes 'Pictons' or 'Pictavi'), territorial tribelands were along the Bay of Biscay in the present-day Départements of Vendée, Deux-Sèvres and Vienne in western France, then known as Gallia Celtica, and their main settlement was at *Lemonum* (modern-day Poitiers). It was here and on the south bank of the estuary of the lower Liger (the River Loire) that they developed a thriving shipbuilding industry. Caesar considered them one of the more civilised of the Gallic tribes and commissioned their ships for the Roman navy. Even so, despite being regarded as allies by the Romans, the Pictones sent 8000 warriors to support Vercingetorix in his rebellion. In defeat, following a long siege, the settlement of Lemonum was burned to the ground and rebuilt as a city under Roman occupation and the administration of the Roman province of Gallia Aquitania.

Quadiates

The Quadiates, (sometimes 'Quariates'), were an Alpine tribe who had the distinction of being the last on the list of Alpine tribes that were subdued by Marcus Julius Cottius as recorded on the Arch at Susa in 9 BC, (also known as the Arch of Augustus), in the Piedmont region of Italy. They were mentioned by Pliny as Quariates and lived in the Queyras River valley in the French Hautes-Alpes. The twelfth-century castle of Quadratum near Queyras was named after the tribe.

Remi

By the first century BC, the Remi tribe had grown to become the largest of all the Belgic tribes. They had originally crossed the Rhine into northern Gaul in the sixth century BC, accompanied by other migrating tribes including the Caleti, Catuvellauni, Meldi, Suessiones and Veliocasses. Their settlements were in a region between the Mosa (the River Meuse) and Matrona (the River Marne), in the Aisne, Vesle and Suippe valleys, in the present-day Champagne region bordering the Ardennes. Their chief city was at *Durocortum* (present-day Reims), which after their subjugation became the capital of the Roman province of Gallia Belgica.

The city of Reims takes its name from their tribal name and in around 400 AD it was designated a Roman *Civitate Remorum*. The Remi supported Julius Caesar in his conquest of Gaul during the Gallic Wars, refusing to join in the rebellion of Vercingetorix, instead asking the protection of Rome in 57 BC, thereby retaining their independence throughout the wars. Their tribal name comes from the Gaulish word 'remos', meaning 'the first ones'. The Remi's chief deity was *Camulus* (or 'Camulos'), a Celtic god of war that the Romans identified with Mars. Camulus was also an important deity of Roman Britain and was venerated widely among the Belgae tribes. In the year 1284 their capital was named 'Rems'.

Ruteni

The Ruteni, (sometimes 'Rutenes' or 'Ruthenes'), were a Gallic tribe dwelling in the southern part of the Massif Central of France, around the present-day town of Rodez, (then known as *Segodunum*), in the region of Aveyron. Present-day inhabitants of Rodez are still called 'Ruthénois', after the Ruteni. Their tribal name translates as 'the blond or red-headed ones'. They were supporters of Vercingetorix and fought alongside him in the rebellion against Rome. In 121 BC, as part of a confederation with the Allobroges, they confronted Consul Quintus Fabius Maximus, and a force of 12,000 fought his troops at the confluence of the rivers Rhône and the Isère. The confederate army was defeated and Ruteni territory was seized, half becoming part of a Roman province, based at their former capital, Albi. Little more is known about the tribe other than the fact that they mined lead and silver, and their early adoption of coinage. An impressive hoard of 20,000 minted Ruteni coins, dating from the first century BC, has been found about fifteen miles from Rodez in the village of Goutrens.

Salassi

The Salassi tribe, (sometimes 'Salasses'), were a Gallic tribe dwelling in the upper valley of the River Dora Baltea. They were one of the most powerful and reputedly warlike of the Alpine tribes living around the border between modern-day France and Switzerland. Cassius Dio described them as constantly plundering Roman convoys and harassing troops. The tribe controlled the St Bernard pass route into the Po valley of northern Italy from about 100 BC, and even the Romans had to pay a toll for passage through their territory.

The tribe developed thriving gold and iron mining industries, which were acquired by Rome in 143 BC. During the reign of Augustus Caesar, in 25 BC, large numbers of the Salassi were destroyed by Roman legions commanded by Consul Appius Claudius. According to Dio, the Romans lost 5000 men in two engagements, while somewhere between 36,000 and 50,000 Salassi were killed or sold into slavery. Subsequently, Augustus created the civitas of *Augusta Praetoria Salassorum*, (modern-day Aosta), and named it after himself: it had previously been the tribe's main settlement. The 'Sal-' element of their tribal name may be an indication that they also specialised in salt mining.

Salyans

The Salyans, (sometimes known as 'Salyes', 'Salyi' or 'Saluvii'), were a Celtic Ligurian tribe that held territory around Arles and Marseilles in the south of France. In the sixth century BC they established their main settlement and capital at Entremont, near present-day Aix-en-Provence, between the Druentia (the River Durance) and the Greek colony of Massalia (Marseilles). Ptolemy identified at least five oppidum (settlements) of the Salyans: at Tarascaon, Glanum, Arelatum, Aquae Sextiae and Ernaginum. Although earlier writers identified them as 'Ligurian', Strabo insisted that they were 'Celto-ligurian', and described them as a warlike people who were ferocious fighters on foot and on horseback. The Salyans were notorious devotees of the cult of the *tête coupée* (the 'severed head'), in keeping with a widespread practice among many Celtic tribes of decapitating captured enemies. In 123 BC, they were defeated in a battle by General Sextius Calvinus, whose troops sacked their hill-fort at Entremont, and the entire population were sold as slaves. In 49 BC, Marseilles was besieged and eventually surrendered to Julius Caesar, at which point all rebellion against Roman rule was finally crushed in the region. From this time the Salyes tribe disappeared from all historical record.

Santoni

The Santoni tribe, (sometimes 'Santones'), originally migrated sometime in the ninth century BC, from around the Main and Neckar rivers in Germany. By the Roman era they had settled around Saintonage, north of the River Gironde in western Gaul. Their main settlement was at *Mediolanum Santonum* (modern-day Saintes), which is based on the tribe's name. They allied and traded with Rome, and 12,000 Santoni auxiliaries formed part of Caesar's fleet against the Helvetii in 56 BC. That year, as allies of Rome, the Santoni had been ordered to supply ships to the Romans, yet four years later they had turned coat and supplied 12,000 warriors to fight the Romans at the Battle of Alesia.

Savincates

The Savincates, (or 'Savincats'), lived in the Ubaye Valley of the Cottian Alps and were one of the Alpine tribes of the Caturiges federation that were subdued by Cottius in 9 AD and listed on the Triumphal Arch of Susa in the Piedmont region of Italy, near Turin. The town of Savine in the Hautes-Alpes Département was named after the tribe.

Seduni

The Seduni, (sometimes 'Sedunes'), were a small Celtic tribe who established a territory at Valais, in western Switzerland and the border with France, as part of the Vallenses, a group of tribes including the Nantuates and Uberi who lived between Lake Geneva and the Pennine Alps. Their capital city (oppidum) was at Sedunum in the upper Rhône Valley (present-day Sion in Switzerland).

Their territory was located on an important route through the St Bernard pass from northern Europe to Italy, and together with other Alpine tribes, the Seduni applied toll charges to all merchandise that was passing through. In 56 BC, realising its strategic value, the Romans sent Servius Galba (who later became Emperor) to open up the pass as a free trade route through the mountains, in the process of which he captured much of the region and forced out its inhabitants. Faced with this Roman occupation, the Seduni joined forces with the Veragri and counter-attacked with a fierce battle in which many Celtic warriors were slain. Despite heavy losses, reportedly amounting to some 30,000 men, their dogged resistance eventually succeeded in driving the Romans from their territory. Galba then burned down several neighbouring settlements and returned back to Rome.

The Seduni were finally subdued in 15 BC, and during the reign of the Emperor Claudius (42–54 AD) their settlement was created as *Civitas Vallensium* as part of the Roman Empire.

Segni

During the Iron Age, the Segni were a small Belgian tribe who held territory in the Luxemburg and Ardennes region between the valleys of the Meuse and the Moselle. Their name did not appear among the tribes that took part in the Belgic coalition against Rome in 57 BC and it is not certain if they were truly Belgae or Germanic in origin. Certainly Caesar was informed that they were the Germani of Belgian Gaul, and they were referred to as the *Germani Cisrhenani*, (Germans on the west side), to distinguish them from Germani living on the east of the Rhine, and outside of the Roman area of influence. The name of the Segni is preserved in the present-day town of Sinei (or 'Signei'), located on the River Meuse, in the Belgian province of Namur.

Segobrigii

The Segobrigii, (or 'Segobriges'), were a Celtic-Ligurian people who lived around Massalia (present-day Marseilles), an area known as the 'Bouches du Rhone', in south-east France. According to Greek accounts, the tribe founded the settlement of Massalia in about 600 BC. The remains of the seventh-century fortifications at Saint-Blaise in Provence are thought to be the site of the Segobrigii chief city.

Segovellauni

The Segovellauni, (also known as the 'Segalauni'), were a small Celtic tribe that held territory in the Drôme region between the River Rhône in France and Lake Geneva on the Swiss border in what the Romans called Gallia Narbonensis. Their main settlement was in the present-day city of Valence, which became a Roman colony during the time of Julius Caesar. The modern-day city of Soynos was probably another one of their settlements.

The tribal name comes from a Gaulish word, 'Segouellaunoi', which means 'chiefs of victory'. Their territory was annexed to the province of Gallia Transalpina by the Roman Republic in 121 BC, and in 62 BC, their settlement at Ventia was destroyed by the Roman army under the command of Legate Manlius Lentinus during the revolt of the Allobroges. Towards the end of the first century BC, the Segovellauni were integrated into the Roman Colonia Valentia, which had been founded either by Julius Caesar or the Emperor Augustus.

Senones

The Senones, (sometimes 'Semnones'), were one of the oldest known Celtic tribes, as evidenced by their tribal name, which translates loosely as 'the elders' or 'the sages'. Their capital was at *Agedincum* (modern-day Sens in France). During the reign of Julius Caesar they occupied territory around the River Seine basin. They were one of the leading tribes that captured Rome in 390 BC, led by their chief, Brennus, before looting Delphi in Greece in 279 BC. A group of the Senones went on to resettle in Galatia. The tribe was a constant menace to Roman authority for more than a century until they were finally subjugated by an army led by the Roman Consul Dola-Bella. A second tribe settled in Gallia Lugdunensis. Little more is heard of them thereafter.

Sequani

In the first century BC, the Gallic Sequani's territorial tribelands lay between the rivers Saône, Rhône and Rhine with their major settlement at *Vesontio* (present-day Besançon). It roughly equates to the present-day Franche-Comté region and a section of Burgundy, in an area that the Romans knew as Gallia Belgica.

Their tribal name comes from Sequana, the goddess of the River Seine; it was also the Celtic name for that river. They were frequently at war with the neighbouring Aedui tribe, and sought assistance from Ariovistus, the chief of the Germanic Suebi, whose territory was in the nearby Alsace region. However, once in Sequani territory, Ariovistus turned on them and soon began to take over their landholdings for himself, subjugating many Sequani as virtual slaves in the process. Consequently, the Sequani were forced to appeal to Caesar for help in reclaiming their lands and driving out the interlopers. The Suebi were finally defeated in the Battle of Vosges and driven back over the Rhine in 58 BC by Julius Caesar.

Unfortunately, though Rome initially restored the territory to the Sequani, their liberation was only partial, as by 51 BC their lands had become an integrated part of the Roman Empire.

Sogionti

During the Iron Age and in Roman times, Sogionti (or 'Sogiontii') territory was in the River Durance valley around *Segustero*, (modern-day Sisteron), in the Provence-Alpes-Cote d'Azur region of France. It is thought that they were part of the Vocontii federation. They were one of the tribes that were conquered by Rome in 15 BC and their tribal name is engraved on the *Tropaeum Alpium*, (the 'Trophy of the Alps'), which celebrated Augustus's victory over the Alpine tribes.

Sontiati

The territory of the Aquitanian Sontiati tribe, (sometimes 'Sontiates' or 'Sotiates'), was south of the River Garonne where it meets the Lot and the Aveyron. Their main settlement and capital was at Sotium, known to the Romans as *Oppidum Sotiatum* (modern-day Sos), which is located at the confluence of the Gueyze and Gélise rivers. The Sontiati, one of the strongest of the Aquitanian tribes, rose up against the invading Romans as part of Vercingetorix's rebellion in 56 BC, led by their chieftain, Adiatunnus (or 'Adiatuanos'). Initially his army made great inroads into the Roman legions by employing their main strength, mounted cavalry, but as things began to favour the Romans, Adiatunnus fled the field in disorder and withdrew with his warriors into their fortified stronghold at Sotium, which immediately came under siege. The Sontiati ploy was to feign capitulation and to send representatives to sue for peace, so that while the Roman commander, Licinius Crassus, was distracted, Adiatunnus and some 600 of his trained *soldurii* (bodyguards) planned to escape via newly dug tunnels beneath the walls of the oppidum. The plan failed; they were driven back into the town, which was eventually captured, and the Sontiati were forced to surrender.

Sordones

According to Strabo and Polybuis, the Iberian Sordones tribe, (also known as 'Sordes' and 'Sardons'), were a sub-tribe of the Volques, who had territory in Roussillon, France. Both historians located their main settlement at *Ruscino*, (present-day Chateau-Roussillon near Perpignan), in a region of the Eastern Pyrenees and the Aude, immediately north of the Spanish border, which the Romans called Gallia Narbonensis. Julius Caesar wrote that the Sordones were '... of the same race as the Aquitanians'.

Suessiones

By the first century BC, the Suessiones, (sometimes known as the 'Suaeuconi'), held territories in north-eastern Gaul, located between the River Marne and the River Oise, around present-day Soissons. Their main settlement and capital, founded around 20 BC, was at *Noviodunum*, (which translates as 'new hill fort'), now the Commune of Pommiers in the Départment of Rhône. Before the Roman Conquest, their main settlement had been at present-day Villeneuve-Saint-Germain, and stood on a plain near the River Aisne. Soissons became a Roman garrison some time after the Conquest.

In his *Gallic Wars*, Julius Caesar recorded that the Suessiones possessed extensive fertile lands and in his own lifetime had been under the control of Diviciacus, reputedly a powerful man who ruled over many of the Belgic tribes of Gaul, as well as parts of Britain.

The Suessiones were culturally closely related to the neighbouring Remi tribe. However, despite the advice of the Remi, who had already sworn allegiance to Caesar, some 15,000 Suessiones tribesmen, together with the Parisii, led by Galba, chieftain of the Suessiones, took part in the revolt of Vercingetorix against Julius Caesar in 52 BC. As well as 4000 men for the Battle of Alesia, they also contributed 10,000 warriors to help the Nervi fight against Rome. However, their resistance to Roman advances proved ultimately ineffectual and Noviodunum was eventually besieged by Caesar in 57 BC; its inhabitants surrendered the civic leaders, as well as two sons of King Galba as hostages, to prevent wholesale slaughter of their citizens. The city of Soissons, known as *Augusta Suessionum* in the fourth century AD, is named after the tribe.

Suetrii

The Suetrii, (or 'Suetri'), were a Gallic tribe that held territory in the Verdon River valley of the Alpes-de-Haute-Provence region of south-east France during Roman times. Their tribal name translates as 'good birds'. Their capital and main settlement was at a place called *Salinae*, (modern-day Castellane), named by the Romans on account of its local salt deposits. They were one of the Alpine tribes conquered by Rome in 15 BC, and listed on the *Tropaeum Alpium* monument (the 'Trophy of the Alps'), located a few miles from Monaco and celebrating the triumph of Emperor Augustus over the Alpine tribes.

Tarbelli

The Tarbelli were a small Aquitanian tribe, part of a confederacy of four Basque tribes, related to the Vascones and were sometimes known as the 'Tarbelles' or the 'Tarus'. Their tribal name translates as 'tribe of Taurus' and their capital was Dax, which was known to the Romans as *Aquae Tarbellicae*. They occupied territory on the Atlantic coast, from the south of Landes, to the current French Basque Country, from Chalosse, to the valleys of the Adour, the Gaves de Pau and Oloron. In his *Geographia*, Strabo describes the Tarbelli gold industry of the Gallatic Gulf: '...the gulf is held by the Tarbelli, in whose land the gold mines are most important of all; for in pits dug only to a slight depth they find slabs of gold as big as the hand can hold'.

Unlike many other Celtic tribes, the Tarbelli did not join in the rebellion against Roman invasion during the Gallic Wars but chose to be allies of Rome. Together with the Auscii tribe, they constituted one of the most powerful peoples of Aquitania. However, when the Romans tried to requisition scarce food supplies from the tribe, they rebelled and sprung a trap on the Fourth Cohort commanded by Tribunus Lucius Varro. Three cohorts of legionaries were immediately despatched to punish the tribe, and despite the Tarbelli's previously long and peaceful association with Rome, they were finally subjugated by a Roman army led by Legatus Licinius Crassus in 56 BC.

Taurini

It is generally thought that the Taurini were part of a confederation of small tribes, which according to Strabo and Pliny was made up of Ligurians who had integrated with invading Hallstatt Celtic tribes to become what by the third century were known as 'Celto-Ligurians'. Their settlements were around the upper valley of the River Po in the Piedmont region of northern Italy.

There is an opinion that the Taurini tribal name derives from the Celtic word 'tauros', meaning 'bull'. Hence, 'the tribe of the bull'. However, this has been disputed, despite the fact that the name of modern-day Turin is taken to mean 'little bull', and it has been proposed that it more likely comes from the word 'montanus', meaning 'mountaineer', a reflection of the Alpine region in which they lived.

Their capital of Taurasia was destroyed during the Second Punic War, following a three-day siege by Hannibal's army as it passed through their territory in 218 BC, but was rebuilt in 25 BC by the Romans as *Colonia Augusta Taurinorom*, (modern-day Torino, or Turin). The Taurini were finally subjugated by Augustus in 9 BC.

Tencteri

The Tencteri, (sometimes 'Tenchteri' or 'Tenctheri'), were descended from the Celtic La Tène-culture. However, they were first described in 55 BC by Julius Caesar as a Germanic tribe searching for a new homeland across the Rhine, having driven out the resident Celtic tribes who previously occupied the region. Worried by the advance of the Roman legions into their territory, together with the Usipetes, the Tencteri sent representatives to Caesar in the hope of making a peace treaty, but Caesar would only grant such an alliance if the Germanic tribes left Gaul. They refused the condition and took the initiative, attacking the legions head on and forcing a humiliating Roman retreat. Caesar immediately mounted a new force of eight legions to counter attack and massacred the entire Tencteri army to a man, a fact that he recorded in his *Gallic Wars*. Dispassionately, he wrote that he '...ordered his men to attack the camp. Men, women, and children all tried to escape, but they had been killed, or had thrown themselves into the rivers.' In fact, archaeological evidence from the site has revealed that thousands were slain, which is evidenced by quantities of weapons and armour, as well as women's belt clasps and children's leather boots. Words like 'genocide' are often used to describe the event.

Tigurini

The Tigurini were a branch of the Helvetii, whose traditional homeland was in the present-day Canton of Vaud, near Lausanne in Switzerland. The tribe joined the Cimbri and the Teutones under the command of Diviciacus of the Helvetii (known as 'Divico'), in invading and looting the territory of the Gaulish Allobroges tribe, which lay between the River Rhône and the Alps as part of their migration south. In 107 BC the Roman Consul Lucius Cassius Longinus was sent to Gaul to prevent the migration of the Tigurini and the other Germanic tribes. He is said to have pursued the Tigurini as far as the Atlantic Ocean around present-day Bordeaux. But, failing to drive the Gallic tribesmen back, the Roman army was defeated at Burdigala.

Cassius began to make his way back to Gaul and was killed in a surprise ambush by the Tigurini, which, according to Livy, took place in the territory of the Nitiobriges tribe (around the River Garonne); he recorded that Cassius Longinus was massacred along with his entire army.

The Helvetii, among them the Tigurini, were eventually defeated by six Roman legions under Julius Caesar at the Battle of Bibracte in 58 BC. According to Caesar, more than 300,000 of the Helvetii and their allies had fought in the battle. However, destitute, starving and unsupported in defeat, only an estimated 110,000 warriors of the Helvetii tribes, including the Tigurini, made it back to their homelands. They had left due to famine – back home certain famine awaited them.

Tolosates

The Tolosates were a Celtic tribe of the Haute Garonne region of France, a region known to the Romans as Gallia Transalpina, whose main centre was at *Tolosa* (present-day Toulouse). They were probably a sept or client group of the Volques Tectosage tribe and are believed to have arrived in the area early in the second century BC. They were a Germanic tribe, possibly related to the Cimbri, who originated in the Rhône Valley and invaded the lands south of the River Garonne. Tolosa was captured by the Romans under the command of General Quintus Serveries Campio (or Caepio), whom Rome had sent to conquer and punish the tribe in 106 BC. The city became a Roman military outpost and in time developed as a civitas of Gallia Narbonensis.

Tornates

The Tornates, (or 'Turnates'), were an Aquitainian tribe who held territory in Tournay, near Bagneres de Bigorre in the Hautes-Pyrénées Département in the Occitanie region of south-west France, a region the Romans called Gallia Aquitania. Little is known of the tribe other than a brief mention in Pliny the Elder's *Natural History.* Their main centre may have been in the present-day city of Tournai, on the River Arros, a tributary of the Adour, and this could be the origin of their tribal name.

Toxandri

Sometimes known as the 'Texuandri', 'Taxandri' or 'Toxandrians', these were a Germanic people whose territory of Toxandria (or 'Texandria') lay in the south of modern-day Netherlands and northern Belgium, between the rivers Scheldt and Rhine at the time of the Romans. The place-name Toxandria translates as 'land of the southerners.' By the mid-fourth century AD, Frankish tribes had begun to cross the Rhine and settle in Toxandria, possibly having gained permission to settle there from the Roman Emperor Julianus Apostata in 358 AD.

It remains a matter of conjecture whether the Franks actually drove the Toxandri from their tribal lands, as by the end of that century they had become the dominant force in the region. Alternatively, the Toxandi tribe may simply have been incorporated into the Frankish Federation.

An inscription mentioning 'Texandri' exists on an altar in the Temple of Mithras at the Roman Carrowburgh Fort near Hadrian's Wall, suggesting that at least some Toxandri warriors may have acted as mercenaries in the Roman Army and served for a time in northern Britain.

Treveri

Julius Caesar said of the Treveri that although they spoke a Celtic language, they claimed to be descended from the Germans. But the Treveri were a tribe of Belgae Celts. They had settled in the Ardennes Mountains on both banks of the River Moselle and the River Rhine, possibly as early as the ninth century BC. Its chief settlement was at Trier (or possibly Titelberg), which the Romans renamed as *Augusta Treverorum* after the Emperor Augustus in the first century AD.

Although their language was Celtic, according to Tacitus they claimed Germanic descent. In fact, at least culturally, they were probably a mixture of Celtic and Germanic influences and cultures. Despite the fact that their leader, Indutiomarus, led them in the rebellion against Julius Caesar during the Gallic Wars, after their subjugation many Treveri warriors joined the Roman army and were noted cavalrymen, serving under their leader Cingetorix as Roman auxiliaries.

In the year 30 BC, a Treveri revolt was put down by Marcus Nonius Gallus, and their capital became a garrison of the Roman army. The family of Germanicus, which included the future Emperor Caligula, lived for a time in the city of Augusta Treverorum. In 16 BC, under an edict by Augustus, Treveri territory became part of the Roman province of Gallia Belgica.

Tricasses

In the first century BC the Gallic Tricasses tribe lived on the right bank of the Sequana (the River Seine) near the present-day River Aube in the Roman province of Gallia Lugdunensis, now the Champagne region of France. Their tribal name is thought by some to translate as 'three groups of warriors', while others prefer 'those with three locks of hair'.

According to Pliny in his *Natural History* and Ptolemy in *Geography*, they were a sub-division of one of the bigger tribes, possibly the Senones, and had their main capital at *Tricasses* (present-day Troyes). The Romans knew the place as *Augustobona*, which was named in honour of Caesar Augustus. In the third century the city was renamed Tricassium, and then in the fifth century, as Trecae.

There is an ancient inscription near Mainz in the Rhineland that records an unknown tribe called Cassii or Casses, and it is thought that they may have been the forebears of several other Gallic tribes like the Tricasses. For example, the Veliocasses, Viducasses and Baiocasses all show similar name derivations. The Tricasses tribe converted to Christianity in the third century.

Tricastini

The Tricastini (or 'Tricastii') were a small Celto-Ligurian tribe, possibly part of the Cavarum confederation, dwelling in the Alpine region of western Switzerland

and the French-Italian border in the modern Tricastin region of the Département of the Drôme, near present-day Montelimar. They are thought to have settled in the region sometime in the sixth century BC. The tribe rated a mention in Ptolemy's *Geographia*, and he located them in what the Romans called Gallia Narbonensis, and recorded that their capital (oppidum) was at *Neomagus*. Later, in the Christian era the place was known as the ancient diocese of Saint-Paul-Trois-Chateaux, (after the Tricastini name, which translates as 'three castles'), and now the Commune of Nyons. The Romans called the city *Augusta Tricastinorum*, after the Emperor Augustus.

Livy placed the tribe's main settlement along the east bank of the River Rhône, just north of Arausio (present-day Orange). Historical records have the Tricastini subdued by the Roman Second Gallic Legion in 40 BC. They had arrived and established a base at *Colonia Julia Secundanorum Arausio* in 35 BC on the instructions of Vespasian. Their best land was ceded to the retired legionaries, while the Tricastini were left with the poorest, least fertile areas.

Strabo described the Tricastini as the most Romanised tribe in southern Gaul. However, others maintain that they were eventually integrated into the Segovellauni tribe and thereafter disappear from historical record. Despite this latter hypothesis, the Segalauni were included by Livy among the Tricastini. Strabo associated both tribes among the Cavares, leaving us more questions than answers regarding their true lineage and history.

Tungri

The Tungri, (sometimes 'Tongri', or 'Tungrians'), were a group of tribes who lived in northern Gaul, somewhere north of what the Romans called 'Arduenna Silva', now known as the Ardennes Forest. They had probably migrated from beyond the Rhine to become the dominant tribe in the region following the extermination of the Eburones by Julius Caesar, and the territory was later formally ceded to them by Augustus. As newcomers they established their main settlement on the site of the former stronghold of the Atuatuci tribe, who had been driven out after a prolonged siege and their capitulation to the Roman army. It became their main settlement and capital and was thereafter called *Atuatuca Tungrorum*, (modern-day Tongeren in the Limburg Province of Belgium).

Under Roman rule, the Tungri capital became known as *Civitas Tungrorum*, and was initially part of the Roman province of Gallia Belgica, and later became Germania Inferior. The tribe was designated as 'Germani' by Tacitus, thus: 'The first people to cross the Rhine and appropriate Gallic territory, though they are known nowadays as Tungri, were at that time called Germani.' However, some historians regard them as a Celtic tribe. In reality they may have been a Celto-Germanic people, a mixture of both, as inter-tribal unions and marriages were not uncommon.

The Tungri retained an amicable relationship with their Roman conquerors and in 69 AD they came to the aid of the Romans during the Batavi uprising, in which the Batavi tribe had initially defeated two Roman legions. Tungri warriors also served in the Roman army, and a group were based at the Carrawburgh fort where several inscriptions mention them, as well as at Housesteads and Vindolanda, where a carved tablet records that a thousand men of the *Cohors Primae Tungrorum* (the First Tungri Cohort) served on Hadrian's Wall under the command of Gaius Silvius Auspex between 122 and 138 AD. Other similar inscriptions have been found in Chester and in York. The Cohort also served for a time on the Antonine Wall. Another memorial stone at Birrens in Dumfries & Galloway records that some of the tribe served as auxiliaries in Scotland. The dedication reads: 'To Mars and the Emperor's Victory, the Raetian tribesmen serving in the Second Cohort of Tungrians'.

The tribal name might be derived from an archaic word 'tungrisch' (meaning 'tongue'), to describe a group of people who speak the same or similar dialects. This would make sense if, as is widely believed, the Tungri were made up of several tribes who were closely related, friendly neighbours or some kind of loose federation.

Turones

The Turones, (or 'Turoni'), were a Gallic tribe, possibly a Celto-Germanic people, who settled in territory along the south bank of the Liger (the River Loire) around Touraine, in the Indre-et-Loire Département of France. According to Ptolemy, their main settlement and former capital was at Turones, which in Roman times was named *Caesarodunum* (modern-day Tours). Initially the tribe made no resistance to the Roman invasion, but later became supporters of Vercingetorix's revolt of 52 BC. Julius Caesar estimated the number of Turoni warriors engaged against his troops at around 8000. The tribe also joined the Aedui and Treveri when they rebelled again in 21 BC, in the so-called Revolt of Sacrovir, led by Julius Sacrovir, a former Roman soldier. Tacitus recorded that the rebel army was defeated by two Roman legions from the Upper Rhine under Senator Gaius Silius. Together with many of his warriors, Sacrovir committed suicide rather than be taken prisoner. In 24 AD, Gaius Silius was tried in Rome for having sympathy with the rebels, and also committed suicide.

Uberi

Together with the Nantuaten, the Veragri and the Sedunas tribes, the Uberi, (sometimes spelled 'Viberi'), were one of the Vallenses, the four Celtic tribes living in the modern Canton of Valais in the Alpine region of modern-day Switzerland during the Roman period. Pliny said that the Uberi were a sub-group of the Lepontii tribe, an ancient Celtic people occupying areas of Rhaetia (in Switzerland and Northern Italy), and lived around the source of the River Rhône, while Ptolemy locates their territory in the Cottian Alps on the border with France. After the Romans conquered the region in around 15 BC, their territory was integrated into the 'Alpes Graiae et Poeninae' (a small province of the Roman Empire), by the Emperor Claudius. It was a single civitas shared with the other Vallensian tribes living between Lake Geneva and the Pennine Alps.

Vangiones

The Vangiones were a Germanic tribe who invaded Gaul and fought in the army of the Suebian chief Ariovistus before being defeated by Julius Caesar at the Battle of Vosges and driven back over the Rhine in 58 BC. Vanagiones territory was in the southern Black Forest of Germany, and their capital was at *Argentorate* (present-day Strasbourg). Following their subjugation, they were integrated into the Roman Empire between the first century BC and the third century AD. It is recorded that more than a thousand Vangiones warriors joined the Roman army as auxiliaries and were formed into the *Cohors Primae Vangionum* (the First Cohort of Vangiones), a unit of horse and foot soldiers, with postings at Condercum (Newcastle upon Tyne), as well as the Chesters and the Benwell forts on Hadrian's Wall.

Veliocasses

The Veliocasses were a Gallic tribe that settled in the lands between Rouen and Paris on the lower Sequana (the River Seine) in the present-day Seine-Maritime Département of Normandy, known to the Romans as Gallia Lugdunensis. The main tribal settlement was called *Ratumacos*, which was renamed later by the Romans after the reign of Augustus (27 BC–14 AD), as Rotomagus and is now the site of the city of Rouen. In 52 BC they raised 3000 men in support of Vercingetorix's rebellion against the Romans. The tribal name, Veliocasses, is thought to mean 'the curly ones', undoubtedly a reference to their typical hairstyle.

Vellavi

The Vellavi were also known as the 'Vellaves', 'Vélaunes', 'Vellaunes' or 'Vellavii'. According to Caesar, this small tribe were probably a client sub-group of the Arverni and were part of the Arvernes confederation. By the middle of the first century BC, they occupied territory in the Auvergne around Le Puy-en-Velay. Their main city (oppidum) was at *Ruessium*, now better known as Saint-Paulien. Their tribal name means 'mountain dwellers'. Later, the Roman base in Le-Puy-en-Velay was renamed as Anicium. Sometime around 400 AD, the city of Le Puy was named as *Civitas Villavorum* (meaning 'city of the Vellavii').

Venelli

By the middle of the first century BC, the Venelli tribe, (also known as 'Unelli', and in Gaulish, 'Uenelli'), had settled in the Cotentin Peninsula in north-west Normandy and their capital was at *Cosedia* (modern-day Coutances). In 57 BC, led by Viridovix, the tribe rebelled against Roman occupation and were finally defeated by the Seventh Legion under the command of Publius Licinius Crassus. However, the following year the remaining tribe rebelled again and sent troops to join a tribal confederation under the leadership of Vercingetorix at the Battle of Alesia. The allied tribes suffered a crashing defeat and Rome imposed heavy punishments on the survivors, taking many into slavery. The tribal subjugation finally brought the whole of northern Gaul under Roman rule.

Vergunni

The Vergunni lived in the River Riou Valley near Verdon in the Hautes-Alpes de Provence in south-eastern France during the Iron Age. They were one of the tribes who were subdued by Rome in 15 BC and whose name is listed among the Alpine tribes subjugated by Augustus on the *Tropaeum Alpium*, the 'Trophy of the Alps', (also known as the 'Trophy of Augustus'), at La Turbie.

Vindelici

The Vindelici were a Celtic people who lived in the Alpine foothills of Bavaria, in the Roman province of Rhaetia, around Lake Constance; the region was known by the geographer Ptolemy as *Vindelicia*. Their main settlement was at a place known to the Romans as *Augusta Vindelicum*, (present-day Augsburg), and they built at least two forts there that formed the administrative headquarters for the whole province. According to Pliny the Elder the Vindelici were one of several Alpine tribes that were conquered by Rome in around 16 BC. Groups of Vindelici warriors are known to have served later as auxiliaries in the Roman army.

Vocates

The Vocates were a Celtic tribe of Aquitania and were sometimes known as 'Vocats' or 'Vocati'. Their territory was based near the border with Spain, south of the neighbouring Cocosates tribeland, on the banks of the River Garonne in south-west France. Their capital settlement was at *Cossium*, later known as Vasatae and now Bazas, a commune in the Gironde Département. Together with the Tarusates tribe they fought two major battles, the second in 56 BC, against a Roman army led by Publius Crassus. Their defeat saw the end of any viable resistance of the Aquitani tribes of south-west Gaul. According to Caesar, the Vocates, Tarusates and their allies fielded 50,000 men, while Crassus had a legion of infantry and auxiliaries of a mere 5000. Despite their superior numbers, the encamped Gallic warriors were taken by surprise and fled, pursued by Roman cavalry, and suffered an overwhelming defeat.

It is thought that the Vasates or Vasatae tribes were probably the same people as the Vocates mentioned by Caesar. This adds to an already existing confusion, as some regard the Basavocates of Pliny and the Vasarii of Ptolemy, as well as other obscure references to the Vasates and Volcates, as alternative names for the Vocates.

Vocontii

The Vocontii tribal name translates as 'twenty', suggesting that it was actually a confederation or sub-grouping of twenty tribes or clans. Their territory was along the Rodonos (the River Rhône) located between the present-day cities of Valence and Avignon in the western foothills of the Alps, in the Roman province of Narbonensis. They were subjugated by Roman General Marcus Fulvius Flaccus in 125 BC. Their chief settlement was called *Vasio Vocontiorum*, after which the present-day town of Vasio la Romaine is named. It was originally simply called Vasio, and the 'la Romaine' element was only added in 1924, following which the town was designated as a historic monument by the Vichy government in 1942.

By the middle of the first century AD, Vasio had become one of the wealthiest cities in Gallia Narbonensis. During Roman times the Vocontii became a so-called semi-autonomous 'allied community', (a *civitas foederatae*), under Roman rule. Unlike many Celtic tribes, they flourished, being granted a degree of autonomy and the retention of their territorial tribeland well into medieval times. Some scholars claim that the historian Tacitus was born in Vasio Vocontiorum. Elements of the tribe were conscripted as mercenaries in the Roman army, where they were known as the *Ala Augusta Vocontiorum* (the August Wing of Vocontii). While accompanying Hadrian to Britain, they were stationed on the Scottish borders at Newstead and like several other Gallic tribes they may have had a part in the construction of Hadrian's Wall.

Volques

The Volques, (also known as 'Volcae' or 'Volgae'), were possibly a confederation of tribes that included the Tectosages and the Arecomices. Others argue that the Volques and the Tectosages actually were the same tribe. Whichever is true, contemporary sources, including Livy, maintained that they originated in the Hercynian Forest region, around the River Danube, and that during the third century BC they migrated into an area that would eventually become the Transalpine province of the Roman Empire.

The Volques were allies of Hannibal and sent mercenaries to fight in his army during the Punic Wars. Their tribal name is taken to mean either 'wolves' or 'falcons'. During the reign of Augustus, (c.37 BC to 14 AD), the Volques became Romanised and began to adopt Latin as their first language, which around the Perpignan and Barcelona region evolved into Catalan.

Chapter Six

The Tribes of the Iberian Peninsula

The Iberian Peninsula has known human inhabitation for at least two and a half million years, and over many centuries it has been subjected to repeated waves of migrating people. By the early Bronze Age, from the eighth to the sixth centuries, Iberia saw Celtic migrants arriving from the north and from Eastern Europe into what would become modern-day Spain and Portugal. Though their invasions were not always peaceful, eventually the indigenous Iberians of the north-eastern Meseta Central plateau, Catalonia and Aragon, formed closer bonds and accommodations with the new Celtic arrivals, through trade, through alliances and often through intermarriage, to become what were known as 'Celtiberians'.

Both Strabo and Pliny saw them as Celts. Herodotus referred to the same people as 'Celtici'. The Romans generally identified these tribes as 'Centiberes' or 'Celtiberi'. The term 'Celtiberian' refers to the inter-mixing of these tribes from the sixth century BC until the Roman period, and the way that became closely linked – geographically, socially, linguistically and culturally. The language that emerged on the peninsula would have been a fusion of early proto-Celtic and Iberian, often referred to as Hispano-Celtic or Iberian Celtic.

Initially, they inhabited the hill country between the sources of the Tajo (River Tagus) and the Iberus (River Ebro), and are thought to have settled in the north and central area alongside the Iberians, who may have taken their name from the Ebro.

It remains a matter of continuing speculation as to what routes the migrating tribes actually took, but it is most likely that they crossed the Pyrenees during several waves and moved into the regions of Navarre and Aragon, while others pressed on further into Galicia, Asturias, and Cantabria. Some have argued that some may even have crossed the Strait of Gibraltar from North Africa.

Julius Caesar also identified a third group of people who occupied Hispania; he called them 'Aquitanians'. His account reads: 'All Gaul is divided into three parts, one of which the Belgae inhabit, the Aquitani another, those who in their own language are called Celts, in ours Gauls, the third. All these differ from each other in language, customs and laws. The River Garonne separates the Gauls from the Aquitani.' The name Aquitani translates as 'long haired Gaul'. In fact, the Aquitani were more closely related to the Iberians than the Celts, and during the Roman period some twenty Aquitanian tribes occupied the northern parts of the Pyrenees in the present-day French regions of Aquitaine and Gascony and the Basque Country of Spain.

Among the Iberian tribes, mention must be made of the Lusitani, ('Lusitanos' in Portuguese), a people who were living in the Beira Alta area, surrounded by the Serra da Estrela mountains, a region that we know today as Portugal, as well as parts of Spain's Extremadura region. People were probably already occupying the land from around 1600 BC, long before the Celtic migrations began between 800 and 700 BC, but they very soon became what some writers call 'Celticised'. Like the other tribes of Iberia, the Lusitanians resisted Roman encroachment and in 194 BC they joined the Celtiberians to mount stiff resistance to the Roman presence in their territorial tribelands. However, despite the valiant leadership of their legendary chief Viriato (Viriatus) and the defeat of several legions, the might of the Roman army prevailed and the Lusitanians were subdued. Viriatus was assassinated and the Romanisation of the Lusitani began. As a result, the Roman province of Lusitania was established in central Portugal in the year 27 BC.

In 218 BC, the whole of the Iberian Peninsula was faced with a Carthaginian occupation and it was to take two Punic Wars to drive them out. Many Celtiberian mercenaries were counted among the Carthaginian army and for much of the third century BC the peninsula was a battleground in the war between Carthage and Rome. However, in 146 BC, Carthage finally succumbed to Rome's military superiority, and Iberia came entirely under Roman domination, which resulted in the deaths of several thousand Iberian and Celtiberian mercenaries who had been employed by the Carthaginians.

In the year 133 BC, following a Celtiberian revolt against Rome, General Scipio, supported by a combined force of 60,000 legionaries and mercenaries, besieged the fortified Celtiberian settlement of *Numantia*, (now known as Garray), which was located on a hill known as Cerro de la Muela, near modern Soria, on the River Douro, in the modern-day Spanish region of Castile and León. Numantia was one of a number of hill-forts that have been discovered in the region, and was typical of defensive systems found widely throughout the British Isles and Europe.

The city refused to surrender to Scipio, but after a prolonged siege and without supplies the population began to starve and cannibalism was rife. Many Numantian families committed suicide rather than be taken into captivity, or worse, but the remainder of the population surrendered, setting fire to the settlement before abandoning it. Scipio razed what remained to the ground so that it could not be reoccupied.

The subjugation of the Celtic tribes of the peninsula continued during the reign of Caesar Augustus (63 BC to 14 AD). It was much later that the Emperor Diocletian (284 AD, until his abdication in 305 AD), established a region called Gallaeci and the Romanisation of the remainder of Iberia began at a pace. Gallaeci covered present-day Asturias, Galicia, León and Zamora, as well as a substantial part of northern Portugal. Following their incorporation into the Roman Empire, many Celtiberians served as mercenaries in the legions.

Over time the Iberians in the east and south of the country and the Celts in the centre gradually assumed Roman ways of life and assimilated the Latin language. Both peoples were subsequently Romanised and eventually ceased to exist as identifiable groups.

THE TRIBES

Allotriges

The Allotriges were said by Strabo to have settlements in the mountains north of the River Arlanzon, between Bilbao and the Orinon Estuary, in what became the modern-day Spanish region of Rioja. Little is known about their origin or history, other than that they seemed set on retaining tribal sovereignty, refusing requests to join the confederacy of the neighbouring Cantabi, Autrigones and Turmodigi tribes, finally choosing to form an alliance with Rome. It has been suggested that they were the same people as the Autigones. However, Ptolemy was of a different opinion; he wrote that the Allotriges may have been a sub-group of the Vascones, or else they were a separate people who spoke the same language.

Albiones

The Albiones, (sometimes 'Albioni'), were part of a confederation of Gallaecian tribes whose territory was on the west bank of the River Navia, in western Asturias and eastern Galicia. Their name may have come from the proto-Celtic word 'albiyu', which translates as 'the upper world', which would be a reference to their geographical location on the west bank of the River Navia some way north-east of Lugo, on the northern coast of Spain. Alternatively, the name may derive from the Latin word 'albus', which translates directly as 'white'. In this case the tribal name might mean 'those who are white', a possible distinction from the southern Iberian tribes, especially those around the Mediterranean whose skin would have been darker. Very little else is known about the tribe.

Andosini

The Andosini tribe, or the 'Andosins', as they were called by the Greek historian Polybuis, are the first recorded inhabitants of the Pyreneean state of Andorra. Their remote territorial tribeland was on the southern slopes of the East Pyrenees, in the

River Segre basin. Their tribal name may be derived from 'handia', a Basque word meaning 'big' or 'gigantic'. In 218 BC, the Androsini were confronted by some 90,000 infantry and about 12,000 cavalry of the Carthaginian army led by Hannibal as they made their way through the Pyrenees towards Italy during the Punic Wars. Together with the neighbouring Aerenosii, the Andosini were subdued and their lands confiscated.

Arevaci

The Arevaci were a Celtiberian tribe whose capital of Numantia was in the upper Douro basin, east of the Meseta Central Plateau in the western province of Soria, a region that the Romans called Hispania Tarraconensis. They were much admired by neighbouring tribes for the quality of their horsemanship, fighting and metalworking. Several large stone sculptures of bulls have been found in their territory, strongly suggesting that their tribal name probably relates to their keeping of cattle, given that the Spanish word for a cow is 'vaca'.

Together with the Belli, Titii and Lusones tribes, the Arevaci were the most influential of the ethnic Celtiberian tribal confederation that dominated neighbouring tribes from their hill-fort strongholds. Under their chieftain, Avaros, they were at the forefront of the resistance to the Roman invasion of the Iberian Peninsula and mounted stiff resistance for some twenty years during what became known as the Numantine Wars, which lasted from 154 BC until the surrender of Numantia in 133 BC. After fifteen months of siege, rather than submit to the Romans, some 20,000 men, women and children of the Arevaci were reported to have committed mass suicide.

Artabri

According to Strabo, the Artabri (or in Latin, 'Arotrebae') were an ancient Celtic tribe that lived in the extreme north-west of Lusitania, known to the Romans as Hispania Tarraconensis, located around a bay called Artabrorum Sinus, in the modern-day Spanish province of Galicia. Ptolemy stated that their capital town was *Lucus Augusti* (now Lugo). In his *Geographia*, Strabo asserted that '... they inhabit the promontory called *Nerium* (modern Cape Finisterre), which is the boundary (of Iberia) on its western and northern sides', which seems to have been a glaring geographical inaccuracy. Pliny denied that the Artabri existed as a separate tribal entity at all, stating that the name was a misspelling of 'Arrotrebas'. Some historians agree with his conclusion that the Artabros and the Arrotrebas tribes were one and the same. The present-day Port of Artabri takes its name after the tribe.

Astures

The Astures were a Celtic tribe who held territory in the north-west region of modern-day Asturias, which gets its name from the tribe. Their capital was *Lucus Asturium* (modern-day Orviedo). It has been suggested that their name might be derived from the Phoenician goddess Astarte. They fought alongside Hannibal's Carthaginian army during the Punic Wars, (between 264 and 146 BC), and together with many other Celtic tribes in northern Spain, they were subdued by the Romans during the Cantabrian Wars (29–19 BC).

Sometimes called the Asturian Wars, these conflicts were the final stage in the conquest of Hispania. Both the Cantabri and Astures tribes were the last surviving independent Celtic tribes in Spain to be subdued during the reign of Emperor Augustus. Later, Asturean warriors even served as Roman legionaries, and the Second Cohort of Astures amounted to a 500-strong regiment and was stationed in South Wales during the first and second centuries AD. They were also recorded as rebuilding the granary at Great Chesters fort on Hadrian's Wall in the fourth century AD.

Ausetani

The Ausetani territory was in the modern-day province of Barcelona, situated between La Plana de Vic and the Montseny Massif in Catalonia. The tribe established a fortified town settlement called *Sebeldunum*, later known as Gerunda, which became modern-day Girona. The Ausetani spoke an Iberian language and the Roman city of Ausa (present-day 'Vic') is named after the tribe. Under their leader Amusicus, the Ausetani revolted against Roman occupation and were only subdued after a thirty-day siege by a force led by Roman General Scipio. In his *History of Rome*, Livy described the engagement, remarking that the Ausetani had supported the Carthaginian army and that the Romans, who had driven Hannibal out of Iberia, then sought to bring the Celtic tribes under Roman rule. He wrote that Scipio '...brought ninety thousand infantry and twelve thousand cavalry over the River Ebro. His next step was to reduce to submission the Ausetani, and also the district of Lacetania, which lies at the foot of the Pyrenees.' The Ilergetes and Bergusii tribes suffered a similar fate.

Autrigones

The Autrigones, possibly a sub-group of the Vascones tribe, lived around the River Ebro in Spain, and held a territory that covered the north of the Iberian Peninsula, La Rioja in the present-day Basque Country, and stretched as far as the East of Cantabria and northern Burgos. In his *Geographica*, Strabo regarded the tribe as Basques and referred to them as Allotrigones, a word that is derived from the Greek, meaning 'strange people'. The Autrigones built the town settlement of *Segisamunculum*, (present-day Cerezo de Río Tirón in the province of Burgos). They had other settlements at Deobriga and Uxama Barca. By the first century AD, the Autrigones had become Romanised, and many of their warriors joined the Roman Imperial army as auxiliary troops.

Bastetani

The ancient Iberian Bastetani tribe, (sometimes 'Bastuli'), were a tribal confederation whose territory included large tracts of the Mediterranean coast and the Sierra Nevada in the present-day provinces of Murcia, Albacete, Jaen, Almería, Granada and Málaga. Their capital and main settlement was at *Basti* (nowadays Baza, in the province of Granada); the Romans gave them the name 'Bastetani' after the town. In common with other neighbouring tribes, the Bastetani are usually grouped together as 'Tartessian', after Tartessos, the name that the Greeks called the region. The Bastetani were one of the most powerful Iberian tribes and dominated the eastern part of Hispania in the fourth and third centuries BC. They may have been the first to establish a settlement in what would become the city of Malaga. They also had a settlement at Mastia in Murcia, which was taken from them by the Carthaginians, who renamed it *Novo Carthago*, (New Cartagena).

Belli

The Belli, (sometimes 'Beli' or 'Belaiscos'), were a Celtiberian tribe whose most important settlement was at Segeda, in the valley of the Jalón in the province of Zaragoza from around the third century BC. They established a large Celtiberian confederacy, together with the Arevaci, Lusones and Titii tribes, and mounted a fierce resistance to Rome in what became known as the Celtiberian War, which lasted from 153 BC to 133 BC. They were defeated by an army led by Proconsul Quintus Caecilius Metellus Macedonicus in 143 BC. The confederation collapsed and the tribe, together with their territory, were incorporated into the Roman Empire, after which nothing more is heard of them.

Bergistani

The Bergistani, (in Latin, 'Bargusii'), were an ancient tribe of the Iberian Peninsula, who inhabited the Saiarra River Valley in the northern part of the Roman province of Hispania Tarraconensis during the first century AD. They established their capital at *Vergneum*, (modern-day Berga) in Catalonia. The Romans later renamed the Beristani capital *'Castrum Bergium'*. The tribe was first conquered by Hannibal during the Punic Wars in 218 BC. They rebelled twice against Roman occupation. First, during the Sertorian War, which took place between 80 and 72 BC, when the Bergistani joined a coalition of Roman rebels. These included Celtic, Aquitanian and other Iberian tribes, led by former Roman Governor Quintus Sertorius. The war broke out because of the rivalry between Cornelius Sulla and Gaius Marius, both of whom vied for the Governorship of Hispania. Sertorius was finally defeated by Pompey and Metellus Pius.

In the second rebellion, in 195 BC, the Bergistani were savagely defeated by the army of Marcus Porcius Cato, (also known as Cato the Censor), when many of the city's occupants were put to death and others were sold into slavery. Cato was convinced that the Bergistani uprising would convince other Iberian tribes to follow suit and decided to disarm the whole of the Iberian Peninsula north of the River Ebro. His edict was met with defiant responses which he countered by levelling the walls of many tribal cities, bringing about widespread surrender and the final subjugation of the northern Iberian tribes.

Berones

The Berones were a Hispanic Celtic people whose territory around the Ebro River valley encompassed much of modern-day Burgos, La Rioja and Navarra. Their main towns were Tricio, Oliba and Vareia. The strongest of these cities was Vareia, as it stood at a river crossing. They are thought to have been part of the Early Hallstatt migration from the Czech-German region into Gaul before continuing on to Spain. Beronian warriors were sent as auxiliary mercenary horsemen to fight in the Roman army in Italy but were brought back in 76 BC to defend territories against the attempted invasion of Berones territory in northern Celtiberia by Sertorius. The Berones fought alongside the Celtiberians and were defeated at the Battle of Calagurris (present-day Calahorra), a city of the Vascones tribe, in 186 BC. In the brutal conflict the besieged and starving Celtic tribes committed cannibalism and slaughtered their own wives and children, rather than have them taken into captivity and sold into slavery. Their city was eventually taken and destroyed, effectively bringing an end to the Sertorian War.

Bracari

The Celtic Bracari were part of the Callaeci Bracari tribal confederation, whose settlements were around the River Minho and south of the River Douro at Bracara, renamed *Bracara Augusta* in honour of the Emperor Auguatus, (present-day Braga). Another settlement was at Caladunum in the Gallaecia region of north-western Spain and northern Portugal. They had first settled there during the Iron

Age in the seventh century BC and had established several fortified strongholds in the region, many of which were besieged by Roman forces under the command of General Decimus Junius Brutus Albinus in the first century BC.

The Greek historian Appian of Alexandria wrote in his *Historia Romana* that the Bracari were a very warlike people, whose warriors fought to the death in defence of their settlements. His account describes them as '...never turning around, never showing their backs, or screaming, preferring death to captivity'.

After their subjugation, the city of Bracara became a Roman legislative centre and its inhabitants became *Civium Romanorum* (Roman citizens). Livy stated that Bracara Augusta contained 285,000 people at that time. As such, many of its people joined the Roman army and were formed as the *Cohors Callaecorum Bracarum* (the Gallaecian Cohort of Heavy Auxilliaries). Like other conquered Gallic tribes, by the mid-second century AD, Bracari warriors had become the mainstay of Roman cavalry regiments on account of their superb horsemanship. During that century others of the Bracari tribe joined a Lusitani confederation under the leadership of Viriathus, (sometimes spelled 'Viriatus' and also known as 'Viriato'), to fight against further Roman incursions. By the end of the third century, the Emperor Diocletian declared the city of Bracara Augusta to be capital of the newly founded Roman province of Gallaecia (modern-day Galicia).

Cantabri

According to some, the Cantabri were the ancestors of the modern Basques. Their territory lay among the Cantabrian Mountains behind Santander and Bilbao, on the northern coast of Spain. Their tribal name, 'Cantabri', actually means 'mountain people'. Contemporary accounts described them as the most warlike, widely regarded and fiercest people of all the native Celtic tribes on the Iberian Peninsula. It is known that Cantabrian mercenaries fought for Carthage during the Punic Wars, and not until 195 BC did the tribe submit to Rome and were incorporated into the Roman province of Hispania Tarraconensis. Their high mountain settlements were easily defended and consequently they were one of the last surviving independent Celtic tribes in Spain. It had taken eight legions to pacify them and in the end the tribe was almost annihilated. Despite repeatedly revolting against their Roman overlords, they were not finally subdued until 19 BC, during the reign of the Emperor Augustus. The tribe resisted all attempts at Romanisation, a state that continued until the sixth century, when they were finally converted to Christianity.

Capori

According to Ptolemy the chief town of the otherwise obscure Gallaecian tribe of Capori was known to the Romans as *Lucus Augusti*, and in 13 BC it was conquered by Paullus Fabius Maximus and became a Roman military camp. Nowadays, it is the city of Lugo in the A Coruña province of north-eastern Spain. It became one of the two Roman administrative capitals of Gallaecia. The tribe had a coastal settlement called Iria, a port city located at the confluence of the Ulla and Sar rivers, which was later renamed 'Iria Flavia'.

Caristii

The Caristii, (sometimes 'Caristes' or 'Caristios' in Spanish), were a pre-Roman people who settled in the west of the present-day Basque Autonomous region. Together with the Autrigones and the Varduli, they were one of the three great Basque tribes and were some of the first people to inhabit what would become the Basque Country. Pliny the Elder called them Carietes and identified their territory as the Basque interior, while Ptolemy had recorded that they had settlements between the River Deba and the River Nervion, in today's provinces of Biscay and Gipuzkoa. They established another major settlement at *Suessatio*, (which translates as 'well settled'), which could be present-day Arkaia, as well as others at Tullica, (thought to be present-day Tuyo), at Erriberagoitia on the banks of the River Zadorra, and at Veleiam located in the Municipality of Iruña de Oca, a few miles west of Vitoria. It is not exactly clear what the relationship was between these three tribes, but it is probable that they formed a political collaboration and there may have been a degree of ethnic mixing among them. According to some sources, the fate of the Caristii and the Autrigones was to be eventually assimilated into the more powerful Varduli tribe. It is therefore quite probable that elements of the Caristii tribe served in Roman cohorts in Britain, given that Varduli auxiliaries are recorded in an inscription on a Roman altar at Rochester and at Milecastle Nineteen on Hadrian's Wall.

Carpetani

By the third century BC, the Carpetani had formed a loose confederation with the Lusitani tribe, and their territory, known to the Romans as Carpetania, covered lands from the Sierra de Alcaraz in the south to the Guardiana Mountains in the north of Spain. Their domain incorporated the modern provinces of Guadalajara, Toledo, Madrid and Ciudad Real. Their main settlement and capital was at *Toletum* (Toledo) and they had a fortified settlement at Caraca (Caracas), and another in Alcalá de Henares, a Spanish city in the Community of Madrid.

In 221 BC, Hannibal defeated the Carpetani in a battle around the Tagus River, and following the defeat, many Carpetani warriors joined the Carthaginian army. In 218 BC, 3000 Carpetani men deserted and Hannibal was so worried by the episode that, fearing more widespread desertions, he let it be known that he had dismissed them himself.

Livy describes the battle between the Carpetani and the Roman legions during the Punic Wars. According to his account, the Roman praetors Gaius Calpurnius Piso and Lucius Quinctius led their forces into battle at Toletum in 193 BC. There was heavy fighting, and the Carpetani were cut to pieces by Roman cavalry, while Roman casualties were comparatively light. The Carpetani had finally been subdued by the Roman Republic and was incorporated into the Empire as a *civitas stipendiaria*, a so-called tributary or tax-paying community, the lowest status of towns and communities under Roman rule.

Celeni

The Celini (or 'Cileni') were an ancient Gallaecian Celtic tribe, living in the west of present-day Galicia, northern Portugal and the Spanish regions of western Asturias and León. Their territory was incorporated into the Roman province of Hispania Tarraconensis at the time of Caesar Augustus, at which time the entire Gallaeci adopted Roman culture.

Celtiberes

According to Diodorus Siculus writing in his *Histories*, the 'Celtiberes are a fusion of two peoples, and the combination of Celts and Iberes (that) took place after long and bloody wars'. In his words, they were a mixed hybrid race. The Roman historian Appian of Alexandria wrote that the Celtic tribes had crossed the Pyrenees sometime earlier and had 'mingled with the natives', and the name 'Celtiberia' had originated in this way. In fact, both accounts were probably largely fictional rationalisms, and the Celts and Iberes lived side by side in a neighbourly fashion, separate, but sharing a common Celtic language, religion, social structure and culture.

Sometimes referred to as the Celtiberi or Celtiberians, by the time of the Roman invasion, their territory encompassed the present-day Spanish regions of Castile, as well as land east of Burgos, west of Zaragoza, Teruel, and much of the present-day provinces of Soria and Guadalajara and La Rioja. The Celtiberi confederation included elements of the Arevaci, the Titti, the Belli and the Lusones, as well as the Vaccei, the Pelendones and the Berones tribes.

In 133 BC, their main settlement and capital at Numantia was besieged for eight months by the Roman General Scipio ahead of an army reportedly amounting to 60,000 men, of which two-thirds were mercenaries and auxiliaries. The Celtiberian tribes of Hispania Citerior had been engaged for the previous twenty years in conflict with Rome in what became known as the Numantine Wars. The Numantian leaders eventually sued for peace but refused Scipio's Draconian terms of surrender and resisted further, descending into cannibalism and starvation before finally giving in. Many Celts committed suicide. Finally the city was burnt to the ground, which ended all effective resistance to Rome in Celtiberian tribelands. The city of Numantia was eventually rebuilt by the Emperor Claudius, and was not finally abandoned until the fourth century AD.

Celtici

The Celtici were a group of tribes that inhabited several areas of the Iberian Peninsula: in the Algarve in Portugal, in the province of Badajoz north of the province of Huelva and along the coast of Galicia. The group also included the Neri, the Artabri and the Cileni tribes. They were a proto-Celtic-speaking people who may have been the first migrants into the peninsula, gradually travelling to the far western coast around the Algarve region of Portugal. According to Pliny, based purely on their religious rites, their language and the names of their settlements, in his opinion the Celtici were a tribe of the Lusitanians. His view was shared by Strabo. The Celtici were conquered by the Carthaginians under Hannibal before the Second Punic War. However, their independence following the Carthaginian withdrawal from Iberia was short-lived; they were subsequently subdued by the Romans in 179 BC.

Ceretani

The Ceretani (or 'Cerretani') people were an Iberian tribe that settled in the southern Pyrenees and established their territory in what became modern-day Cerdanya in the Segre Valley in the province of Cerona. Their main settlement and capital was at *Julia libyca*, (present-day Llivia). They were famous for the quality of their air-dried ham, which is named after them and is still known today as Serrano ham. The tribe was ultimately defeated by Consul General Gnaeus Domitius Calvinus. Sometime around 40 BC he had defeated Sextus Pompey during the Civil War with Caesar, which earned him the governorship of Hispania. He went on to subjugate the Ceretani and executed their chieftains. Calvinus was granted a triumphal procession on his return to Rome.

Cessetani

Also known as the Cossetani, this tribe lived in the Tarraco region (the present-day province of Tarragona), on the Mediterranean coast of Catalonia, with Kese, (sometimes 'Cissa', known to the Romans as *Tarraco*), as their main settlement. An archaeological dig at the turn of the century unearthed the ancient city of Banyeres del Penedes near Tarragon, a 25-hectare site, built by the Cessetani sometime during the fourth century BC. As was the fate of many Celtic tribes in Iberia, the Cessetani were vanquished by the Romans when Tarraco was taken by the Roman Consul Scipio in 218 BC and they abandoned the city around 200 AD, after which the tribe's name vanishes into the obscurity of the Roman Republic.

Cilbiceni

The Cilbiceni, (also known as the 'Cilbiaeni', 'Cilbiceans' and 'Selbyssini'), were a sub-group of the Turdetani tribe, closely related to the Iberians, which included the Elbisini, Etmanei, Ileates and the Tartessii. Their territory was on the Atlantic coastal region corresponding to the present-day province of Càdiz. The tribe may have been the one that Herodotus had called Elbysini, and which the sixth-century author and geographer Stephen of Byzantium identified as Olbysini, although some authorities dispute this. Their town of Cilbiceni (or Kilbikeni), has a name that means 'the town of Las Columnas' or 'people who live next to the Pillars', both being references to the ancient Pillars of Hercules (thought to be modern-day Gibraltar). Some of the oldest sources maintain that the Cilbiceni were actually Tartessians, which would identify them as a Celtic people.

Conii

Conii territory lay along the northern banks of the Anas (the River Guadiana in the present-day), west of the Extremadura region and the north of Portugal. Their settlement of *Conimbriga,* (also known as 'Conistorgis'), was the most important Conii 'castro' (a fortified tribal settlement), and was established in the ninth century BC; it later became a major Roman city. Located south of Ciomba in Portugal, the site has been the subject of extensive archaeological research, and many significant and exquisite mosaics have been unearthed there. In 1910 it was designated as a National Monument.

After 139 BC the city had been occupied by the Roman army, probably commanded by Decimus Lunius Brutus, and a military encampment was set up nearby. The Romans found the Conii tribe to be a friendly, peaceful people and in time as allies they adopted a Roman lifestyle. Their city became a *municipium*, (the second-highest rank of Roman city after 'colonia'). This new status gave the Conii all the privileges of Roman citizenship, after which the city was renamed *Flavia Conimbriga.* It remains the best preserved Roman site in Portugal.

Part of the Low Alentejo region and the Algarve on the coast of southern Portugal was also known to have been occupied by the Conii sometime before the sixth century BC. Together with Strabo, some argue that the Conii were also known by the name Cynetes (or 'Cynesi'), while others dismiss the argument, maintaining that the two tribes were quite different. (See also: 'Cynetes'.)

Contestani

The Contestani (or 'Contestans') were an Iberian tribe whose territory was on the banks of the River Segura, and their lands were sometimes referred to as *Constantania* and encompassed areas of eastern Murcia, Alicante and Valencia, in a region that the Romans called Hispania Tarraconensis. An important Contestani city was *Saetabis* (the present-day Spanish town of Xativa). The tribe was one of the wealthiest of the Iberian peoples, thanks to their mining of precious metals from the nearby mountains. They were permanently at odds with the neighbouring Bastitani, who occupied the centre of Murcia, and the two tribes were constantly disputing territorial boundaries. It is thought that the Contestani spoke the Iberian language.

Cynetes

The Cynetes, (identified by some as 'Conii'), lived in a territory that spread across the present-day Algarve and Lower Alentejo regions of southern Portugal, part of Badajoz and north-western provinces Cordoba and Ciudad Real, in what became the Roman province of Lusitania. The tribe had arrived in the region sometime during the sixth century BC. According to Strabo, who identified them as Celts, their capital was *Conistorgis*, which probably translates as 'City of the Conii'. During the Sertorian War (80 BC to 72 BC), the tribe aligned themselves with Rome against the Lusitanians; as an act of retribution their settlement at Conistorgis was subsequently overrun and ransacked by Lusitani tribes. Various Roman attempts to retake the city failed, and it was only after negotiations that it was returned.

It should be said that some scholars maintain that the Cynetes and the Conii were two quite different tribes.

Dragani

The Dragani were a tribe of the Ligurian culture who settled in Spain and France, north of the Bay of Biscay, beside the Pyrenees sometime in the sixth century BC. Their tribal name is thought to mean 'tribe (or people) of the dragons'. Little is known about the Dragani, but tradition has it that they established a territory in the region that the Greeks called Ophiussa. It is widely thought that they were possibly the first wave of Indo-European migrations into the Iberian Peninsula, and were direct descendants of the proto-Celtic Urnfield culture.

Edetani

The Edetani were one of the largest of the Iberian tribes with territory around the Sucro (the Xuquer/Jucar River) on the east coast of the Iberian Peninsula, in today's

Guadalaviar region in the province of Cordoba, and includes the modern-day cities of Valencia and Zaragoza. They are believed to have spoken a form of the Iberian language and were known for their fine metalworking skills. The main Edetani settlement and capital since the seventh century BC was Edeta, which now lies buried beneath the city of Liria, (sometimes, 'Lliria'). The archaeological sites of Tossal de Sant Miquel and Castellet de Bernabe have been unearthed nearby. Edetania was conquered by the Romans by 19 BC, and eventually became a Roman province.

Elbisini

The Elbisini were a sub-group of the Turdetani tribe, closely related to the Iberians, which also included the Cilbiceni, Etmanei, Ileates and the Tartessii. Their territory was on the Atlantic coastal region corresponding to the present-day province of Cadiz. According to the Greek historian and geographer Hecataeus of Miletus writing at the end of the sixth century BC, the Elbisini (whom he also called the Eloesti), had established settlements on the southern plains of Portugal, alongside other Lusitanian and Celtic tribes, but there is no mention of the tribe in later sources and little else is known about them.

Etmanei

The Etmanei were a sub-group of the Turdetani tribe, closely related to the Iberians, which also included the Cilbiceni, Elbisini, Ileates and the Tartessii. Their territory was on the Atlantic coastal region, upstream along the River Tartessos around Cadiz, and roughly corresponding to the present-day province of Huelva.

Gallaeci

The Gaellaeci, (sometimes 'Gallaecians' or 'Callaici'), were a tribal confederation of Spain and Portugal, whose name means 'the Gaulish ones'. Their expansive territory covered much of the north-western corner of the Iberian Peninsula, a region that the Romans called Hispania Tarraconensis, and which included parts of northern Portugal, Galicia, western Asturias and western Castile y León in Spain. They spoke a now extinct branch of the Indo-European language family known as Gallaic, Gallaecian, or North-western Hispano-Celtic. They predominantly built their settlements in hill-forts (known as 'castros'), part of what has become known as the Castro Hill-fort Culture. The tribe were eventually conquered in around 136 BC by Decimus Junius Brutus Callaicus, who founded the Roman city of *Portus Cale* (present-day Porto). The name Portugal is derived from the Portus Cale place-name.

Grovii

From the seventh century BC, the Grovii tribe, (occasionally known as 'Gravii'), held territory in the Minho province of northern Portugal and present-day Galicia in Spain, in the Roman province of Hispania Tarraconensis. Their chief fortified stronghold settlement was in Santa Tegra in the present-day municipality of Guarda, but they had other settlements around the rivers Qerez, Ulla, Minho and Douro. The Grovii were a sub-group or clan of the Bracari.

Pliny denied that the Grovii were Celtic, and argued that they had their origins in Greece. In the year 219 BC, warriors from the Grovii tribe fought as auxiliaries for Hannibal during the Second Punic War. By the time of the Roman invasion, they had joined the Lusitani confederation and fought the Romans under Viriatus, (also known as 'Viriathus').

In 1988, archaeological excavations were made near the town of Guarda, at the site of the original Grovii castro, which revealed an extensive settlement that included granaries, stores, workshops and houses for a resident population of between 3000 and 5000. The site was a centre for controlling sea traffic until the Romans arrived, after which its importance declined.

Iacetani

The Iacetani tribe, (sometimes 'Jacetani'), settled in the River Ebro Valley around Iaca (present-day Jaca), which became their capital city, in the southern slopes of the Pyrenees, north of Aragon. It is thought that they may have been related to the Aquitanes and could have mixed and intermarried with other neighbouring tribes, possibly including the Arenosii and Garunni, to become what have been identified as 'Celtiberians'. Ptolemy associated the tribe with the Vascones. Strabo disagreed with this definition in his *Sertorius Chronicles* and thought them to be quite independent; he described their territory as stretching from the Pyrenees to Lleida and Huesca.

The tribe was defeated by the Romans, supported by the Suessetani tribe, and led by Cato the Elder in 195 BC. Writing in the first century AD, Julius Caesar recorded that, together with the Ausetani and Illurgavoness, the Iacetani were one of the tribes that changed allegiances and fought alongside him in his invasion of the Iberian Peninsula. In the year 19 AD their territory was taken into the Empire, but unusually, they were denied the benefits of Roman citizenship. Thereafter they disappear from all historical records.

Ilercavones

The Ilercavones were an Iberian tribe whose territory extended from the modern-day Spanish province of Tarragona, to the north of Castellon and the east of Teruel, a few miles from Tivissa in present-day Catalonia. The tribe built a walled area with a fortified defensive system at Moleta del Remei on Montsia Mountain, (thought to be present-day Castellet de Banyoles), which they began in the fourth century BC on an original site that had been established earlier, sometime between the seventh and ninth centuries BC. It became their capital, and it was from here that they controlled the estuary region of the River Ebro. The settlement was occupied by around 500 people, with living quarters situated around a central ward. The city of Castellet de Banyoles was destroyed by the Romans after a long siege by an army commanded by Cato the Elder, but its two pentagonal defensive towers still survive.

Ilergetes

The territory of the Ilergetes tribe, (sometimes 'Ilergetae'), was in the plains around the Segre and Cinca rivers in the Roman province of Hispania Tarraconensis. The Ilergetes were one of the biggest Iberian tribal confederations, and had their main settlement and capital at Iltrida, in the modern province of Huesca in Catalonia. In 49 BC, a civil war battle took place there between Julius Caesar and his main rival and adversary, Pompey. The tribe played an important role in the Carthaginian army against Rome during the Second Punic War. They were finally defeated by the Roman Consul Scipio, at which time Iltrida fell into Roman hands. Later the city was proclaimed the Roman Municipium of Ilerda – today it is known as Lerida.

Indigetes

Also known as the 'Indigetae', and sometimes as 'Indiketes', they were a confederation of four tribes who lived in the north-east of the Iberian Peninsula around the gulf of the ancient Greek Colony of Empuries (Ampurias) and Rhoda (Rosas) on the Costa Brava, an area roughly corresponding to the present-day province of Girona. The Iberian settlement of El Puig de Sant Andreu was constructed by them as their capital and main settlement in the sixth century BC, and remained inhabited until the second century BC. In 218 BC they were conquered by Rome and in 195 BC they mounted a rebellion that was put down by the Consul Marcus Porcius Cato. Like many other conquered tribes, the Indigetes gradually adopted Roman ways, abandoning their traditional homes for Roman villas and lifestyles.

Interamici

The Interamici (or 'Interamnici') were one of the Gallaeci tribes that lived in southern Galicia in the Ourense province of Spain and parts of the northern province

A Roman coin depicting Julius Caesar.

Lusitanian Burial Pot. Urnfield Culture, Central Europe c.1300 - 500 BC.

Ceramaic Burial Pot with lid, Lusitanian Urnfield Culture c.1300 - 500 BC.

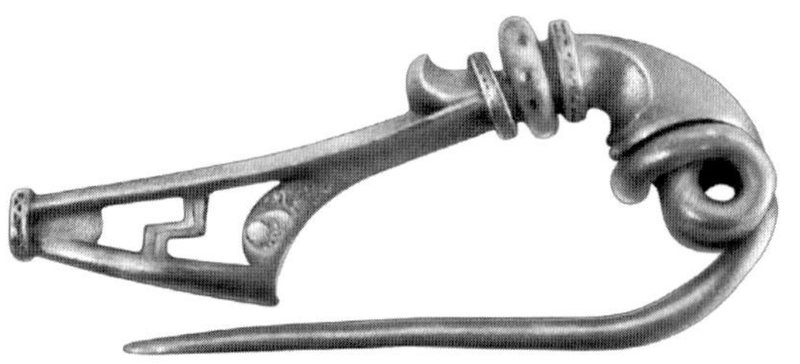

The Market Rasen gold brooch, 'Birdlip' style. La Tène, 1st century AD.

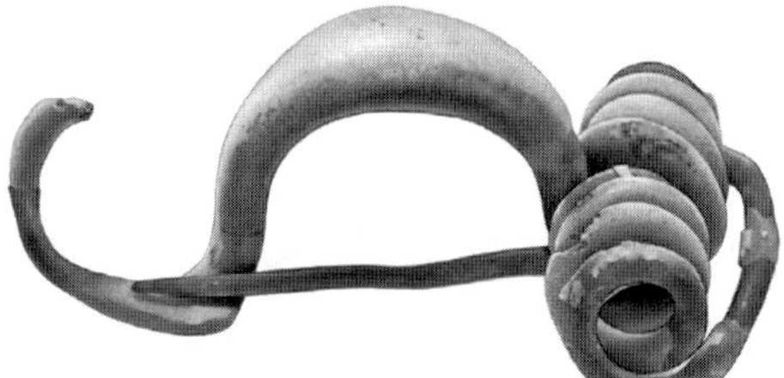

Copper Bow Brooch, 4th-2nd century BC.

Iron Age Shields discovered in the River Thames, London:

Above left: The Battersea Shield.

Above right: The Wandsworth Shield.

High status warrior chief, 1st century AD.

Depiction of Ambiorix from the monument at Tongeren, Belgium.

Depiction of the head of Brennus. Musée National de la Marine, Paris.

Depiction of Vercingetorix at Alise-Sainte-Reine, Côte-d'Or, Burgundy, France.

The Morrigan, Triad of Goddesses discovered at Bath, England. Roman era.

Two British stone carved goddess figurines. 3rd - 1st century BC.

Shrine plaque to Coventina found at Carrawburgh near Hadrian's Wall.

Stone carving of a Celtic Warrior, late 3rd to early 2nd century BC. Czech Republic.

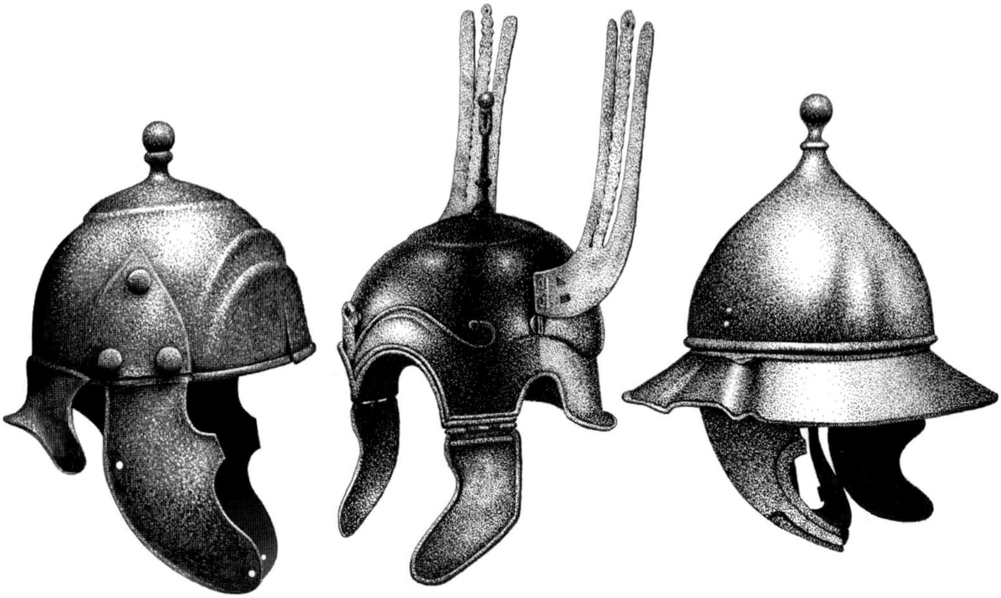

Celtic armoured helmets:

Above left: Eastern Celtic La Tène Helmet, 3rd - 2nd century BC.

Above centre: Celtiberian Helmet, Zaragossa, Spain, 3rd - 1st century BC.

Above right: Celtic Horseman's Helmet, 1st century AD.

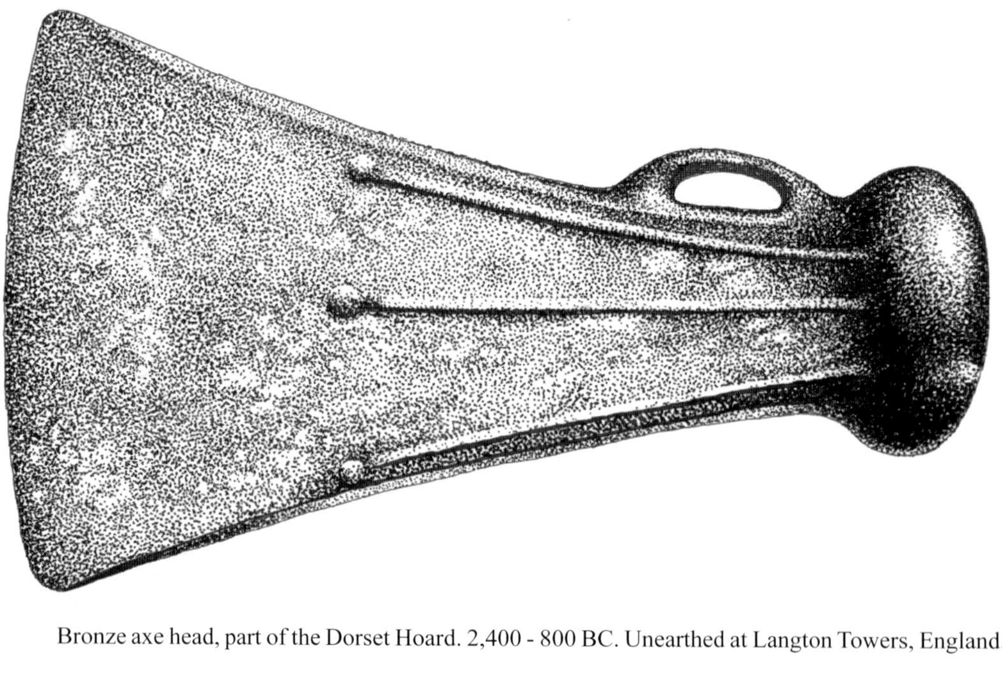

Bronze axe head, part of the Dorset Hoard. 2,400 - 800 BC. Unearthed at Langton Towers, England.

Roman coin depicting the head of the Emperor Claudius.

The Emperor Hadrian depicted on a Roman coin.

Depiction of Augustus Caesar on a Roman coin.

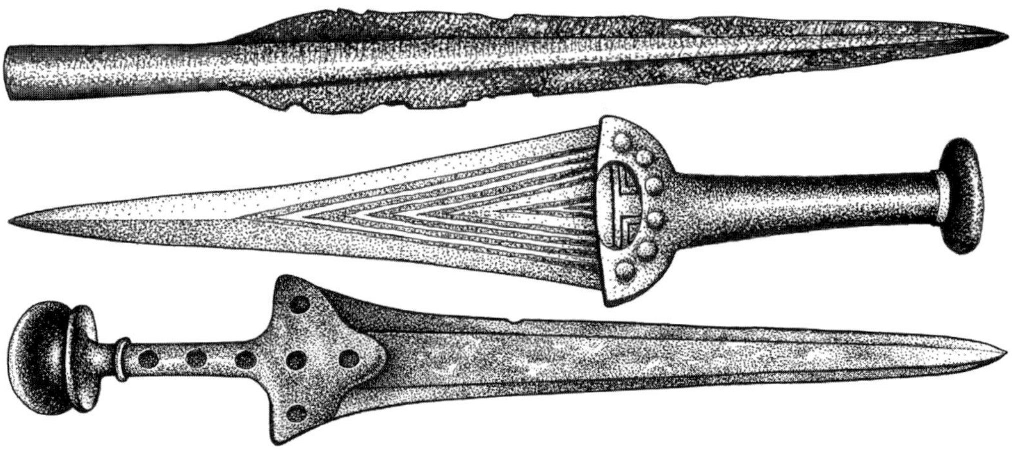

BronzeAgeWeapons:

Top: Javelin Head. *Middle*: Hallstatt period dagger. *Bottom*: Bronze Age short sword.

An Iceni gold coin, part of the Snettisham Hoard, British Museum.

Medal depicting Tranis, the Celtic god of thunder.

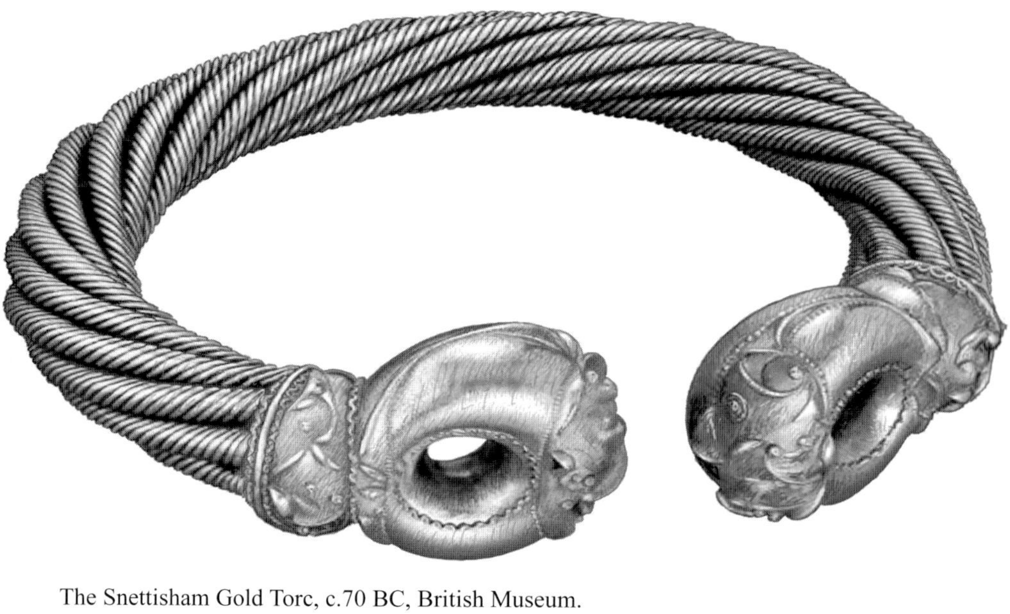

The Snettisham Gold Torc, c.70 BC, British Museum.

of Tras-os-Montes in the present-day north-east of Portugal. Their territory lay between the Minho and Sil rivers – hence their tribal name meaning 'between rivers'. Little more is known.

Laietani

The Laietani (or 'Layetani') occupied the lands around the present-day town of Badalona, a few miles south of Barcelona, from the third century BC until the arrival of the Romans. Early ancestors of the Laietani tribe first settled the region sometime in the fifth century BC. According to Strabo, Laietani territory lay between the River Llobregat and the town of *Blandae* (Blanes), and there is later evidence that the tribe lived in two settlements in Barcelona – one located on Montjuic Hill and the other on Taber Hill. Another archaeological dig at Poblat Iber de Ca n'Oliver revealed that between the sixth century BC and the first century AD it had also been one of their settlements. It is thought that they spoke a dialect of an Iberian language.

Lancienses

The Lancienses were a Lusitanian sub-tribe of the Astures, in the Hispania Tarraconensis region. Lancia, (sometimes 'Lanciatum'), was their main settlement and capital city. The exact location of Lancia is not clear, but it has been associated with the Villasabariego castro, close to Mansilla de la Mulas in the present-day Municipality of León. Despite being strongly fortified, the city was destroyed by the Roman Seventh Gemini Legion (*Legio VII Gemina*), before it was rebuilt and became a Roman-occupied city. According to classical sources, the Lancienses were the last Iberian tribe to be subdued by the Romans.

Limici

The Limici were a Celtic tribe of Gallaeci, who occupied territory in the swampy region around the River Lima, in the border region between Minho in Portugal and Galicia in Spain. Together with the Copori and Helleni, the Limici were part of a larger Gallaeci alliance. The tribe had a hill-fort at Talabriga, which was located near Aveiro, one of the oldest towns in Portugal, which saw stiff resistance to the Roman invasion of the second century BC. Following the subjugation of the tribe by an army led by Quinto Fulvio Flaco in 181 BC, Talabriga was renamed *Caesarobriga* (present-day Talavera de la Reina), and became the Roman capital of the Vouga region from about 30 BC to 300 AD.

Lobetani

The Lobetani were a small Iberian tribe whose territory was around the present-day Sierra de Albarracin mountain range in the south-west of Teruel province in Spain. Their chief city was called Lobetum, but its precise whereabouts is unknown. The tribe clashed with the Celtiberian Belli tribe and became allies of Rome at the time of the Second Punic War (218–201 BC), before being incorporated into the Roman province of Hispania Citerior in 156 BC. By the first century AD the tribe had become fully Romanised.

Lusitanians

The Lusitanians, (or 'Lusitani'), lived south of the Douro and Tagus rivers in Portugal and in the north-west Extremadura region of Spain. They were also sometimes called 'Belitanians'. Technically, the Lusitanians are not considered to be Celts, although their language bears a clear resemblance to Celtic. It is generally accepted that they were a pre-Celtic Indo-European-speaking culture, closely related to that of the Vettones, who were a neighbouring tribal confederation, and may have been related to the Lusones tribe of north-east Iberia. The Lusitanians fought under Viriathus in their war against the Romans. During the Second Punic War against Rome (218 to 201 BC), the Lusitanians supported Hannibal's Carthaginian army. They were finally defeated by Praetor Servius Galba (later Emperor) in 150 BC, when some 9000 Lusitani were killed and 20,000 sold into slavery. After the death of Viriatus, resistance to Rome gradually declined and the Lusitani began to adopt Roman culture and gained Roman citizenship. Lusitania became a Roman province in central Portugal in 27 BC. In the sixteenth century, 'Lusitanian' became a common reference to the modern-day Portuguese people.

Lusones

The Lusones were a Celtiberian tribe who settled around 1000 BC in the Meseta Plateau area of central Iberia, an area that the Romans called Hispania Citerior. They were the smallest of the four tribes that made up the Celtiberians. The tribe came into conflict with the Romans, whose legions were led by Quintus Fulvius Flaccus, during the third and second centuries BC. In 181 BC they were joined by other Celtiberians in rebellion against Roman rule and massed an army of 35,000 to join them in battle. Despite several early successes, they were eventually subdued, first by Tiberius Gracchus and finally by Consul Scipio.

During the first century AD, under the Emperor Augustus, the territory came under Roman administrative rule and a *municipium* was founded at Bilbilis, the tribe's main settlement and capital, which was renamed *Augusta Bilbilis* to reflect the name of the Emperor, at which time the inhabitants were granted Roman citizenship.

Meidubrigenses

The Meidubrigenses, (sometimes 'Meidubrigensis'), were a Lusitani tribe whose main settlement was at Meidubriga or Medobriga, (modern-day Castro de Ranhados) in the province of Lusitania. The town lay at the foot of the Mons Herminius (the present-day Serra de Estrela), a few miles north of Meda. The Romans knew the place as *Civitas Meidubrigensium* after it was captured in 48 BC by Quintus Cassius Longinus, the Roman Governor of Spain at that time. Records show that the Meidobrigenses were involved in the building of the stone arched Tagus Bridge in Alcantara in Extramadura around 105 AD, during the reign of Trajan, which is asserted by an inscription on the bridge stonework. According to Pliny, the inhabitants of Meidubriga were also known as the 'Meidubrigenses Plumbari', on account of their lead mines.

Nemetati

The Nemetati were a Celtic Gallaecian tribe who settled between the Cavado and Ave rivers in the province of Minho, north of the River Douro in present-day Portugal in the seventh century BC. The tribe may have been allied to or possibly a sub-tribe or sept of the Bracari. They established a capital city at *Nemetobriga*; like most tribal oppida whose names end in the suffix '-briga', it derives from the proto-Celtic word 'brixs', which means 'hill', and often relates to a hill-fort. However, it is thought that their main hill-fort was at the Citania de Sanfins in Paços de Ferreira.

In September 493 AD, an army of 25,000 thousand Nemetati warriors set out to wage war on the Massilians, who at that time were allies of Rome. In response, General Publius Scipio immediately despatched the Sixth Legion (the *Legio VI*) under the command of Consul Cornelius Blasio to the Massilian's aid. The Roman force arrived late to the conflict, which the Massilians had been fighting for some time. However, the combined Roman-Massilian force prevailed and by mid-November the Nemetati had been defeated, reportedly having lost 10,000 of their warriors. The surviving Nemetati fled to seek shelter among the Allobroges tribe, before moving eastwards. Blasio pursued them across the Alps and finally confronted them in Liguria. A vicious engagement took place during which what remained of a once great Nemetati army was virtually exterminated. Little more information seems to exist about the tribe thereafter.

Olcades

The Olcades were an Iberian tribe that occupied the Spanish region of La Mancha, in the south-eastern fringe of the Iberian mountains, and their major settlement was at Althea. They formed the ruling elite and settled at least twelve cities in the present-day Castille-y-La Mancha province. During the Second Punic War, the Olcades, along with a confederation of the Vaccaei and Carpetani tribes, resisted Carthaginian expansion into their territories, only to be defeated eventually by Hannibal at the Battle of the River Tagus in 221 BC. For a time they were subject to Carthaginian rule and groups of Olcades warriors were forced to serve as mercenaries in their armies. Following Hannibal's departure from Iberia, the tribe was aligned with Rome and were granted a degree of independence, until the late second or early first centuries BC when they finally lost their tribal lands and were subsumed into the Roman Empire.

Oretani

The Oretani, (sometimes 'Oretoni' or 'Oretanii'), were an Iberian tribe whose territory stretched from the northern slope of the Sierra Morena and Murcia to southern La Mancha. The name Oretani means ‘highlanders’, a reference to their territory in the Andalusian mountains. Recent archaeological excavations at the ancient site of Cástulo, in Linares, Jaén, have revealed that it had been occupied since the sixth century BC and was probably one of several major settlements of the Oretani, with human evidence unearthed dating back to the Neolithic period. The Oretani are thought by some to have spoken an Iberian language, but others claim they spoke a Celtic language similar to the Celtiberians. Pliny regarded the tribe as Germani, but they are generally taken to be a mixed confederacy of Iberian and Celtic tribes. In 156 BC, they were incorporated into the Hispania Citerior province of the Roman Empire.

Paesuri

It is thought that the Paesuri, (sometimes ‘Paesures’), were a dependant sub-group of the Lusitani. What is known for certain is that they held territory near Carquere, (Caceres) between the Douro and Vacua (Vouga) rivers in northern and central Portugal, in the Roman province of Hispania Citerior, where they had settled in the fifth century BC. Some suggest that they were of Thracian origin and were probably Celticised by the neighbouring Lusitani.

Archaeological digs have found human skeletal remains, including skulls bearing tooth marks, suggesting that the Paesuri may have been cannibals. The tribe was forcibly incorporated into the Hispania Ulterior province by Julius Caesar in 60 BC, and by 13 BC their former territory became part of the province of Lusitania by the order of the Emperor Augustus. Their tribal name translates as ‘flowing (or white) river’.

Pelendones

The Pelendones, (sometimes ‘Pellendones’, and occasionally, ‘Cerindones’), were possibly of mixed Illyrian and Celtic origin, and are thought to have migrated to the Iberian Peninsula sometime in the fourth century BC. They settled in the area between the River Duero and the Moncayo Mountains. Together with the Arevaci, Tittos (Titii), Lusones and Bellos, they are counted as one of the five Celtiberian tribal groups. They are believed to have originally migrated from Belgium or the lower Rhineland in the fourth century BC and established four major towns and settlements at Numantia, Visontium, Augustobriga and Savia. However, they lost these lands when they opposed the Romans in what became known as the Fourth Celtiberian War. In the late first century BC, the Emperor Augustus created a Roman colony in Pelendones territory and the tribe were incorporated into the Roman province of Hispania Tarraconensis.

Plentauri

Sometimes known as the 'Pleutauri', the small Plentauri tribe lived in the mountainous Cantabrian range around the River Ebro, in the present-day region of La Rioja. Even under the threat of Roman invasion, the Plentauri resisted all requests from the Cantabri and Autrigones to join them in a tribal confederation, and ultimately, the tribe sought the protection of Rome.

Quaquerni

The Quaquerni, (sometimes 'Querquerni), were a minor ancient Celtic tribe of Gallaecia, that lived in the mountains and around the estuaries of the Cavado and Tamega rivers in the province of Minho in present-day northern Portugal. In his *Geographia* the Greek geographer Ptolemy called them Kouakernoi (*Κουακερνοί*). Their tribal name may be derived from the Latin word *quercus*, meaning 'oak', and it may be translated as 'oak people'. It is thought that they may heve been a sub-group or sept of the Gallaeci Bracarii tribe.

Sedetani

The Sedetani were an ancient Iberian group that some scholars identify as either closely related to or even the same people as the Edetani. Their territory extended from central to southern Aragon and they had major settlements stretching from the River Jalon to the Aguas Vivas, in Salduie in the Zaragoza province and Azaila in Aragon. Like many other Iberian and Celtic tribes, they soon came into conflict with advancing Roman armies and during the Sedetanian War (205 BC – 203 BC), supported by the Belli, Lusones, Arevaci and Vascones tribes, they fought the Romans in the Battle at Barcino (Barcelona). Despite winning several engagements the alliance was eventually defeated and surrendered to Rome in 203 BC. Once subdued, their territories were annexed to the Roman Empire and their settlement at Sagunt became a Roman colony called *Caesaraugusta,* named after the Emperor Augustus, whose bronze statue has dominated the city since it was presented by Benito Mussolini in 1940. The present-day name of Zaragoza is derived from the Roman name, *Caesaraugusta*. The Romans occupied the whole of this territory until the fifth century, when invasions by Gothic tribes marked the fall of the Western Roman Empire.

Silingi

The Silingi, (sometimes 'Silings', and in Latin, 'Silingae'), were a Germanic Vandal tribe who may have originated near the River Silingula in Silesia and migrated to settle in the central Iberian provinces of Lusitania and Carthaginiensis sometime around 409 AD. Sections of the tribe also resettled in the Roman province of Hispania Baetica, (modern-day Andalusia). The name Silesia is most probably a Slavonic literation of the Silingi tribal name, and probably means 'the land of the Silingi'. The tribe were first mentioned by Ptolemy in the second century AD when he wrote that they had lived south of the Suebi-Semnone tribe, north of the Carpathian Mountains. Some scholars have speculated that the Siligi may have been the same people as the Nahanarvali, based largely on the writings of Tacitus, who placed them in the same geographical location as Ptolemy. During the time of Emperor Marcus Aurelius, (161–180 AD), the Silingi lived in what were referred to as 'the Vandal Mountains', which were later part of Sudetenland, and now in the Czech Republic. The Silingi established permanent settlements in Iberia and forged trade relationships with Rome that lasted well into the fourth century AD.

Tamagani

The Tamagani were a Gallaecian tribe that lived near the River Tamega in the present-day Tras-os-Montes in the Chaves region of Portugal. As very little is known about the tribe, they are commonly described as 'one of the lost tribes of Lusitania'.

Titii

The Titii (or 'Tithii'), together with the Arevaci, Belli, Berrones and Lusones, were Celtic-speaking peoples who formed part of the historic Celtiberian tribes, of which they were possibly the smallest. Their tribal lands were along the middle Jalón and upper Tajuña valleys, somewhere between Zaragoza and the Guadalajara provinces. The tribe probably migrated to the Iberian Peninsula around the fourth century BC. They formed an allied confederacy with the Belli and Arevaci against Rome during the Celtiberian Wars of the second century BC before finally signing a peace treaty with the Roman military tribune Tiberius Gracchus in 179 BC. However, they fought alongside the Belli again in 142 BC and were defeated by Proconsul Quintus Caecilius Metellus Macedonicus in 134 BC, when they lost their territories and were incorporated into the province of Hispania Citerior. The Celtiberian tribes became Romanised and nothing else is known about the Titii after this date.

Turdetani

The Turdetani were an Iberian tribe who are thought to have migrated from the Black Sea region into southern Iberia as early as the eighth century BC. Their territory covered a region stretching from the River Guardiana in Andalusia to the

Guadalqutvir in the west, and included a significant part of the Strait of Gibraltar, in the modern-day province of Seville. In his *Geographia*, Strabo maintained that the Turdetani were culturally descendants of the Bronze Age Tartessians. Although the tribe were regarded as the least warlike of the Iberian tribes, during the Punic Wars they employed 10,000 Celtiberian mercenaries to defend their territorial tribelands. Nevertheless, having initially resisted Roman incursions, eventually they rebelled against Rome, before they were defeated in 195 BC by legions under the command of Marcus Porcius Cato the Elder. He was later appointed Consul of Iberia.

Turduli Veteres

The Turduli Veteres, (sometimes simply 'Turduli'), held tribal lands mainly in the south and centre of modern-day Portugal and included parts of the Extremadura coast, northern Huelva and around the River Guadiana in Andalusia. The chief settlement and capital of this Celtiberian tribe was at *Ibolca*, (sometimes 'Obulco'), nowadays the city of Porcuna, in the Roman province of Hispania Baetica. The city of Granada is reputedly the earliest settlement that the Turduli established.

Pliny wrote of *Iponuba*, which had been founded by the tribe in the sixth century BC, and argued that theTurduli were what remained of an ancient Tartessian society that had been based in southern Spain and that had come under the influence of the Iberian tribes that dominated the eastern parts of Andalucia.

As part of their resistance to the Roman advance in Hispania, the Turduli hired a force of 10,000 Celtiberian mercenaries to fight alongside them. Ultimately the tribe was defeated and in 61 BC, sub-groups of the Turduli, (which included the Veteres and the Oppidani), were incorporated into the Roman province of Hispania Ulterior by Julius Caesar.

Turmodigi

The Turmodigi were a Celtic people who settled around the Arlazon and Arlaza river valleys in the Burgos and Palencia provinces of Spain during the fourth century BC. Pliny referred to the tribe as the *Segisamonenses* and their capital as at *Segisama* (modern-day Sasamon); it became the headquarters of Augustus's Roman legions during the Cantabrian Wars from 29–19 BC.

Vaccaei

The Vaccaei were a Celtic tribe whose territory was in the valley of the *Durius*, (the Latin name of the modern-day River Duoro), with *Pallantia* as their major settlement and capital (present-day Palencia, in Castile y Léon province), where they held territory from the third century BC. The classical author Diodorus described them as the most cultured people among all the neighbouring tribes.

In 220 BC the Carthaginian armies of Hannibal attacked the Vaccaei and took the tribal settlement of *Hermandica* (present-day Salamanca). In his *Histories*, Polybuis recorded one of the engagements: '…Hannibal turned the tables on the enemy, and, re-crossing the river, (the Tagus), attacked and put to flight their whole army, to the number of more than a hundred thousand men'.

Later, suffering encroachment from the Roman legions, several tribes rebelled under the leadership of the Vaccaei. In 179 BC, they were defeated by the Romans but were continually rebellious and it was not until the year 29 BC that the Roman Consul Titus Statilius Taurus finally managed to subdue them. Within two years, they were incorporated into the Roman province of Hispania Tarraconensis and became fully Romanised; nothing more is known of the Vaccaei after the third century AD.

Varduli

The Varduli, (sometimes 'Vadulli'), were a Celtic or possibly Aquitanian tribe (opinions vary) who settled in the north of the Iberian Peninsula, in a territory that included the present-day Basque Country and parts of western Navarre, an area now known as Guipuscoa. They had an important settlement at *Donostia*, (modern-day San Sebastian), and probably spoke an early version of what became the Basque language; the dialect of Guipuzcoa, also known as the Central dialect of Euskara, is still spoken today in the region. Their territorial tribeland was known as Vardulia, which translates as 'borderland' or 'limit'. As conscripts in the Roman army, the *Cohort I Fida Vardullorum* (First Cohort of Vardulli) worked on several forts in the north of Britain, including Milecastle Nineteen on Hadrian's Wall, and records exist that place the Vardulli drawing supplies at the fort of Vindolanda. From 138 BC to 61 AD they were recorded further north on the Antonine Wall. The Varduli were assimilated by the Vascones tribe in the sixth and seventh centuries AD.

Vascones

The territory of the Vascones, (or 'Vascons'), covered the whole of Navarre and part of Alava, Guipuzcoa, an area of the province of Zaragoza, and La Rioja in north-eastern Spain. The tribe's migrations into Iberia took place in the late sixth century BC and they settled in the region that the Romans called *Novempopulana* or *Aquitania Tertia*.The present-day cities of Calahorra, Tudela and Pamplona all began life as Vascones settlements. The Vascones tribal name roughly translates as 'highlanders'. It is thought that their language may have been an early precursor of the modern-day Basque language and the tribe is often considered the true ancestors of the Basque people. The old province of Gascony in south-west France derives its name from the Vascones. Unlike their neighbouring Aquitanian and Cantabrian tribes, the Vascones were peacefully assimilated into the Roman Empire.

Vescetani

The Iberian Vescetani tribe, (sometimes 'Oscenses'), held territories in northern Aragon and around the Cinca River valley. Their capital and main settlement was at Bolskan (present-day Huesca). For some time it was held by the renegade Roman General Quintus Sertorius, an Iberian hero who defeated all the Roman attempts to remove him. He was finally assassinated in 72 BC and in 37 BC the city became the Roman colony of *Urbs Victrix Osca*. Vescetani territory and possessions were destroyed in 179 BC by the Roman Consul Gaius Terentius Varro, after which the city was refounded and given the name Osca.

Vettones

The Vettones were a pre-Roman Celtic tribe of the Iberian Peninsula who had migrated into the area during the ninth century BC and intermarried with the indigenous Ligurians. Their territorial tribelands were between the Douro and Tagus rivers south of Salamanca in western Spain as well as the Serra de Mogadouro and Serra de Lapa in modern-day Portugal. The ancient capital of the Vettones was at Castro de Ulaca in the Spanish province of Castilla y León, which they established well before the arrival of the Romans in Iberia, and was not abandoned until the first century AD.

They were a cattle-herding people, best known for their stone-sculptured representations of bulls and pigs, known as 'verracos' in Spanish and 'berrão' in Portuguese, of which more than 400 examples are known to exist, a significant number of which are located in the Ambles Valley.

The tribe controlled the area around present-day Avila, which they heavily fortified as a stronghold in the second century BC and which they named *Obila*, which translates as 'high mountain'. The Vettones formed an alliance with the Lusitani during the so-called Lusitanian War of 155 AD, when 6000 Roman soldiers were killed, including their commander, General Marcus Terentius Varro. For their part in the invasion of Britain in 43 AD, a Vettones auxiliary cavalry regiment, the *Ala Hispanorum Vettonum*, were all granted Roman citizenship by the Emperor Vespasian. Stone monuments that mention the regiment are found in the British cities of Bath, Carleon, Brecon and Durham.

Zoelae

The Zoelae people, (sometimes 'Zelas' or 'Zoelas'), were a Celtic tribal confederacy of Gallaecia that probably included elements of the Desonci and the Tridiavi tribes, who may have migrated into Iberia from the Hallstatt culture of central Europe. Some maintain that that the origin of the Zoelas is uncertain, but many authors consider them one of the oldest ethnic groups in the Iberian Peninsula. The precise location of their tribal territory is also unclear, but it has been suggested that it likely lay between the border of Zamora (modern-day León) and Tras-os-Montes in northern Portugal, between the mountains of Serra da Nogueira and Mogadouro. They also established settlements along the Duoro, Sabor and Angueira rivers. Some historians have their capital in *Ocellum Galaicorum* (present-day Ouselle), in the Lugo municipality of Becerrea, but most think that the present-day city of Curunda is more likely. The tribe was finally subdued by Rome early in the second century BC.

Chapter Seven

The Tribes of Galatia

The story of the Galatians, whom the Greeks called *Galatai*, began when an inter-tribal confederation of around 150,000 Celtic warriors undertook one of several mass migrations to the east, led by Brennus, the Gallic war chieftain of the Senones tribe. They invaded Greece in the third century BC, but despite several victories, the army of Brennus was ultimately defeated at Delphi and his armies scattered. However, three tribes of that confederation (the Tolistobogii, the Tectosages, and Trocmi), led by two chiefs, Leonorius and Lutarius, went on to besiege Byzantium. From here they migrated through the Balkans into Thrace and moved on into the territory of ancient Phrygia in the centre of Anatolia (modern-day Turkey). The three tribes finally established settlements in land that became known as Galatia, which translates as 'land of the Gauls'. They split the land into three parts, and founded the cities of Ancyra, Tabia and Pessinus.

All tribal differences that hitherto existed between the three tribes were set aside, and a new administrative and political order based on a cross-tribal council was established. Strabo called this council a *drynemetum*, a word that loosely translates as 'the sacred oak grove', harking back to the traditional Celtic councils or woodland meeting places. In this council each of the three tribes supplied representatives. In his *Geographia* Strabo wrote that 'The Council of the twelve tetrarchs consisted of three hundred men, who assembled at Drynemetum, as it was called.'

Galatia grew to become one of the most powerful states in Asia Minor under this new system. However, the acquisition and settlement of Anatolia by the Galatian tribes was a far from peaceful process. Livy recorded that '…so great was the terror of their name, their numbers being also enlarged by great natural increase, that in the end even the kings of Syria did not refuse to pay them tribute'. These reputedly fierce warriors continued to ravage and pillage the neighbouring people of their newly acquired territory, while still maintaining a distinctive Celtic identity in the preservation of their language, religion and customs.

However, both Livy and Diodorus suggested that the cultural identity of the Galatians had changed due to their interaction with the surrounding Hellenes. Over time, these former western Celtic people had become eastern Celts, and it was inevitable that they would begin to adopt some of the Hellenic customs of their neighbours and eventually became known as 'Hellenic-Celtic' or 'Gallo-Greeks', or as the Romans called them, *Gallograeci*. Despite these strong external influences on Galatian culture, their language preserved a Gallic identity that distinguished them from the other peoples of Asia Minor.

The Romans conquered the Galatians in 64 BC, and in 25 BC, during the reign of Augustus Caesar, it was established as a Roman province. Following their annexation, many Galatian warriors were integrated into the army by governor Marcus Lollius, and formed the Roman *Legio XXII Deiotariana*, (the Twenty-Second Legion of Deiotarus), named after the Celtic king of Galatia and ally of Rome.

The Galatians were the first non-Jewish people to convert to Christianity, though elements of the old pagan religion often persisted alongside it. For this reason, in the first century AD, St Paul the Apostle made missionary journeys into Galatia and was disturbed by the way that many old Celtic practices were still in common use. This prompted him to write his *Epistle to the Galatians*, in which he urged them to forego their 'pagan' Celtic practices and stay faithful to Christianity.

THE TRIBES

Aigosages

The Aigosages, a sub-group of the Tectosages, were a Galatian-Celtic tribe dwelling on both sides of the narrow passage between the Aegean Sea and the Sea of Marmara, (the Hellespont, known today as the Dardanelles), first in Thrace and then in Troas and Mysia on the Asian side. In 218 BC, King Attalus II Philadelphus of Pergamum employed Aigosages mercenaries to fight in his campaigns in Aeolis and Phrygia, granting them extensive territorial holdings in Phrygia as payment. However, the coastal region was given to the Trocmi, Aeolis and Ionia were ceded to the Tolistobogii, and the Tectosagi were granted the inland region. The Aigosages tribe carried out many raids against these other neighbouring tribes and met their end after attempting a takeover of the territory of Abydos and the town of Arisba, where they were finally defeated by King Prusias I of Bithynia in 217 BC. The whole tribe, including the women and children, were put to the sword.

Ambituti

The Ambituti, (sometimes 'Ambitouti'), were a tribe of Gallic-Illyrian warriors and a sub-group or clan of the Tolistoboii tribe, who had settled near Breda in the south of Galatia and went to Turkey as mercenaries in the third century BC. The Ambitouti tribal name comprises two elements: 'ambi-', meaning 'on both sides', and 'touti', which means 'all of the 'folk'. Hence, 'all of the people from all sides'.

Tectosages

The Tectosages tribe (or 'Tectosagii') originated in south-eastern France, which became known as the Roman province of Narbonensis. Polybius called these Galatian peoples Aigosages or Rigosages. Together with the Arecomici they were part of the confederation of the Volcae. The tribal name has two elements: the Celtic prefix 'texto', meaning 'property' or 'possessions', and 'sagi', meaning 'who is seeking'. It can be translated as 'those who seek possessions' or 'striving for possession'. The Greek philosopher Strabo maintained that they originated in the region around Tolosa in southern Gaul (present-day Toulouse). A group of the Tectosages, accompanied by the Tolistobogii and the Trocmi, invaded Greece and migrated to Galatia in the third century BC, where they settled and established their capital at Ancyra (modern-day Ankara, Turkey). Ptolemy listed Tectosages settlements at Corbeus and Aspona. All three tribes were defeated and subjugated by the Roman Consul Gnaeus Manlius Vulso at the battles of Mount Olympus and Mount Magaba in 189 BC.

Teutobodiaci

In the third century BC, the Teutobodiaci tribe settled in Cappadocia, a region of central Anatolia around the Sakarya River in present-day Turkey. Pliny refers to the Teutobodiaci as a Gallic tribe, one of the four clans (or septs) of the Tectosages, which also included the Voturi, Ambituti, Tosiopes and the Tolistobogii, with whom they shared the most fertile parts of the territory.

Tolistobogii

The Tolistobogii (or 'Tolistoboii') main settlement and capital was at Pessinos (or Pessinus – modern-day Ballihisar), which later became the capital of the Roman province of Galatia. According to Livy, the Tolistobogii were one of the three ancient Gallic tribes of Galatia who were subdued by Manlius Vulso. When he arrived at their settlement, its inhabitants had taken refuge in a stronghold on Mount Olympus. However, they were overcome and their Roman victors slaughtered hundreds of them and reputedly sold some 40,000 men, women and children into slavery. Manlius Vulso earned great wealth on the strength of his successful campaigns against the three tribes during the Galatian War, and was granted a triumphal procession on his return to Rome.

Tosiopes

In the third century BC, the obscure Tosiopes were a Gallic tribe that along with the Voturi and the Ambituti, were one of the three clans of the Tolistobogii tribe.

Trocmi

The Trocmi, (sometimes 'Trogmi'), were one of three ancient tribes of Galatia, and according to some, Tavium, (or Tavia), was their chief city. Others maintain that the tribe settled by the River Halys (Kizilirmak) with their chief settlement at *Eccobriga,* on the road from Ancyra to Tavium. They called their territory Galatia and formed into three tribes. Their territory had at various times been occupied by Hittites, Persians, Greeks and Ottoman Turks. Owing to its position on an ancient commercial highway at the crossroads of a caravan route, and located at a place where five or six great roads met, it became an important and prosperous trading centre. In common with the other Galatian tribes in 189 BC they allied themselves with the Carthaginians during the Punic War and following a siege of their stronghold at Mount Magaba, the Trocmi were completely subdued by the Roman Consul Manlius Vulso. Following their surrender, the fort was pillaged by Roman soldiers.

Voturi

In the third century BC, the Voturi were a Gallic tribe that settled in Cappadocia, an area in present-day Turkey, and were one of the three clans or sub-groups of the Tolistoboii tribe. The tribal name, Voturi, probably derives from the proto-Celtic 'wor-tero', which loosely translates as 'the nobles'. According to Pliny, together with the Tolistoboii, their territory stretched from the *Sangarius* (the River Sakarya) to its tributary, the Alander River.

Chapter Eight

The Tribes of Brittany

The peninsula of Brittany, located at the north-western extremity of Gaul, was known to the Romans by its Latin name, Armorica, (sometimes spelled 'Aremorica'), and at that time it also included the western part of Normandy as far eastwards as present-day Dieppe. The name derives from the Gaulish 'are-morici', which is taken by some to mean 'those living east of the sea' and by others as 'place in front of the sea', reflecting coastal lands stretching from the mouth of the Loire to the Seine estuary. Ancient Armorica corresponded to the Départements of Finistère, Côtes-du-Nord, Morbihan, Ille-et-Vilaine and the Lower Loire, with its capital at *Lugdunum* (modern-day Lyon).

Celtic tribes had arrived in Armorica as early as the sixth century BC. In his *Natural History,* Pliny the Elder claimed that Armorica was the older name for Aquitania, and that its land stretched as far as the Pyrenees in south-west France. Strabo and Poseidonius both described the Armoricani people as belonging to the Belgae. In his *History of the Kings of Britain*, Geoffrey of Monmouth called its people 'Armorici Britones' (Armorican Britons).

According to Diodorus Siculus, the supply of Cornish gold as well as tin for making bronze had been a trade between Armorica and Britain long before the arrival of the Romans, and an alliance between the Celtic tribes of southern Britain and Brittany was firmly established.

When Julius Caesar invaded northern Gaul in 56 BC, Armorica became part of the Roman province of Gallia Lugdunensis. The region had a strategic value to the Romans because it gave them control over the Atlantic and the English Channel, and after subduing the native Veneti tribe, it would become a launching place for Caesar's planned invasion of Britannia (Britain). It would be the last place in Gaul to fall to the Romans.

In 57 BC, serving under the command of Caesar, Publius Crassus embarked on a campaign to put down the continued resistance to Roman rule in Armorica, which was still being supported by allied Celtic tribes in Britain. Caesar's invasion of Britain was in part intended to break that supportive alliance and a number of uprisings took place before Armorica was finally integrated into the Roman Empire. One took place by peasant insurgents in the third century, which led to unrest, followed by a punitive Roman response in which many villages were destroyed.

However, following the withdrawal of the Roman legions from Britannia in 407 AD, Armorica rebelled against its Romanised governance, just as its British allies had done. In his *Historia Nova*, the sixth-century Greek historian Zosimos described how Celtic peoples had defected from Roman rule, and wrote that '…all Armorica and the other Gallic provinces followed their example, freed themselves in the same way, expelling the Roman officials and setting up a constitution such as they pleased.'

In the fourth century AD, mass migrations into Brittany from south Wales, Devon and Cornwall began, probably by native Celtic people fleeing the westward advance of the Anglo-Saxons.

The two peoples, Britons and Bretons, had much in common: their spoken language was very similar and they were genetically closely related. These new Celtic migrants called the place 'Corouaille', which translates as 'peninsula people', and derives from the Celtic word 'kernou', meaning 'horn' or 'headland'; it has the same root as the Cornish name for Cornwall, 'Kernow'.

Settled in Armorica, the Britons became Bretons, and their new land became known to the Romans as Britannia Minor, or Bretagne, which means 'Little Britain', while the old motherland became Grande-Bretagne, ('Great Britain'), a name still used by the French to describe Britain. These new arrivals became permanent settlers and contributed to the development of Breton, locally known as 'Brezhoneg', a language closely related to Welsh and Cornish.

In his *Historia Brittonum,* (History of Britain), the ninth-century monk Nennius recorded that during the fourth century AD, sections of the Roman army were stationed in Armorica. He wrote that Magnus Maximus, the military commander of Britannia, withdrew Romano-British forces from Britain to Armorica. Writing much later, Geoffrey of Monmouth credited Maximus with setting up Conan Meriadoc as king in Armorica. Later, in around 409 AD, Constantine III ordered the complete withdrawal of the Roman army from Britain and Gaul to protect Rome from serious incursions in Italy and direct threats to Rome by barbarian tribes.

Clearly, these migrants from Britannia still regarded themselves as British. Their tribal leaders called themselves 'Bretenanwelde', meaning 'ruler of the Britons'. Their spoken language, which eventually emerged as Breton, was a form of Brittonic Celtic, like that spoken in Cornwall and Wales, and remains closely linked to these dialects even today.

THE TRIBES

Abricatui

Sometime between the sixth and fifth centuries BC, the Abricatui tribe migrated from their homeland south-east of present-day Cologne on the Abrinca, (the River Vinxtbach), a small stream that was once the border between the Roman provinces of Germania Inferior and Germania Superior. They settled in Aremorica on the River See around present-day Avranches in the Manche Département of Normandy in north-western France.

Alauni

The Alauni were a Celto-Scythian tribe that settled on the west coast of Brittany with a centre at Alauna on the present-day River Aulne by the first century BC. The tribal name derives either from a Gaulish word 'alauna', meaning 'stream', or from 'albho', meaning 'shining' or 'white', as in 'shining (river)'. Some of the tribe also settled another territory in south-eastern Gaul at Alaunium.

Ambiliati

The Ambiliati, (or 'Ambiliates'), Pliny called them 'Ambilatri', held territory along the southern reaches of the River Loire. They received the briefest of mentions in Caesar's *Commentaries*, where he calls them 'Ambianos'. Together with the Morini, they were allies of the Veneti and fought alongside them against the Roman invasion led by Publius Licinius Crassus and the Seventh Gemina Legion into Armorica, who came in search of corn supplies in 56 BC. This caused the Ambiliati and other tribes, including the Diablintes, Lexovii and Menapii among others, to rise up in revolt. In the confrontation that ensued the confederation was destroyed and Roman rule was firmly established in the region. The prefix 'ambi-' in the tribal name translates as 'both sides' (possibly of the Loire?), an element it shares with the Ambibari tribe, suggesting some connection between the two. They may even have been the same tribe. Another suggestion is that the tribal name could mean 'those who live on both sides of the Ile', a reference to the Département of Ile-et-Vilaine.

Armorici

The Armorici, (sometimes 'Aremoricani'), were early Celtic settlers to the territory and either took their name from or gave their name to the territory, which meant 'country by the sea'. By the time of the Roman conquest of Gaul in the first century BC, the Armorici, supported by the Menapii and the Morini, had come to dominate most of Armorica. According to Hagith Sivan's account in his *The Appropriation of Roman Law*, the Armorici were located north-west of the River Loire, and he characterises them as '...recent British migrants and descendants of the Romano-British soldiers of Magnus Maximus'. It is known that sometime around the year 380 AD a large number of Roman troops from Britain were settled in Armorica.

The Byzantine historian Procopius, (c.325–366), more or less agreed with Sivan's conclusion and recorded that 'Roman soldiers had been stationed at the frontiers of Gaul to serve as guards. And these soldiers, having no means of returning to Rome, gave themselves, together with their military standards and the land which they had long been guarding for the Romans, to the Armorici.' As a result, by the fifth century AD the Armorican Peninsula had been settled by numbers of Romano-Britons from across the English Channel.

Andecavi

These Gaulish people, (also known as the 'Andes', 'Andecavos' or 'Andegavi'), were a clan or sept of the Aulerci tribe. Sometime between the sixth and fifth centuries BC they settled in a territory located around the River Loire in Armorica, an area that corresponds with Anjou, in the present-day French Département of Maine-et-Loire. The tribe was forced to feed and to billet wintering Roman legions in 57 BC, which led to severe food shortages, resulting in a tribal uprising to support Vercingetorix. Led by Dumnacus, the Andecavi continued to resist Roman occupation, even after the defeat of Vercingetorix at Alesia. However, despite a number of Andecavi victories, they were eventually overcome in battle by a Roman relief force under the command of Gaius Caninius Rebilus, and sustained heavy losses of around 12,000 warriors. Dumnacus is thought to have fled from the battlefield before going into self-imposed exile.

Atesuii

The tribal territory of the Atesuii was around the headwaters of the River Orne in Normandy. Together with the Esubii tribe, (sometimes called 'Esuvii'), with whom they were closely related, the Atesuii claimed direct descent from the god Esus, who was associated with ritualistic bloodshed and human sacrifice. The similarity in the two tribal names might suggest that they were the same people.

Baiocasses

The Brythonic-speaking Baiocasses, (sometimes 'Bodiocasses', or 'Bellocassi' as Julius Caesar called them), were related to the Cassi, Di Casses, Tricasses, Veliocasses, and Viducasses tribes. Their tribal name is similar to the Middle Irish expression 'buidechas', which means 'blond-haired', a physical characteristic of many northern Gallic tribes. They had migrated from their German homeland in the sixth century BC and settled around the mouth of the River Orne in the Le Bessin region of Normandy, and on the west bank of the Sequana (the River Seine), in the Roman province of Gallia Lugdunensis.

In the first century AD their capital was named by Ptolemy as *Noviomagus Badiocassium*, (meaning 'the new market of the Badiocassi'), and was renamed by the Romans as *Augustodurum*; it is now the modern-day city of Bayeux.

The Baiocasses are thought to have developed the natural harbour at Port-en-Bessin-Huppain a few miles north-east of Bayeux. Excavations performed in 2010 on Mount Castel, which overlooks the port, revealed a number of military items from the late Roman period, which suggests that a Roman garrison was built on the site of an earlier Celtic fortified settlement.

Curiosolitae

The Curiosolitae, (sometimes 'Coriosolites'), were a small Gallic tribe that occupied territory at the north-western tip of Brittany. Their tribal name translates as 'lovers of slaughter'. They were named by Pliny as 'Cariosvelite'. Their capital oppidum and chief settlement was formerly at Arvil, though its original Gallic name is unknown, but during Roman times it was moved to *Fanum Martis* (which translates as 'Temple of Mars'), now the small town of Corseul on the Côtes du Nord, (clearly already under the influence of Roman culture). A bad harvest and the scarcity of corn during 57 and 56 BC prompted the Roman General Publius Crassus, whose Seventh Legion were quartered in the region, to send one of his officers, Marcus Trebuis Gallus, to acquire provisions from the Curiosolitae. Due to their location on the Atlantic coast, Caesar called their settlements 'maritimae civitates' (maritime cities).

The tribal name may come from the Gaulish 'corio-soli-tes', which loosely translates as the 'troop-watchers' or 'those who watch over the troop'. The tribe minted a large number of coins, and hordes of more than 20,000 have been found throughout Brittany, as well as in the Channel Island of Jersey.

Diablintes

The Diablintes were a clan of the Aulerci confederation and are sometimes known as the Aulerci-Diablintes. The term 'Aulerci' is a portmanteau word that means 'lesser' or 'smaller' and appears as a qualifying adjective in the names of other tribes within the confederation (e.g. Aulerci Cenomani, Aulerci Eburovices, Aulerci Sesuvi, etc.). Ptolemy called the Diablintes 'Aulerci Diaulitae', and Pliny referred to them as 'Diablindi'. Their chief oppidum, probably a substantial fortress, was at Jublians (or 'Jublains'), situated near the town of Mayenne in the Pays de la Loire region, which by 65 AD the Romans had renamed *Noeodunum*.

In 56 BC the Diablintes sent warriors to help the Veneti fight the invading Romans. Along with the other Aulerci tribes, (which included the Veneti, Ambiliati, Lexovi, Morinii, Menapii and others), their strongholds were attacked by Roman forces and their people were either slaughtered, captured or enslaved, so that the confederation was completely destroyed and Roman rule was firmly installed in the region. The Diablintes were among the north-western Gallic tribes that submitted to Julius Caesar in 57 BC. The town of Jublians became fully Romanised during the reign of the Emperor Tiberius.

Eburovices

In the sixth century BC, the Eburovices, (also known as the 'Aulerci-Eburovices'), migrated from Germany and settled in Aremorica in eastern Normandy around Falaise at the confluence of the Mayenne, Sarthe, Iton and Loire rivers. They established towns at *Mediolanum Aulercorum* (now Evreux), which served as its tribal capital, as well as the town of Gisacum, a few miles away. The first element of their tribal name derives from 'eburo', meaning 'yew', as in the yew tree, which held a sacred and ritualistic significance in many Celtic and Gallic tribes. The second element comes from 'wic' or 'vic', a Celtic word indicating traders or a trading or commercial settlement. Therefore, taken together, the tribal name may be interpreted as something like 'traders who live among the yew trees'.

Five thousand warriors of the Aulerci Cenomani and three thousand of the Aulerci Eburovices attempted to relieve Vercingetorix at the siege of Alesia, but were repulsed by Julius Caesar.

In about 400 AD, their main settlement was named by the Romans as 'Ebroicorum' and declared a civitas; it was renamed 'Ebroicas' in 511 and 'Ebroas' in around 1034, and eventually was to become the present-day city of Evreux.

Esubii

The tribal territory of the Esubii (also known as the 'Esuvii' and the 'Sesuvi'), was between the Sequana (the River Seine) and the River Loire around the present-day town of Sées (sometimes spelled 'Séez'), in the Orne Département of France. They were part of the Aulerci confederation of tribes, and often referred to as the Aulerci-Sesuvi. They were one of several Aremorican tribes that were compelled to supply grain to feed Roman legions that were wintering in the region. Various legions were despatched to be billeted among neighbouring tribes, but Caesar had given command of a legion to Lucius Roscius to set up his camp among the Esubii. This action caused severe hardship and near starvation, which prompted the Esubii to join the Veneti, Lexovii and the Curiosolites in a widespread rebellion in 57 BC. However, in 56 BC they were all subdued and came under Roman control.

Lexovii

The Lexovii were a Celtic people who lived on the western banks of the Sequana River (the Seine) in the Armorican region of Gaul. Lexovii territory may have included land around Lisieux and Bayeux. Their capital and main settlement was at a place the Romans called *Noviomagus*, and later it became *Civitas Lexoviorum*, (present-day Lisieux). They were allied to the powerful Veneti confederation. The origin of their tribal name is obscure, but it is widely thought that as they were a relatively small tribe, who sent only 3000 men to join the Veneti confederation to fight the Romans, it might be derived from 'legu', meaning 'small'. During the Gallic Wars, Caesar commissioned Quintus Titurius Sabinus to seek out and destroy the confederation and after fierce battles they were defeated and eventually surrendered to Sabinus in 56 BC. The coast of Lexovii territory was one of the launching-off points for Julius Caesar's first invasion of Britain in 54 BC.

Menapii

At the time of the Romans the Menapii were a Belgic tribe that held territory around the south bank of the Rhine and the River Maas estuary in south-western Netherlands and northern Belgium, living beside the Scaldis (the River Scheldt). They were one of the tribes who joined the Veneti confederacy against the Roman advance into their territory. In the event, Julius Caesar destroyed most of the Venetti villages and killed untold numbers of confederate warriors. However, the Menapii seem to have avoided the worst of the Roman slaughter, and lived on to fight a guerrilla-type war.

The tribe was at odds with a Germanic confederation of Suebi who were intent on seizing their territory and several engagements took place between them in the surrounding swamps and woodlands. Fortunately for the Menapii, Caesar attacked the Suebi and forced them back across the Rhine. However, as with all the other Gaulish tribes, Menapii rebellion brought them into direct conflict with Caesar, who despatched five legions to attack them, forcing them to hide in the wilderness. Eventually they surrendered to the might of Rome, and were incorporated into the expanding Roman Empire. At some point in their history, a group of Menapii migrated to Ireland. (See 'Chapter 12: The Irish Tribes'.)

Morini

During the Iron Age and Roman period, Morini territory was in the Pas de Calais region around the present-day towns of Calais and Boulogne, bordering the River Canache. Their capital was at a place called *Tarvenna* (modern-day Thérouanne) and they had another settlement at *Gesoriacum* (now Boulogne-sur-Mer). This was a strategically important port city that the Romans knew as *Portus Itius*. Because of their coastal location on the English Channel, within sight of Britain, this was one of Caesar's set-off points for the 54 BC invasion.

The first element of the Morini tribal name derives from the proto-Celtic word 'mori', meaning 'sea', and the whole name is taken to mean 'the people of the sea'.

In the year 57 BC, the Morini sent 25,000 warriors to join a tribal confederation under Galba, the chief of the Suessiones tribe, to fight the Romans. They were one of the tribes who also made last-ditch attempts at resistance to the Roman advance in 33 BC and 30 BC. Finally vanquished, by the end of the first century AD, the Morini had become fully Romanised, and many of its warriors enlisted as auxiliaries in the Roman army to form the *Cohors Primae Morinorum* (The First Cohort of Morini). In the late fourth century, the unit was listed in the *Notitia Dignitatum*, (the so-called 'Register of Dignitaries'), stationed at a garrison of the Ravenglass coastal fort in Cumbria, England.

Namnetes

The Namnetes tribal territory was located around the mouth of the River Liger (the Loire), between the Vilaine and the Semnon rivers, and gave its name to the present-day city of Nantes, now the capital of Loire-Atlantique Département of France. Nantes became an important trade and administrative centre under the Romans. The Namnetes' major settlement (oppidum) was at Contigwic (known to the Romans as *Condivincum*). It was one of the most important townships in the Roman province of Gallia Lugdunensis. During the third century AD, the city became known as *Portus Namnetum*, before acquiring its present-day name of Nantes sometime in the Middle Ages.

The Namnetes tribal name is derived from the common Celtic word 'nemus', meaning 'tree' or 'sacred grove'. In 56 BC, the Namnetes joined the Veneti in a sea battle against a Roman fleet commanded by Decimus Brutus during the Gallic Wars, but were defeated and the tribe was finally subjugated.

Osismii

The Osismii were a warrior tribe who helped defeat tribes of the Ligurian culture in Aremorica during the Iron Age. They settled in the Finistère Peninsula around the River Alaunos (the Aulne), in the extreme north-west coast of Brittany, bordered on the one side by the Bay of Biscay and the English Channel on the other. In the fourth century BC, the Greek geographer Pytheas named them as 'Ostimioi'. Their tribal name means 'those at the end of the world'. Their capital and main city was at *Vorgium*, (in the modern-day Commune of Carhaix-Plouguer). The Osismii also established a stronghold at Paule, (in modern-day Saint Symphorien, near Metz) sometime around 50 BC, which was reckoned to have been one of the strongest fortified oppida of the tribe. In 57 BC they joined the Veneti confederation in a revolt against Roman rule, before the confederation was defeated and along with the other tribes, they eventually submitted to Rome.

Redones

The tribal name of the Redones, (sometimes spelled 'Rhedones'), is a combination of Celtic and Germanic elements. The early Celtic word 'reid' signifies a 'driver' (as of a vehicle), suggesting that the tribe's name may indicate that they were charioteers. The Redones capital was at Condate, (which means 'confluence'), in the eastern part of the Aremorican peninsula, located beside the River Loire, on the site of the present-day city of Rennes, which takes its name for the tribe. After their subjugation, Rennes was known as a *Civitas Redonum* (the 'city of the Redones'). Their territory in eastern Brittany was approximately equivalent to the modern Děpartement of Ille-et-Vilaine, and nowadays its university is an important centre for Breton and Celtic studies. The Redones were one of several tribes that took part in the siege of Alesia as part of Vercingetorix's failed uprising against Julius Caesar's advance into Aremorica in 52 BC. Caesar counted the Redones among the maritime territories that bordered the ocean, which was of particular interest to him as a potential launching point for his planned expedition to Britain.

Sesuvii

See: 'Esuvii'.

Trinovantes

The Trinovantes were one of several tribes that migrated from Thrace to the North Sea, before travelling south to Brittany where they settled on the right bank of the mouth of the Liger (the River Loire) sometime between the fifteenth and the thirteenth centuries BC. A branch of the tribe also settled around the modern-day British counties of Essex and Suffolk. (See also: 'chapter Nine: The British Tribes'.)

Venelli

The Venelli, (sometimes 'Unelli'), came to Gaul from Germany as early Hallstatt Celtic people sometime during the ninth century BC and settled around Contentin, in what is now the Cherbourg Peninsula of north-western Normandy. They established several stronghold settlements in the region, including at Le Petit Celland near Avranches, with their capital city (oppidum) at *Cosedia*, known today as Coutances. The tribe formed an alliance with the Cariosvelites and the Lexovii and under the leadership of Viridovix, faced three Roman legions under the command of Quintus Titurius Sabinus. Their rebellion was crushed by the overwhelming might of the Roman army, and in 57 BC, they surrendered to the Legate Publius Licinius Crassus, who confronted them with twelve cohorts of legionaries. However, the following year they joined the Gallic coalition to support Vercingetorix against Rome, and took part in the Battle of Alesia in 52 BC. It is thought that some of the Venelli tribe from Coutances were the earliest settlers in the Channel Islands of Jersey and Aldernay, just off the western coast of France, where they arrived between 700 and 600 BC.

Veneti

Veneti, (also known as 'Venedi'), were an ancient Celtic people who lived in what is now the Morbihan district of modern Brittany. Ptolemy called them by a Greek name, 'Ouenedai'. They established several coastal strongholds, giving them control of passing maritime traffic; this saw them develop into a major trading group that had a flourishing and lucrative tin trade with British tribes.

Their tribal name seems to derive from an ancient word like 'wenet' or 'vinet', meaning 'white', the kind of term often used to describe the pale-skinned blond northern European Celtic tribes, to distinguish them from the darker-skinned Mediterranean peoples.

In about 56 BC, Caesar besieged the Veneti coastal strongholds, forcing them back into the sea where they boarded their substantial naval fleet, which amounted to around 220 ships. It took many months for the Romans to amass a sufficiently large navy to confront them, but eventually a fierce naval battle ensued, which became known as the Battle of the Bay of Biscay, in which the Romans were victorious.

After the engagement, in common Roman practice, the surviving defeated Veneti warriors were sold into slavery. There were many ancient tribes named Veneti, with instances found in Scotland, around the Adriatic and Anatolia to the Baltic Sea. The Armorican Veneti of Gaul gave their name to the modern city of Vannes.

Viducasses

The Viducasses, (also known as 'Veliocasses'), were a Gallic tribe that lived in the modern-day Calvados Département of north-western France, a region known to the Romans as Gallia Lugdunensis, with their chief town at *Aregenua* (present-day Vieux). In the third century AD, it was named by the Romans as *Civitas Viducassium*, (the city of the Viducasses).

Chapter Nine

The British Tribes

The First Britons

The term 'Ancient Britons' is bandied about as if there actually were a tribal people by that name. In fact, during the Iron Age, before the Romans and written history, all the people who lived in the British Isles and islands were 'ancient' by definition. Therefore, the term 'Britons' is sufficient. What they shared was a common Brittonic language, (sometimes spelled 'Brythonic'). It was not until the Roman Conquest of Britain in the first century AD that the various groups of native inhabitants were given names by the Greeks and Romans who visited Britannia, as the British mainland was known.

But these islands were occupied long before the coming of the Romans. It is thought that the first hunter-gathers may have settled in Britain as far back as 11,000 years ago, when sea levels may have been more than thirty feet lower and the British Isles were still connected to continental Europe by a land bridge called Doggerland.

This period is known as the Mesolithic (Middle) Stone Age, a period between the Old Stone Age (Palaeolithic) and the New Stone Age (Neolithic). These Stone Age Britons subsisted by fishing, hunting and gathering fruit and berries – hence 'hunter-gatherers'. There were not many of them – estimates range from a mere 1000 to up to 10,000 settling in the whole of mainland Britain.

After the last major Ice Age came to an end almost 12,000 years ago, evidence shows that global temperatures gradually increased, the ice sheets that had covered Europe as far south as the Mediterranean began to recede and sea levels began to rise. Finally, around 8000 years ago, a vast quantity of ice-melt water was released from the great North American lake, which together with a massive undersea landslide off Norway caused sea levels to rise to such an extent that the Doggerland Bridge was finally inundated. Low-lying settlements would have been flooded and its people forced to live in areas of higher ground. As a result, Britain became a group of islands, now separated from the continent by the English Channel, and its residential population would become irrevocably divorced from their original European culture.

We cannot be certain what these ancient people were like, but a twentieth-century archaeological excavation offered some clues when the remains of the most ancient known British ancestor were discovered in 1903 at Gough's Cave, in the Cheddar Gorge range. The almost complete skeleton of this Mesolithic man, known as Cheddar Man, who lived about 10,000 years ago, is the oldest specimen of modern man (Homo Sapien) ever found in Britain.

The finds were surprising. First, DNA analysis of Cheddar Man's bones suggested that he probably had the sort of dark skin usually associated with sub-Saharan Africa. Also, further analysis showed that his eyes were probably blue or green and that he had dark brown hair. The kind of pale skin and blond hair normally associated with northern European people in modern times came about as a result of a natural evolutionary process where the body adapts and a paler skin is better at absorbing Vitamin D. Added to this was the later influx of paler people from Eastern Europe.

During the early Neolithic Age (c.4400–c.3300 BC), many long barrows like the one at Silbury Hill began to appear across the British Isles, and even later, from about 2900 BC large stone circles and henges were erected, of which Avebury and Stonehenge are examples. These suggest an advanced society that had already developed a religious or ritualistic culture. Neolithic Britons had also developed tools and funerary practices, and possibly most important of all, a thriving and prodigious production of pottery.

Later Migrations: the Beaker People

Around 4,500 years ago, at the start of the Bronze Age, a new people and culture appeared in Britain: migrants from the Iberian Peninsula of Spain and Portugal. At that time they would have crossed the Channel in small boats. DNA analysis of more than 400 prehistoric skeletons from this time revealed that these migrants almost completely replaced the earlier population. Their skin was paler, blonde hair was more common and their eye pigmentation was lighter. Their earlier ancestors had come from the region of Eurasian Steppes. It has been argued that these were the people who helped spread the Indo-European language, from which the Celtic languages are derived, across the continent and into Britain.

The new immigrants brought with them a particular style of bell-shaped pottery, which earned them the name 'Beaker People', or sometimes the 'Bell Beaker People' on account of the distinctive bell shape of their pottery vessels. They appear to have co-existed alongside and almost certainly intermarried with the Neolithic inhabitants of Britain – the people who are thought to have begun the construction of Stonehenge. In 2017, studies by the Natural History Museum of London revealed that at least ninety percent of the ancestry of British inhabitants were replaced by these new European immigrants.

The Beaker People also spread their culture into Central and Western Europe. Their funeral practices included building large earth mounds, known as barrows, and often burying clay drinking vessels alongside the interred bodies of their dead. These actual clay beakers and vessels were clearly important possessions of the people who were buried with them. Their graves often included jewellery and weapons fashioned from alloys of copper and tin, which made bronze, a metal technology unknown to Neolithic peoples.

Large settlements of the Beaker culture were established, particularly in south-west Britain, which became known as the 'Wessex Culture'. Unearthed graves in the region have revealed a wealth of elaborately decorated daggers and gold ornaments.

During their migration they had brought with them a Bronze Age technology that would virtually replace that of the earlier inhabitants of Britain. It remains somewhat speculative, but there is a body of opinion that suggests the Beaker People may have also completed the building of Stonehenge.

The arrival of the Celtic tribes on British shores marked the end of the dominance of the islands by the Bell Beaker people.

The Arrival of the Celts

The Celts are thought to have arrived in Britain from Continental Europe in around 1000 BC. They were to dominate the landscape during the Iron Age and well into the Roman period, and later. The culture that they established throughout the British Isles would have been a largely uncoordinated, piece-meal affair. There was no single Celtic invasion; they came to Britain as separate tribes who were only loosely related by similar language, religion and culture. Most importantly, they were the people who brought iron-working to Britain.

The origin of the name 'Britain' is derived from the Celtic Pritani tribe who occupied it, and it was the Greek writer Pytheas who referred to them as the 'Pretanic Isles'. Later commentators translated these names incorrectly: they called the inhabitants 'Brittani' and their lands, 'the Britannic Isles'. Later the Romans used the Latin form of 'Britannia'.

The language spoken by these Celtic migrants developed into several varying dialects. In Wales, it developed as Welsh, in the north of Britain the Cumbric language was dominant, while in the south-west the dialect became Cornish in Cornwall and in Gaul (France), it emerged as the Breton language.

Unfortunately for the Celtic tribes, they were more concerned with fighting each other than forming alliances and confederations, a shortcoming that they realised too late. They were easily conquered by the more organised militarism of the Roman legions.

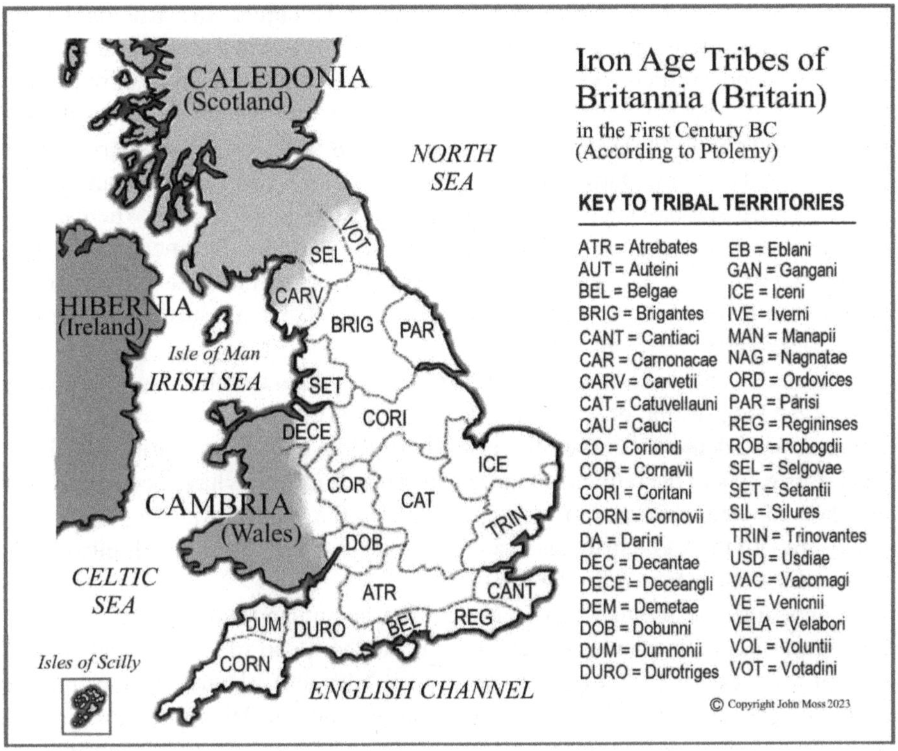

The Arrival of the Romans

In the first century BC, the first of the Roman invasions began. At this time the Celtic tribes were very well established and were producing objects in the La Tène style of Celtic art and speaking a distinctive Celtic language. By the time of Emperor Claudius's invasion in AD 43, they were a loose conglomeration of peoples, ruled by tribal kings and warlords, with no single political or central governing body. The Romans saw them as savage and uncivilised barbarians.

Unlike the two previous more or less abortive attempts at conquest by Julius Caesar in 55 and 54 BC, the Emperor Claudius preferred to make peace treaties wherever possible, to effectively 'Romanise' the Celtic tribes, and in fact, many, like the Atrebates, did sue for peaceful occupation and chose to join the Roman Empire. However, a significant number, (like the Catuvellauni tribe led by Caractacus), refused to pay allegiance or taxes to Rome and resisted the encroachment of their territorial tribelands. As a result, the conquest of Britannia was not a quick affair; it took more than forty years of bloody war before Rome could claim control of Britain, and then only the southern part, which we now call England.

In short, during the protracted invasion of Britannia, the Roman legions viciously slaughtered many hundreds of thousands of Celtic tribesmen, along with their wives and children, or sold them into slavery. Typical of the type of retribution meted out by the Romans against resistant Celts was the way they dealt with fortified hill-forts. There were around forty-seven such forts in Somerset alone, home to the Dubbuni, Durotriges, and Dumnonii tribes. Until the Romans arrived, these fortified settlements were virtually impregnable to all attacks, whether from foreign invaders or warring neighbours, but they were not designed to withstand an attack by the kind of highly trained and equipped army that first-century Roman legions could sustain. They all either fell as their inhabitants surrendered or they were sacked and destroyed.

At least twenty such forts were destroyed by Roman commander Vespasian as part of the subjugation of southern Britain. Evidence of brutal battles and hill-fort sieges is well demonstrated by the Danesbury Ring, an Atrebates tribe hill-fort in Hampshire, where the remains of more than a hundred bodies have been excavated, all showing clear evidence of battle wounds. By the year 48 AD the Romans had conquered all the Celtic tribelands and hill-forts south of the River Humber in the east and the River Severn in the west.

Thereafter, the remnants of Celtic culture in England would only survive in the far north, in Northumbria, Cumbria, the southern part of the Scottish borders, and in the western extremities of the British Isles and islands. By the time the Romans had accomplished their subjugation of southern Britain, the Celtic tribes had virtually disappeared from England, either by Romanisation or extermination, as the fate of the following British tribes illustrates.

THE TRIBES

Ancalites

Together with the Bibroci tribe, the Ancalites were two of the more obscure to be noted by Julius Caesar in his *Commentaries*. They were a minor tribe, possibly one of his so-called 'four tribes of Kent' living in the south-east of England during the first century BC. Later commentators believed they had a settlement around the River Thames, probably near present-day Henley-on-Thames in Oxfordshire. Others place them on the north or south forelands on the Isle of Thanet, or towards Dungeness. Another has suggested that they inhabited parts of Berkshire and Wiltshire at the time of the Roman invasion, but there is little documentary evidence for either hypothesis.

Their tribal name has been associated with the Latin 'ancala', meaning 'bent arm'. It is thought that the Ancalites formed an early treaty with Caesar in 54 BC. Within a century, together with four other tribes: the Bibroci, the Segontiaci, the Cenimagni and the Cassim, the Ancalites had merged to form one single Celtic tribal confederation, the Cantiaci. The confederation eventually surrendered to Caesar and revealed the location of Cassivellaunus's stronghold at Wheathampstead, which Caesar proceeded to put under siege, forcing Cassivellaunus to surrender.

Atrebates

The Atrebates were a Celtic people whose territory covered most of modern-day Sussex, Berkshire and Hampshire during the first and second centuries BC. Sometime earlier, between the third and second centuries BC, they had sailed across the English Channel, accompanied by warriors of the Catuvellauni and Cantii tribes, and settled in south-eastern England. The name Atrebates means 'settlers'.

The Atrebates originally came from *Nemetacum Atrebatum*, (or Nemetocenna), around the modern-day city of Arras on the River Scarpe, south-west of Lille. They were one of several continental Belgic elements that moved into the region and intermarried with earlier Celtic tribes and established a capital at *Noviomagus* (modern-day Chichester in West Sussex). They occupied a region stretching between the Thames, the Test, and West Sussex.

Another important tribal centre was at a hill-fort settlement in the Bracknell Forest in Berkshire, known as 'Caesar's Camp', (the only such fort known to exist in Sussex), which was constructed sometime between 500 BC and 300 BC. During the first century it fell into the hands of Cunobelin, king of the Catavellauni tribe. The Atrebates also established a hill-fort at Old Sarum near Salisbury in Wiltshire sometime around 400 BC, but they were expelled from the place by the Romans, who set up a military garrison within its earthworks in the first century. They renamed it *Sorviodunum*.

An offshoot of the tribe are known to have migrated with King Commius from Gaul sometime before 54 BC, and established a settlement and their capital at *Calleva* (present-day Silchester). After Commius, the tribe were ruled by three kings: Tincommius, Eppillus and Verica.

In 43 AD, the Atrebates were finally subdued by the Romans and their capital was later granted civitas status and thereafter known as *Calleva Atrebatum*. They were one of the last Gallic tribes to surrender to Julius Caesar.

Belgae

The Belgae were a northern Gaulish people, a small group of whom crossed to Britain during the late second or early first century BC. Later, others followed after sustained war with Rome in Continental Europe, and Belgic culture spread to most of southern

Britain. Their three most important settlements were established at Colchester, St Albans and Silchester and their capital was at the later Roman site of *Venta Belgarum* (Winchester). The Belgae were a large confederation of tribes from northern Gaul, around the North Sea or Baltic regions, who gave their name to the Roman province of Gallia Belgica and, much later, to the modern country of Belgium.

It was during the late second or early first century BC, as part of a third wave of Celtic migrants, that a small band of Belgae are thought to have crossed to Britain and established settlements around modern-day Winchester in the county of Hampshire, and perhaps extending into Somerset and Avon.

Bibroci

The Bibroci received only a passing mention by Julius Caesar in his *Commentaries*. They are believed to have held territory around the River Thames, possibly at Bray. Together with four other tribes, (the Ancalites, the Segontiaci, the Cenimagni and the Cassi), the Bibroci sent emissaries to the Roman camp seeking a peace treaty, surrendering as hostages to Caesar, and as a condition of their release were persuaded to reveal details of the whereabouts of Cassivellaunus, the Celtic chieftain and rebel commander, who led the fight against Roman occupation. The tribe finally surrendered to Caesar in 54 BC.

According to some, the tribal name Bibroci stems from the Gaulish word 'bibros', meaning 'beaver', while some prefer the more general interpretation of 'brown animal'. Yet others prefer a Greek word meaning 'to devour', indicating a possible tribal association with gluttony or even cannibalism.

Brigantes

Sometimes called the Briganti, this large tribe was made up of a federation of smaller communities, which at the time of the Roman Conquest included the Setanti, the Lopocares, the Corionototae and the Tectoverdi. They are thought to have migrated to Britain, originally from Turkey, led by the Welsh chieftain, Hu Gardarn, sometime between the fifteenth and thirteenth centuries BC. Other parts of the tribe settled in Upper Bavaria and in Switzerland.

Their tribal name derives directly from the Gallic word 'briga', which simply translates as 'hill', a possible reference to some of the hill-forts that they built in parts of their territory. It has also been argued by some that it may be more broadly interpreted to mean 'superior' or 'elevated ones'. But given the hypothesis that their name more accurately translates as 'hill dwellers', this is the most probable interpretation as the Pennines formed the heart of their northern British territory. The Brigantes venerated the Celtic goddess Brigantia, as did the Brigantii tribe in the Alps and the Brigantes of Ireland.

At the time of the Roman invasion in AD 43, the Brigantes were arguably the most powerful Celtic tribe in Britain. After the conquest, they were formed into very large 'civitates', or administrative units, that covered most of Yorkshire, Cleveland, Durham and Lancashire. It stretched east-west from the North Sea to the Irish Sea.

An important centre for the Brigantes was built at Stanwick in North Yorkshire, though it is thought that their settlement at *Isurium Brigantum*, (Aldborough in North Yorkshire), was probably the capital of Queen Cartimandua, who ruled the Brigantes. The tribe also constructed the sixteen-acre Mam Tor hill-fort in the Derbyshire Peak District, on a much older Late Neolithic site dating from around 2400 BC. Mellor in Greater Manchester was another Brigantian hill-fort with earlier prehistoric origins. Others, like the Wincobank hill-fort, were hastily thrown up in reaction to the advancing Roman conquest of Britain by Julius Agricola.

The Romans invaded and occupied the territory in AD 79 but the Brigantes were never truly Romanised. They broke out in revolt against Roman occupation in 138 AD and again in 154 AD, and were a perpetual problem for the Roman authorities.

There was a Brigantes presence across the sea in Ireland and it has been argued that at least some of the tribe may have migrated there during the sixth century BC and settled around Waterford.

Cantiaci

The Cantiaci tribe, (sometimes 'Cantii'), were an Iron Age people who occupied the whole of modern-day Kent, with the eastern parts of Surrey, East Sussex and Greater London, with their capital located at *Durovernum Cantiacorum*, (present-day Canterbury). At the start of the first century AD, following the Roman invasion, they formed a confederation with the four smaller kingdoms of the Bibroci: the Ancalites, the Segontiaci, the Cenimagni and the Cassi. In his *Gallic Wars*, Caesar said of the tribe that 'of all these, by far the most civilised are they who dwell in Kent, which is entirely a maritime region, and who differ but little from the Gauls in their customs.' From the second century BC, the Cantiaci had occupied Bigbury hill-fort which afforded a commanding position overlooking the heavy marshes upstream from Canterbury.

The Cantiaci were the first to face the Romans in battle as they marched into their tribal territory shortly after their arrival in Britain. The engagement was fierce and the Cantiaci were forced to retreat into the hill-fort, where they were eventually defeated. Caesar recorded the battle thus: 'They had moved with their cavalry and chariots down from the higher ground to a river and were trying to engage us in battle. The Britons came out of the woods in small groups to fight ....but the men of the Seventh Legion holding up their shields to form a protective shell piled up earth against the fortifications and captured the place.' As was their custom, the victorious Romans gave no quarter, and hundreds of Celtic warriors were slain. The present-day city of Canterbury is named after the Cantiaci tribe.

Carvetii

Carvetii tribal territories chiefly included parts of north Lancashire, Cumbria (formerly Cumberland), and south-west Durham, but before county or national barriers existed a part spilled over into what would become the south-east corner of Dumfries & Galloway in Scotland. They were a relatively small tribe, completely overlooked by Ptolemy, and may have originally been part of the larger Brigantes confederation, before striking out as an autonomous tribe in their own right. The name Carvetii translates as 'deer men'. It is possible that the tribe's capital was at *Luguvalio*, the name that the Romans gave to Carlisle when it was granted civitas (municipal) status. What little else is known of the tribe comes from three third and fourth century AD recovered Roman monuments and milestone inscriptions. It is thought that Venutius, the husband of Queen Cartimandua of the Brigantes, may have been a member of the Carvetii tribe.

Cassi

The little we know about the Cassi tribe comes from a brief mention in the writings of Julius Caesar, who identified them as one of the four tribes of Kent. Together with the Ancalites, the Segontiaci, the Cenimagni and the Bibroci, the Cassi are known to have been absorbed into the Catuvellaunian federation, but were one of the tribes that capitulated to the Romans and sent emissaries in an attempt to sue for peace.

Catuvellauni

The Catuvellauni tribe dominated south-eastern Britain and were reputedly one of the most powerful Celtic tribes of the first century BC, occupying territory north of the Tamesis (the River Thames). They were a Belgic tribe from Europe's North Sea or Baltic coastline and may have been related to the Catalauni tribe of Gaul. The main Catuvellauni settlement and capital was located near present-day Wheathampstead in Hertfordshire, but after the decisive defeat of Cassivellaunus by Julius Caesar in 54 BC, they were dispossessed of their capital and forced to resettle at *Verulamium*, near St Albans.

As the third largest Roman town in Britain, Verulamium became a Roman 'municipium' around 50 AD, and the tribe were granted a limited degree of autonomy under Roman law. Following Caesar's return to Rome, the Catuvellauni began to expand their territory widely across the present-day counties of Cambridgeshire,

Northamptonshire, Bedfordshire, Buckinghamshire, Oxfordshire and north-eastern parts of Surrey, to become the largest tribe in southern Britain by the end of the first century AD. The tribal name Catuvellauni probably translates from Gaulish as 'war chiefs' or 'battle leaders'.

Corieltauvi

The Corieltauvi, (sometimes 'Corieltavi'), dominated a territory that covered much of the modern-day East Midlands of England, including the counties of Lincolnshire, Leicestershire, Nottinghamshire, Derbyshire, Rutland and Northamptonshire. In his *Geographia*, Ptolemy referred to them as 'Coritani'. The Romans called their capital *Ratae Corieltauvorum*, (meaning the 'fort of the Coritani'), which is known today as Leicester. It was captured around 44 AD, after which the *Legio IX Hispana* (the Ninth Spanish Legion) occupied it as a garrison and in 50 AD they built a fort on the site. The Roman road known as the Fosse Way passed through Corieltauvi territory at Leicester. The tribe was probably part of a loose confederation of small, largely agricultural and relatively peaceful tribes that offered little resistance to the Roman occupation of their tribelands. This is reflected in the tribe's name, which may translate as 'joined tribes'.

Corionototae

Very little is known about the Corionototae tribe, other than that they apparently inhabited Northern England and were recorded in a Roman stone inscription brought from the village of Corbridge in Northumberland to Hexham Abbey near Hadrian's Wall, but was lost sometime before 1860. The Latin inscription recorded the victory of a cavalryman named as Prefect Quintus Calpurnius Concessinius, over the Corionotatae. Part of the inscription read *caesa corionototarum manu*, which translates as 'after slaughtering a band of Corionototae'. The tribal name Corionototae is thought to translate as 'tribal army', 'people's army', or perhaps 'people of chiefs'. It has been suggested that they may have been a sub-group or sept of the Brigantes federation.

Coritani

The Coritani tribe, (also known as 'Corieltauvi' and 'Corieltavi'), were a group or federation of small tribes that held territories in the East Midlands, across the present-day counties of Leicestershire, Nottinghamshire, Derbyshire and Lincolnshire. Following the withdrawal of the *Legio XIV Gemina* (the Fourteenth Gemini Legion) from their base in Ratae (later Romanised to *Ratae Corieltauvoru*, modern-day Leicester), the tribe seem to have adopted it as their capital city.

In around 46 AD Ratae was captured by the *Legio IX Hispania* (the Ninth Spanish Legion) and the tribe submitted to Roman authority.

Cornovii

The Cornovii tribe lived in northern England on the border with Wales. Their territory covered parts of Shropshire, north Staffordshire and Cheshire, as well as what became known as the Welsh Marches. Their capital before the Roman Age was probably a hill-fort on the Wrekin. However, in his *Geographia* Ptolemy names two of their towns: *Deva Victrix* (modern-day Chester) and *Viroconium Cornoviorum* (Wroxeter), which became their capital under Roman rule.

Their tribal name loosely translates as 'people of the horn', a probable reference to their worship of the Celtic god Cernunnos, whose name meant 'the horned one'. The Cornovii seemed to prefer living in hill-forts, as their territory contained more than any other in Britain. Of all the northern tribes, the Cornovii seemed to be the least warlike as they were defeated in 47 AD at their Wrekin hill-fort in their only battle with the Romans. Their name appeared in Caledonia (Scotland) in around 140 AD, which suggests that at least some part of the tribe had migrated northwards to avoid the worst effects of Roman occupation. In the fifth century AD, warriors of the Cornovii tribe migrated from Lancashire and resettled in Brittany, in a region that became known as 'Cornavia'.

Dobunni

The Dobunni, (also spelled 'Dobuni'), were originally an Iberian tribe whose extensive territories came to include the modern-day counties of Gloucester, Avon, parts of Oxfordshire and north Somerset, along with southern Hereford and Worcester and Warwickshire, a region that would become the Roman province of Britannia Prima. The tribe are known to have created a number of fortified hill-forts within their territory, especially around Bristol and the Avon Gorge, as well as one on Bredon Hill in the Vale of Evesham. The Romans called their main capital *Corinium Dobunnorum*, (present-day Cirencester), and at that time it was the second largest city in Britannia. In 41 AD, Caractacus became the chieftain of the Catuvellauni tribe, and sought to expand his tribal territory by subjugating the Dobunni and the neighbouring Atrebates tribe. This prompted the Atrebates to appeal for aid from Rome, which many believe was the pretext for the subsequent Roman invasion of Britain by Claudius in 43 AD.

It has been suggested that their tribal name may translate as 'dark haired people'. Others maintain that their original name may have been 'Bodunni' and possibly related to the Celtic word 'bouda', technically meaning 'victorious', but in a wider sense taken to mean 'victorious ones'. Yet a third explanation has been offered, that their name is connected to an archaic Irish word that translates as 'people of the river mouth'. Neither one seems more probable than another, so take your pick!

Dumnonii

The Dumnonii, (sometimes 'Dumnones'), were an Iron Age tribe whose territory was in what is now Devon and Cornwall. Their tribal name may be related to the Latin word 'dominus', meaning 'masters' or 'lords', and they gave their name to the county of Devon. Their capital and main settlement was known to the Romans as *Isca Dumnoniorum*, (present-day Exeter). They would have spoken a Brythonic dialect that was the forerunner of modern Cornish and Breton. It was emigrés of the tribe that fled across the English Channel to establish the province of Armorica, (modern-day Brittany), with which the region still continues a close affinity. The Iron Age hill-fort at Cadbury Castle in present-day Somerset was probably constructed by the tribe before they were driven out by the Durotriges. The fort was eventually overtaken by the Romans who destroyed it and burned the surrounding villages to the ground.

The Dumnonii must have been a very pragmatic people as, realising that Roman domination was inevitable, they offered little resistance and came to an early accommodation. The Romans granted Isca Dumnoniorum 'civitas' status and thereafter there is little evidence that the Romans ventured further into the West Country beyond the River Exe.

Durotriges

The Durotriges tribal confederation favoured hill-forts as defensive living quarters and constructed many within their territories in Dorset, south Wiltshire, south Somerset and Devon east of the River Axe. Their hill-fort at Maiden Castle was one of the largest and most complex Iron Age hill-forts in Europe and was the location of the tribe's stubborn resistance to the Second Augustan Legion, (*Legio II Augusta*), commanded by Vespasian in AD 43.

Archaeological digs at Maiden Castle have revealed many insights into the culture and social structure of the Durotriges. For example, a number of unearthed grave pits have revealed the remains of high-status women, some bedecked with rings, necklaces and other jewels, of the kind that would have been found on only the wealthiest elite of the hill-fort inhabitants. Some of these remains contained swords, suggesting that many of the occupants must have been leading women warriors. Further, in her BBC1 television series *Digging for Britain* Professor Alice Roberts mooted the possibility that power in Durotriges society may have descended through the female, rather than the male line, as it had always been thought.

Skeletal analysis has also shown evidence of bone deterioration such as might be found in sufferers of scurvy, which suggests an absence of Vitamin C in their diet, which would have been a common complaint among the wealthier meat-based and fruit- and vegetable-deficient diets of some elite families. There were also widespread examples of bone malformations, almost certainly due to Vitamin D deficiency, a contributing factor in cases of rickets. This opened the possibility that the Maiden Castle findings may be typical of other British tribes, and not just limited to the Durotriges.

Several other Durotriges hill-forts, including those at Abbotsbury Castle on Wears Hill, Spetisbury Rings on the River Stour, Pilsdon Pen near Beaminster, and Hod Hill in Blackmore Vale, suffered similar fates to Maiden Castle. Many of these forts fell to the Roman Second Augustan Legion during the first century AD.

Following their conquest, the Durotriges' main settlement and probable capital was at *Durnovaria* (modern-day Dorchester), which became a civitas in the Roman province of Britannia. The tribal name Durotriges may actually mean 'hill-fort-dwellers', although some have suggested that 'dwellers by water' might be a better interpretation. By 70 AD, the tribe had become Romanised and many may have enlisted in the Roman army. A sandstone inscription in the Chesters Museum shows that members of the Durotriges tribe undertook repair work between the Chesters and Housesteads sections of Hadrian's Wall in the fourth century AD.

Gabrantovices

A debate existed for some time as to whether the Gabrantovices were a sub-group of the Parisii tribe, but the prevailing hypothesis is that they were more likely to have been a sept of the Brigantes tribal federation. Certainly it was one of the three main tribes of present-day Yorkshire, with the Parisii tribe in East Yorkshire and the Gabrantovices in the north of the county. The remainder of the region was ruled by the Brigantes.

In his *Geographia*, Ptolemy described the Gabrantovices as a coastal dwelling people and referred to their 'good harbour'. Their main settlement and capital is thought to be somewhere near the present-day village of Percy Cross Rigg and their tribal name may have meant 'horse-riding fighters' or simply 'cavalrymen'. Conversely, some have argued that their name meant 'goat fighters'.

Iceni

The Iceni tribe, (also known as the 'Eceni'), occupied territory around Norfolk, north-west Suffolk, Essex and eastern parts of Cambridgeshire, in East Anglia. In about 400 BC, the tribe constructed the Wandlebury Ring hill-fort, one of three in the Gog Magog Hills, overlooking the ancient Icknield Way.

Like many of the neighbouring tribes the Iceni originated in the North Sea or Baltic coastal region, and had arrived in a third wave of Celtic migrants to Britain. Tacitus recorded that the tribe had not been conquered in the invasion of 43 AD, but had made a peaceful alliance with the Romans. However, following a dispute about bearing arms, they rebelled against the governor, Publius Scapula, in 47 AD, following which a peaceful state of coexistence was restored and the tribe was granted a measure of independence under their king, Prasutagus.

Then following the king's death in 60 AD, the Romans moved in to take the territory into Republican hands, which set in motion a major revolt led by the tribal queen, Boudicca. Until this time the Iceni had not opposed the Romans. According to Tacitus: '... the Iceni, a powerful community not yet broken in battle, as they had voluntarily acceded to our alliance'. He went on to report that Boudicca was flogged and her daughters raped in reprisal. The account in Tactitus' *Annals* continued to describe how Boudicca '...was subjected to the lash and her daughters violated: all the chief men of the Iceni were stripped of their family estates, and the relatives of the king were treated as slaves'.

Incensed and vengeful, Boudicca led a rebellion that spread throughout the region and a confederation of tribes, including the neighbouring Coritani and Catuvellauni, headed by the Iceni, sacked and burned the cities of *Londinium* (London), *Camulodunum* (Colchester) and *Verulamium* (St Albans). Eventually, the Romans crushed the rebellion, and rather than be taken prisoner and humiliated, Boudicca took her own life. The defeat of the Iceni was instrumental in setting in motion almost 400 years of Roman rule in Britain.

Lopocares

The Lopocares were a Celtic tribe that lived around Corbridge, in the Tyne Valley on the south side of Hadrian's Wall in Northumberland. They are thought to have been among the many sub-groups of the Brigantes federation, but little else is known about them.

Parisi

The Parisi, (sometimes 'Parisii'), had their tribal territory in North Humberside and the East Riding of Yorkshire during the Roman period. Like many other tribes of the region, they probably originated around the North Sea or Baltic coastline. Their capital and main settlement may have been at Brough-on-Humber, which after the Roman invasion became the *Civitas of Petuaria*, as mentioned by the second-century geographer Ptolemy. The Parisi share their name with the people who lived in France around present-day Paris, to which they gave their name, and were most likely to have been a breakaway section that migrated to Britain. The British Parisi were known for their unusual chariot burials and large cemeteries. They are thought to have been a sub-tribe of their neighbours, the Brigantes, although they maintained a distinctly separate culture.

Regni

The Regni, (also known as the 'Regnenses'), were a small tribe whose territory covered parts of Sussex, Surrey and Hampshire, an area that had belonged to the Atrebates before the Roman Conquest. It has been argued that the Regni did not exist as a tribe before the Roman era and that they were created from a smaller tribal group of the Atrebates. Their tribal capital was at *Noviomagus* (present-day Chichester), close to the River Arun in West Sussex. In the first century AD they were ruled by King Tiberius Cogidubnus, who was created 'Rex Britannorum' (King of Britain) when the Regni allied themselves to become a client kingdom of Rome. Tacitus recorded that 'Certain civitates were bestowed as a gift on the king Cogidumnus, whose allegiance lasted up to our own time.' The tribe embraced Romanisation, Cogidubnus built himself a luxurious palace at Fishbourne, near Chichester in 75 AD, and the Regni were subsequently incorporated into the Roman province.

Segontiaci

The Segontiaci were a Celtic tribe who lived in south-east Britain and are thought to have been a small sept of the Ordovices tribe. They may have been the same tribe as that which existed at that time around Caernarfon in North Wales.

(See: 'Segontiaci'. Chapter Eleven: The Tribes of Wales.)

Setantii

The Setantii, (sometimes 'Segantii'), were probably a sept of the larger Brigantes tribal federation, who dominated northern England at the time of the Romans. They were Brythonic Celts who were descended from the Iberian 'beaker folk'. Their most southerly tribal land boundary was *Seteia* (the River Mersey). The main Setantii settlement was at present-day Heysham. In the second century AD, Ptolemy referred to *Portus Setantiorum* (the 'harbour or seaport of the Setantii'), which he located somewhere on the Fylde coast of present-day Lancashire, probably near the mouth of the River Wyre and the fishing port of Fleetwood. This has led some to suggest that the tribe's name might mean 'people of the water'. Others have argued that their tribal name means 'reapers of men', a reference to the Celtic predilection to cutting off the heads of their enemies, a practice of which, apparently, the Setantii were very fond. The tribe was eventually subjugated by the Ninth Legion under the command of Agricola.

Textoverdi

Also known as the 'Tectoverdi', the Textoverdi name appears in the upper valley of the South Tyne River in present-day Northumberland. They were probably a client or sub-tribe of the Brigantian confederation. A local goddess, patron and protector of the tribe was Satiada (or Sattada), known from a single altar stone found in a churchyard at Beltingham, near Bardon Mill, but may have been brought there from Vindolanda fort on Hadrian's Wall. Others suggest that the ground on which the churchyard was built may have had some ritualistic or religious significance for the tribe. The inscription reads: 'To the goddess Satiada, the council of the Textoverdi willingly and deservedly fulfilled their vow'. It is possible that the Vindolanda site was some sort of tribal centre or assembly place, as neither the tribe nor the goddess are known to have existed elsewhere. There is a body of opinion that suggests that the Textoverdi tribal name may be derived from a Gallic word distantly related to the modern word 'textile', indicating that the tribe may have been weavers, but this is somewhat speculative.

Trinovantes

The Trinovantes, (sometimes 'Trinobates' or 'Trinobantes', and 'Trinowanti' in the Brittonic Celtic language), was the name that the Romans gave to the Celtic tribe that dominated the northern Thames Estuary, from the area around London to the east coast and northwards into lower Suffolk during the Iron Age, a region corresponding to the present-day county of Essex. They were probably a Belgic tribe that had originally migrated from the North Sea or Baltic coastlines. Their capital was named after Llud Llaw Ereint, a high king of Britain, and became known as 'Lud Dun', meaning 'Llud's fort (or settlement)', from which the Romans extrapolated the Latin name *Londinium* (modern-day London).

Loughton Camp, a small hill-fort in Epping Forest just north of London, was probably constructed by the tribe sometime around 500 BC as a defence against their warring neighbours, the Catevellauni tribe.

Shortly after Julius Caesar's second invasion of Britain in 54 BC, the Trinovantes made a treaty to assist the Romans against the Catuvellauni tribe, which was led by Cassivellaunus, encouraging other tribes to join their alliance with Rome. For a time, the tribe flourished under Roman governance. However, things changed in 49 AD, when the Romans seized Trinovantes land to establish the *Colonia of Camulodunum* (modern-day Colchester). A Colonia was the highest level of all Roman settlements and it became the capital and administrative centre of Roman Britain.

The loss of their tribal territory caused the Trinovantes to ally with Boudicca of the Iceni in her revolt against the seizure of their land. The rebellious tribes went on first to sack Colchester and then London. The revolt failed, it was quickly supressed and the rebels were severely punished. Nothing more is known of the Trinovantes thereafter.

Venicones

This tribe lived in what is today Tayside. The Roman army campaigned several times in the territory of this people, but they were never permanently conquered and occupied. The archaeological evidence shows that the Venicones and their northern neighbours, the Taexali, had much in common. The tribe were one of the few groups in northern Britain at this time that buried their dead in stone-lined graves; such graves and cremation burials were very rare in other parts of Britain before the Roman period. Archaeologists suspect many Iron Age peoples often practised complex funeral rituals in which bodies were naturally allowed to decompose. The Venicones and Taexali also made offerings of prestigious decorated locally made metal objects in bogs and lakes, including massive bronze armlets. Only the Venicones and Taexali wore these unusual ornaments, which could weigh more than 1.5 kg each and were worn one on each arm.

Chapter Ten

The Scottish & Pictish Tribes

The Roman Invasion

In the year 71 AD, led by two generals, Gnaeus Julius Agricola and Quintus Petillius Cerialis, the Romans arrived in Scotland, the lands north of the River Forth, which they called *Caledonia.* It was to be the first of three abortive attempts they made to subdue the fierce warriors of the Caledonian and Pictish tribes. By 83 AD, Agricola had been appointed as the Roman Governor of Britain and was determined to conquer southern Scotland. As the Roman historian Tacitus recorded, the Caledonians '...turned to armed resistance on a large scale'. According to his account in his *Life of Julius Agricola*, despite the severe weather conditions, '...the third year of the expedition brought to light new tribes, which we attacked even as far as the Tyne estuary. The enemy was thoroughly terrified by this attack.'

Agricola had marched northwards and in 84 AD his army, said by Tacitus to amount to 30,000 legionaries, confronted a combined Caledonian and Pictish tribal army of 60,000 warriors. The numbers may have been grossly exaggerated, and different accounts put the figures much lower, but whatever the true numbers were, the outcome was a resounding victory for Agricola and a defeat for the Caledonian confederacy.

Reportedly, the two armies formed up in battle order and a major engagement occurred at a place that became known as Mons Graupius, a hill that has been (arguably) identified as Bennachie in Aberdeenshire. Tacitus claimed that 10,000 Caledonians were killed with the loss of a mere 360 Roman soldiers. Despite their apparently overwhelming military success, the victory yielded very little tactical value for Rome. The surviving Caledonians and Picts had scattered into the forests where despite a bloody and decimating rout, its tribesmen quickly reformed.

Ultimately they were not subdued, as faced with determined and continual guerrilla-type raiding attacks, Roman battle tactics proved largely ineffective. Further, this was to be Agricola's only actual battlefield engagement in Scotland; strict regimented Roman army tactics were no match for the Caledonians, especially among their forested and mountainous territories, and the cost to Roman resources was reckoned too expensive for any potential benefit. As a result, Rome did not keep a hold on the territory for long and gradually began to relinquish any ground that had been taken. Within a year of the battle, Agricola withdrew to the south and was recalled to Rome.

The Roman Walls

In 85 AD, realising the impracticability of conquering the Caledonian tribes, Rome embarked on a series of defensive barriers and walls to limit the continual raids and incursions by Pictish tribesmen into northern Britannia. First, they constructed the most northerly Roman frontier system in Britain, an 11-mile-long turf-built barrier, known as the Gask Ridge. It was complete with forts at Ardoch and Strageath, as well as two watchtowers at Kaims Castle. The Ridge barrier was constructed on high ground between Perth and Crieff. It was abandoned in about 88 AD, as the Romans withdrew further from Scotland.

Hadrian's Wall was the second barrier, and unquestionably the most impressive permanent marker of the northern limits of the Roman Empire in Britain. The Emperor Hadrian came to Britain in 122 AD and according to his biographer, 'He was the first to build a wall, eighty miles long, to separate the Romans from the barbarians.' The wall extended across the width of northern Britain, actually running as a continuous barrier for seventy-three miles, from Wallsend on the River Tyne in the east to Bowness on the Solway Firth in the west.

The wall was built entirely of locally quarried stone and stood around twelve feet high and in places up to ten feet wide, with watchtowers, mile castles and forts interspersed along its length. It was constructed by men of the three legions of Britain, and manned by the auxiliary troops drawn from around the Empire, many from subjugated Gaulish tribes. The wall remained in constant use until the Romans withdrew from Britain in around 410 AD, and in modern times has been designated as a World Heritage Site.

In the year 140 AD, the Roman Emperor Antoninus Pius ordered the building of a third frontier barrier, the Antonine Wall, which was named after him. Having already witnessed Hadrian's great enterprise, the envious Antonius felt the need to leave his mark on history. His wall was located north of Hadrian's and stretched east to west for thirty-seven miles from present-day Bo'ness on the Firth of Forth to Old Kilpatrick on the River Clyde. The barrier comprised a bank of turf almost seven feet high and five feet wide. A wooden palisade was constructed on top, with about nineteen forts along its length to billet several hundred Roman soldiers. However, the wall failed to hold back the continual raiding parties that persistently harried the English-Scottish borderlands. The Picts continually attacked the wall, which was lost and regained twice by the Romans before they finally quit and retreated back to Hadrian's Wall. The Antonine Wall was finally abandoned in about 165 AD, a little over twenty years after its construction. The superstitious Picts called it the Devil's Dyke, because they could not believe that such an enormous project could have been been built by human hands.

Ptolemy's Map of the
Scottish & Pictish Tribes
of Caledonia, 1st Century BC
NORTH ATLANTIC
OCEAN
ORCADES
SMERTAE
CORNOVII
NORTH
SEA
The Minch
LUGI
CAERENI
DECANTAE
Moray Firth
VACOMAGI
CALEDONII
EBUDAE
CREONES
TAEXALI
VENICONES
EPIDII
Antonine
Wall
Firth of Forth
VOTADINI
DAMNONII
SELGOVAE
Hadrian's Wall
IRISH SEA
NOVANTAE
BRIGANTES

The Picts

The unvanquished Pictish tribes were a 'painted people', whose name comes from the Latin word 'picti', meaning 'painted'. The Romans used it as a pejorative term, regarding them as a barbarian, savage and uncivilised people. Other than the fact that they inhabited the north and east of Scotland, we know very little about them. What we do know comes from Roman and Greek writers, as in common with many ancient peoples, they left no written language, and there remains only a profusion of intricately carved standing stones, many decorated with mysterious symbols whose meaning is not fully known.

The Picts were distinguished from the other Scottish and British tribes by this widespread practice of body painting and tattooing. Julius Caesar recorded that they '...dye themselves with woad, which produces a blue colour, and makes their appearance in battle more terrible. They wear long hair, and shave every part of the body save the head and the upper lip.' Many other writers commented on their love of body painting and tattooing.

A later recorded historical account of the Picts appeared in the third century AD, when the Roman writer Eumenius described the 'Pictus' as fierce and skilled in battle. Eumenius' characterisation of the Picts as an inordinately aggressive people was fully justified by events, as they are known to have fought numerous battles with the migrant Scotti. They were also at war with King Edwin, (sometimes 'Ecgfrith'), of the Northumbrians, whose territory was just south of what must have been an ill-defined border with Britannia at that time. Edwin had taken possession of southern Pictish territory as far north as the River Forth and he had established a fortified settlement there, which he called 'Din Eidyn', meaning 'Edwin's fort'. It later became 'Edwin's burgh', and finally Edinburgh. The Picts, led by King Bridei MacBili, defeated Edwin at the village of Dun Nechtain in Angus in 685 AD, and drove his army back to Northumbria.

According to some sources, the Picts probably originated in Scandinavia, while others see them as an indigenous population who had been there throughout the various periods of the Stone Age. Tacitus used the word 'Caledonii' to identify them.

The Picts were not one single people, but a group of quite separate tribes, who were frequently at inter-tribal war with each other, but came together to fight Vikings, Angles and Romans as a common foe.

By the tenth century AD, the Picts had apparently disappeared, having intermixed and intermarried with Scots and Gael immigrants from Ireland. They may be gone, but they are not forgotten; many Scottish towns like Pittenweem and Pitlochry, among others, still retain vestiges of Pictish ancestry in their placenames.

The Scotti

Scotti (or 'Scoti') was the Latin name for the Gaels, a people who had migrated from Hibernia (Ireland) into Caledonia (Scotland) in around 500 AD. They are thought to have originated from the Dal Riata (or 'Dalriada'), one of more than a hundred petty Hibernian tribal kingdoms, whose territory was in present-day County Antrim in Northern Ireland, and a branch of whom crossed the Irish Sea to settle in the Argyl and Bute region of Scotland.

The Scotti spoke a Q-Celtic language and they called themselves Goidil (or Gaels). These invading Gaelic migrants expanded further east and drove out Pictish tribes from their newly conquered territory, which they probably began to refer to as 'Scotia'. By the ninth century, through association and intermarriage, under the rule of Kenneth MacAlpine, (the *Rex Pictorum*, or King of the Picts), faced with increasing Viking incursions, 'Scotti-land' and 'Pict-land' had evolved into a unified Gaelic-Pictish kingdom, which they called Alba and MacAlpine given the title 'King of Alba'.

The Angles had arrived on the British mainland earlier, from around 700 AD, and their culture began to influence the Scottish borderlands. A century later the Vikings established settlements in Orkney and the Outer Hebrides. These later invasions were frequently hostile, and were a contributory factor in the unification of Scotti and Pictish tribes in 844 AD. By this time, the lands of Caledonia had undergone a multi-ethnic transformation to become the nation we now call Scotland. MacAlpine was probably crowned at the Iron Age hill-fort at Dunadd in Argyle, which became the capital of the Scotti kingdom. From that time on, the language of the Picts died out to be replaced by Scottish Gaelic.

THE TRIBES

Boresti

The Boresti, or the 'Voresti' as Tacitus called them, were a Caledonian tribe whose territory was in the Great Glen around Strathmore in east-central Scotland. They were the only Caledonian tribe to be named by Tacitus. It is not clear if the Boresti actually fought in the Battle of Mons Graupius, as in his work *The Life of Agricola*, Tacitus stated that Agricola's foray into Boresti territory ('*...in fines Borstorum*') was primarily to find winter quarters, but in the process he had taken hostages. He annexed their territory a year after the battle in 84 AD.

Their tribal name probably derives from the Latin word 'boreas', meaning 'north', and has been interpreted to mean 'north mountain', a reflection of their lands that were arguably located between the Grampian Mountains and the Sidlaws. Some translate the name Boresti as meaning 'boar people'. It is also possible that the tribal name is a corruption of the Celtic 'Horesti' or 'Horreii', whom Ptolemy placed at a settlement called Horrea, somewhere in Fife. Other investigators also place Boresti tribelands in the Lomond Hills of the Fife Peninsula. However, their precise location continues to be the subject of debate. Together with the Vacomagi and Verturiones, the Boresti are thought to have been part of the Maetae

Confederation of tribes. Of the Boresti, Tacitus was of the opinion that, like other Caledonian tribes, 'The red hair and large limbs of the inhabitants of Caledonia point clearly to a German origin.'

Caereni

The Caerini, (sometimes 'Carini' or 'Caberini' as the Romans called them), were a minor Iron Age tribe that held territory in the western Highlands of Sutherland in the north of Scotland, probably somewhere around the estuary of the River Naver. Their main settlement may have been a place called *Ceberenion.* Their tribal name has been interpreted to mean 'sheep people', suggesting they were predominantly shepherds.

Cait

The Cait, or 'Cat' tribe, were an Iron Age Pictish kingdom that lived around Caithness and Sutherland in northern Scotland. The name Caithness derives from the tribe. The tribal name is also enshrined in the Gaelic name for Sutherland ('Cataibh', which means 'among the cats'). Also, the name of the Shetland Islands, (in Gaelic, 'Inse Catt'), includes a reference to this Pictish tribe, and translates as 'islands of the Cat people'.

Pictish legend has it that the kingdom had been originally founded by Cait, one of the seven sons of Cruithne, son of Cinge, who according to an account recorded in the ancient Irish *Book of Lecain,* was the first king of the Picts.

A large carved Pictish stone, known as the St Martin Pictish Stone, possibly dating to between the fifth and seventh centuries, has been found in a cemetery at Ulbster in Caithness, showing early examples of intricately decorated Pictish art. Archaeologists from the University of Aberdeen have uncovered the remains of an ancient Pictish settlement at Wag of Forse in Caithness, which includes a cemetery and a longhouse, (known as a 'Wag'), and is thought to date from about 1400 years ago.

Caithness is part of the Highland Pictish Trail, which includes thirty-two known sites as well as several intricately carved Pictish standing stones.

Caledones

The Caledones, (also known as 'Caledonii' and 'Caledonians'), were a confederacy of indigenous Brittonic Celtic speaking tribes that occupied the Highlands region of present-day western Scotland. Cassius Dio remarked on the hardiness and apparent ability of the Caledonians to endure cold, hunger and other privations. The tribal name Caledonii may derive from the Brittonic word element 'caled', meaning 'hard' or 'tough', and may be interpreted as 'hard (or tough) people'. The Romans used the name 'Caledonii', not just to identify the tribe, but as a portmanteau name for all the tribes living in the north of Scotland.

The Confederation may have included the Vacomagi, Taexali and Venicones tribes. Ptolemy also counted the Cornovii, Caereni, Smertae, Lugi, Epidii, Decantae, Carnonacae and Creones among their number. As with many such confederations, these allied tribes were frequently at war with each other, but faced with the kind of common threat that the Romans posed, inter-tribal differences were often laid aside in a common cause. The Battle of Mons Graupius was one such occasion. Tacitus records one of their leaders, Calgacus, delivering a rousing speech to the assembled confederate warriors before the battle began in 84 AD. It was a resounding defeat for the Caledonii, though the Highlands would never be completely conquered, and Agricola withdrew his troops back to Hadrian's Wall shortly afterwards.

Despite their defeat, the tribes were in a constant state of rebellion against Roman occupation of their tribelands and continued to fight against Agricola during the first century. They continued to resist a later renewed attempt at domination by Roman legions during the reign of the Emperor Septimus Severus in the third century. Severus launched his invasion ahead of an army of 40,000 in 208 AD but was constantly dogged by the guerrilla tactics of Caledonian war parties and suffered heavy losses of men and equipment. Severus died in *Eboracum* (York) in 211 AD, at which point the invasion was abandoned and the legions were withdrawn back behind the relative security of Hadrian's Wall, even though by then it was unmanned.

Earlier, in the year 180 AD, the Caledones had attempted an invasion of Britannia by breaching Hadrian's Wall, and it was only after a peace treaty that was agreed with the Roman Governor Ulpius Marcellus that they withdrew back beyond the River Forth into their own territories. After the legions were withdrawn from the Wall in 197 AD, the Caledonians joined the Maetae and Brigantes in further forays into Britannia. Despite their decisive defeat at Mons Graupius, and their confrontation with Severus in the third century, with rumours of their defeat and eradication by him, all attempts at their complete subjugation seem ultimately to have failed.

Carnonacae

It is open to question whether the Creones, Caereni, and Carnonacae tribes were actually one and the same people whose tribal name has had several different spellings, or if they could have descended from a common, single tribe. Rome generally grouped all these tribes together as Calendonii. The Carnonacae were said to be a fierce tribe and reputedly customarily smeared their faces with the blood of their slain enemies. Ptolemy placed them on the western Highlands, on the coast of modern-day Ross-shire, located between the territories of the Creones and the Careni. The names and locations of their main cities are unknown, but it had been suggested that their main centre may have been at a place called *Carnonacion*, where the first name element 'car' has been interpreted by some as 'steep hill', which could have been a reference to a hill-fort settlement. Others prefer to translate the first element, 'Carn', as a variant of the word 'cairn', a pile of stones, often used as way markers or to identify ritually sacred places. Hence, in this case, suggesting an overall placename meaning of 'people who dwell among the stones'.

Cornovii

It has been argued that the Cornovii tribe of Scotland were a branch of the same tribe that inhabited western Cornwall and a district in Brittany. Of all the northern tribes, the Cornovii seemed to be the least warlike as they were defeated in 47 AD at their Wrekin hill-fort (in the present-day English county of Shropshire) in their only battle with the Romans. The tribe is recorded in Scotland by around 140 AD, which suggests that at least some of their number had migrated northwards to avoid the worst effects of Roman occupation. They settled at the extreme northern tip in Caithness. In the fifth century AD, warriors of the Cornovii tribe migrated from Lancashire and resettled in Brittany, in a region that became known as 'Cornavia'.

Creones

The tribal name of the Creones, (sometimes 'Cerones'), was either derived from Cernunnos, the horned god, or from a tribal chieftain who was named after the god. It has been argued that they were possibly a sub-group or sept of the Carnonacae tribe. The only historical reference to them is found in Ptolemy's *Geographia*, where he placed their territory on the west coast of Scotland, south of Skye and north of Mull.

Damnonii

The Damnonii (or 'Damnoni') held territory around southern Strathclyde, which before twentieth-century boundary changes included much of the counties of Renfrewshire, Lanarkshire and Ayrshire. Following the Roman invasion, from 82 AD they established a friendly alliance and spent some time under the governance of the Roman occupation forces, governed by Quintilius Clemens. Tribes by the name Damnoni are known to have had territories in Devon, Brittany and Ireland, though it is not clear whether they were offshoots of the original Caledonian tribe or were perhaps a quite separate people who coincidentally had the sane tribal name. On the balance of probability, they were likely to have been the same people. Damnoni literally means 'men under care of the goddess of the deep', suggesting that they were originally miners. They spoke a Celtic language similar to Welsh.

Decantae

Some authorities maintain that the Pictish Decantae (or 'Decanti') tribal name is derived from 'derc', a word that translates as 'summit' or 'steep hill', and is taken to be a reference to their hill-fort settlement at Craig Phadrig near Inverness. Others prefer the Celtic root word element 'deko', meaning 'best', or even 'dekan', meaning 'ten', indicating that they may have been a minor sub-tribe in an allied ten-tribe confederacy. The last element of their name suggests that they may have been a sept of the Cantae or Cantii tribe of southern Britain. Yet another possibility is that the '-cant' element of their name, in common with modern Welsh, indicates a rim, and may have referred to a people who lived on both sides (or rims) of the Moray Firth. Alternatively, it has been suggested that their tribal name means 'noble folk', as their leaders were sometimes referred to as 'Lairds of the Great Loch'.

Ptolemy only mentioned the Decantae in passing and located their territory around the Black Isle on the western coast of the Moray Firth. Another incident of the Decantae tribal name occurs around the foothills of Snowdonia in North Wales, where the name of the town of Deganwy in the Conway Estuary translates as 'town of the Decantae'. Their presence in these two regions might have come about when an original, larger tribe split into smaller sub-groups and established settlements elsewhere – but this is only speculative.

Epidii

The Epidii, (sometimes called 'Equidii'), were a tribe of Islay, Jura and Kintyre in the Western Isles of modern Argyll, whose name has its roots in the Brittonic Celtic word 'epos', meaning 'horse'. Their veneration of horse gods earned them the name 'the horsemen' or 'horse people'. Such devotion to horses was a fairly widespread cult among Celtic and Gaelic tribes, and their superb horsemanship was celebrated even among the Romans. Goddesses like Epona were adopted by Roman cavalry brigades, who helped spread her worship across Europe and into Britain. After Romanisation, warriors of many Celtic and Gaulish tribes served as mercenaries or auxiliaries in the Roman army.

In the second century, Ptolemy listed the Epidii among 'the minor northern tribes of Britain' and described their tribal territory as a promontory on the west coast, called 'Epidion Akron', which has been identified as Kintyre. The Epidii were conquered and their lands overrun by Scotti invaders from Hibernia who displaced them some time during the fifth century AD. Thereafter, the Gaelic-speaking Kingdom of Dal Riata dominated the land of Argyll and north-eastern Ireland, and the Epidii may have been one of the smaller tribes to become part of the Pictish Kingdom that became known as Pictland. Their tribal name effectively disappears from recorded history after this time.

Fortriu

Fortriu was probably the most powerful of the early Pictish kingdoms of Scotland. Its major settlement stretched from the Moray Firth to Fife. It was one of the two great kingdoms that dominated Scotland in the ninth century. Fortriu, the land of the Caledonian Picts, lay in the east, and Dal Raita, the land of the Gaelic Scots, in the west.

A series of excavations on the Tarbat Peninsula in Ross-shire made by the University of Aberdeen in October 2012 revealed that the site was an important Pictish stronghold.

In the mid-seventh century King Ecgfrith of the Northumbrians began to invade Pictish territory, overrunning Fife and forcing the Picts to pay tribute money. However, the Pictish tribes rebelled in 670 AD, and after several setbacks, under the leadership of King Bride MacBile of the Fortriu, in 685 AD they defeated the Northumbrians at the Battle of Nechtansmere near Dunnichen in Angus. Their victory gained them independence from the Northumbrians and emboldened them to go on to retake their lost lands and to expand their territory south into northern England.

The church at Portmahmomack is counted as one of the most important churches of the Kingdom of Fortriu and one of Britain's earliest known Christian sites. It was destroyed by Norse raiders between 780 and 830 AD. The dominance of the Fortriu over eastern Scotland came to a temporary end in 839 AD, when they were defeated by the Vikings. However, they seem to have re-emerged as a dominant force later, having survived a series of bloody inter-clan conflicts around 1115 AD to emerge as victors, ruling virtually all the Pictish tribes. By 1203, they headed a Clan Council and renamed the region 'New Pictavia', which survived until the period of Highland Clearances by the British in the eighteenth century.

Maeatae

The Maeatae were a second-century confederation of Celtic tribes, possibly including the Boresti, Vacomagi and Verturiones, who lived in land between the Firth of Forth and the Firth of Tay, in parts of present-day Clackmannanshire, Fife and Stirlingshire. They established a prominent hilltop stronghold in Stirling known as Dun Maeatae, which means 'the fort of the Maeatae'.

Torwood Broch was another Maeatae site, reputedly the largest prehistoric building in southern Scotland, whose remaining Celtic tower still survives at almost ten feet tall.

In his *Roman History*, Cassius Dio asserted that 'there are two principal races of the Britons, the Caledonians and the Maeatae, and the names of the others have been merged in these two'. He went on to say that 'The Maeatae live next to the cross-wall which cuts the island in half, and the Caledonians are beyond them.' His reference to a 'cross-wall' is reckoned to have been the Antonine Wall. He went on to describe that in the light of Maeatae constant aggression, the Roman Governor Virius Lupus had been '...compelled to purchase peace from the Maeatae for a large sum'. However, the peace failed to last and when the Maeatae finally rebelled in 210 AD the Emperor Septimus Severus ordered their extermination. This had the effect of encouraging the Caledonian tribes to join in the Maeatae revolt. After this date, Roman records show no trace of tribal names, but simply refer to tribes like the Maeatae as 'southern Picts'.

Novantae

The geographer Ptolemy made the only known reference to this tribe in his *Geographia* of 150 AD, where he recorded that the Novantae lived in the region of present-day Dumfries and Galloway, which he called the *Novantarum Peninsula*, (the peninsula of the Novantae). He particularly specifies their territory in *Novantarum Cheronesus* (the modern-day Rhins of Galloway). This used to be part of the former counties of Kircudbrightshire, Wigtown and Ayrshire. He also named their two main towns as *Locopibium* and *Rerigonium*, though the precise location of the former is unknown. As for the latter, it is thought that the city was established by the Novantae on the eastern side of Loch Ryan in Galloway, but its location also remains a mystery.

Originally, they were a Caledonian tribe, but due to territorial changes forced upon them by the Damnonii in the second century, they were absorbed into Pictish lands and became known as the Novantae Picts. Like the Damnonii and Votadini, the Novantae formed an agreeable relationship with the Roman occupiers and apart from a relatively few regional confrontations, neither tribe was ever involved in major conflicts with Rome. The Novantae seem to have been a peace-loving people who were primarily involved with farming and agriculture.

There was a small Roman fort established at Gatehouse of Fleet in Novantae territory, and it was from here that Roman legionaries were sent to deal with tribal incursions against Hadrian's Wall. Iron Age earth ramparts have been discovered at Rispain Camp, a fortified Novantae farmstead, which contains a double rampart and ditch surrounding three roundhouses. Until the 1970s it was thought to be a Roman construction, but archaeological excavations since then have established its Novantae heritage. The site has been designated as a Historic Monument of Scotland.

Scotti

The name of the Scotti, (or 'Scoti'), tribe was a Latin word that originally referred to the Gaels of Hibernia (Ireland), but later referred only to the Gaels of Scotland. As such, the Gaels descended from the Dal Riata (or Dalraida) tribe of Antrim in north-eastern Ireland. According to tradition, Fergus Mor mac Eirc established a new Dal Riata when he migrated across the Irish Sea and settled in County Argyll sometime around 500 AD, at the beginning of the Christian era, displacing the resident Pictish population. These new Dal Riata immigrants to Britain were known to early medieval writers as 'Scoti Brittaniae'. They spoke a Q-Celtic form of Gaelic language, which qualifies as the original Scottish tongue.

The ancient medieval manuscript *Annals of Ulster* (the 'Annala Uladh') records the history of the Dal Raita kings from the fifth century AD to 1540 and confirms their attempts to incorporate much of eastern Pictland into their kingdom. Their new settlements were established in what had been the territory of the Epidii tribe during the Roman period, but the Dal Raita soon founded their own kingdom, with Dunadd in Kilmartin Glen in Kintyre as their capital.

According to legend, Fergus was the founder of Scotland and his tribal name became that of the country, first as 'Scotti-land' and finally as Scotland. At this time, other Irish migrants were landing in Cornwall and South Wales. In around 900 AD the Dal Riata and the southern Pictish kingdoms merged so that by the twelfth century the name 'Scotia' had become widely accepted as the territory of the Gaelic kingdom of Alba.

Selgovae

The Selgovae, (sometimes 'Seglovae' or 'Segloves'), were a somewhat obscure tribe that occupied areas of southern Scotland, between the Cheviot Hills and Dumfries as well as parts of Northumbria, during the Iron Age and the Roman era. Their territory would have included the ancient counties of Roxburgh, Selkirk and Peebles. They received a brief mention in Ptolemy's *Geographia*, but apart from that, there seems to be no other historical record of them. It is possible that they were part of the large Brigantes confederation, and probably referred to themselves by the Brittonic Celtic name 'Selgowi', which translates as 'the hunters'.

The main settlement, or opiddum, and probable capital was at the Eildon Hill North hill-fort near present-day Melrose, which they had occupied since around 1000 BC, and abandoned in 79 AD in the face of the advancing Twentieth or Ninth

Roman legions under the command of Julius Agricola. This forty-acre hilltop fortification would have been occupied by an estimated 3000 to 6000 people, but was eventually replaced at the foot of the hill by the Roman fort of *Trimontium* on the banks of the River Tweed, named after the three peaks of the Eildons (present-day Newstead).

The Selgovae were apparently fiercely anti-Roman in their attitude, judging by several other hill-fort settlements that they established, including those at Cademuir Hill near Peebles, Whiteside Hill near Romannobridge, at Rubers Law and at Tamshiel Rigg near Hawick, and at Dreva Craig near Broughton in the Borders region. There were others.

According to Roman records, together with the Votadini tribe, the Selgovae were conquered by Rome in 80 AD. Following their subjugation, elements of the Selgovae tribe are known to have served as auxiliaries in the Roman army. In the post-Roman period, towards the end of the fourth century, their territory was seized by the Alt Clut, a British tribe who are thought to have been descendants of the Damnonii.

Smertae

According to Ptolemy, the Pictish Smertae tribe, (whom he called 'Mertae'), held territory around the River Oykel on the border of Ross and Sutherland, and probably in the adjoining Carron Valley in the Scottish Highlands. They have a name that comes from the Celtic or Gaulish language and means 'smeared people'. This is thought to be a reference to their practice of sacrificially smearing their bodies with the blood of their slain or captures enemies. They may have venerated Rosmerta, the Celtic 'great smeared goddess'. As with most tribes who lived in the Highlands and islands of Scotland, the Romans tended to group them all together as 'Calendonii'. The Smertae submitted to Roman rule in 84 AD, following Agricola's victory over the Caledonian tribal confederation.

Taexali

Very little is known about the Taexali tribe, (sometimes 'Taezali' or 'Taxali'), and most of what we do know comes from Ptolemy's *Geographia*, where in his brief account he recorded that '… toward the east are the Taezali and the town, Devana.' Their chief settlement of Devana was located near Kinnaird Head, at the mouth of the River Dee, and is the present-day city of Aberdeen. Apart from that we know that their tribal territory was in the south Grampian and north-east Tayside region of Scotland, and included Buchan Ness, which Ptolemy called the *Taexlon Promontory*. The tribe was finally defeated by the Romans at the Battle of Mons Graupius in 84 AD, but their territory was never fully occupied.

Vacomagi

Vacomagi territory was in the ancient counties of Banffshire, Elginshire, Nairnshire and part of Inverness-shire, between the River Tay and the Moray Firth. Ptolemy called them *Ouakomagoi* and named their principal settlements at places he called Bannatia, Tamia, and Tuesis: Their tribal name has been interpreted as a combination of two Gaelic word elements: 'vaco', indicating a bay or a firth, and 'magh', a plain. Hence, 'people of the plain of the bay'. Another explanation maintains that it more probably means 'inhabitants of the curved fields', while yet another cites 'vaco' as indicating a cow, and 'magh' could refer to 'power', in which case it might suggest the tribe were either cattle herders or rustlers. However, in light of so many different interpretations, it is not possible to say with any certainty exactly what their name signified. The Vacomagi were one of the rebellious Pictish tribes who were defeated by the Romans at the Battle of Mons Graupius in 84 AD.

Burghead Fort on the Moray coastal plain is believed to have been built as their main stronghold and may have been one of the earliest of its kind to have been constructed in Scotland. The eight-acre Iron Age hill-fort at Clunie Hills, on the east side of the present-day township of Forres, is also attributed to the tribe. Vacomagi territory later became the clan lands of the Macphersons.

Venicones

The Venicones received only a brief mention as one of the sixteen tribes that inhabited Caledonia by Ptolemy in his *Geographia* of 150 AD. He located their main settlement and probable capital at 'Orrea', which has been identified as the Roman fort of *Horrea Classis*, (present-day Monifieth), located some six miles east of Dundee. They also had established an important hill-fort settlement and burial site at East Lomond Hill, which, after the collapse of the Roman Empire around 410 AD, was inhabited by Pictish kings as part of the Kingdom of Fib, from which Fife takes its name.

The Venicones tribal name has been interpreted to mean 'hunting hounds' and their territory was around the River Tay in modern-day Fife. Venicones operated the Pictish navy. Unlike other more typical Caledonian and Pictish burials, they were one of the few tribes that buried their dead in stone-lined graves at this time. Venicones territory came under threat when the Roman Twentieth Legion Valeria occupied the region and built the fortress of *Pinnata Castra* near present-day Inchtuthill in 85 AD. When General Agricola decided to create the so-called Gask Ridge, a defensive barrier to keep the warring Pictish tribes at bay, he chose a line that formed the border between the pre-existing territories of the Venicones and the Caledonii. By the second century AD, the Venicones had come under Roman rule and by the fifth century that had been incorporated into the Pictish population. Little is heard of them thereafter.

Verturiones

The southern Pictish Verturiones, sometimes known as the 'Verturiones of Fortrui', and occasionally as 'the Southern Maeatae', have a tribal name that is often interpreted to mean 'the destroyers', based on the Latin word 'verturio'. According to others the word has been taken to suggest a fortress. Hence, 'fortress people'.

The Roman soldier and historian Ammianus Marcellinus, writing in the late fourth century AD, (when the northern tribes attacked the Roman province), described the Verturiones and the Dicalydones (both subsequently identified as the Caledonii) as the two most important Pictish tribes. They lived in the valley of the River Earn in Perthshire.

The tribe of sea raiders of Fife, known as the Fortriu, were evidently the same people as the Venicones. In fact, Fortriu was a later form of Verturiones.

By the late seventh century, the Fortriu had developed a powerful kingdom that came to dominate most of the Scottish midlands, so that in contemporary chronicles, terms like 'King of Fortriu' and 'King of the Picts' meant virtually one and the same thing. The tribe established strongholds in fertile lowland regions, at places like Burghead, Ruthven Barracks, Rothiemurchus and Turriff.

By the ninth century, Scotland was divided into just two kingdoms: Fortiu, the land of the Picts, and Dal Raita, the land of the Scots. The title given to the kings of Fortriu were thereafter known as 'Mormaer', a Gaelic term meaning 'great steward'.

Votadini

The Votadini, (also known as the Wotadini, or by Ptolemy as the 'Otadini'), were a large Iron Age tribe whose territory was in Lothian, in south-east Scotland and north-east England, stretching from the Firth of Forth as far as Brigantes territory around the River Tyne. Their name is a Latin version of the Brittonic Celtic form of the name 'Goutodin' or 'Gododdin' and could be translated as 'hill dwellers'. Their settlements were chiefly in hill-forts, with three known within their territory: at Traprain Law, Yeavering Bell and Eildon Seat. Their capital was probably the Traprain Law hill-fort in East Lothian, which they abandoned in the early fifth century before they moved to settle in a place they called *Din Eidyn* (present-day Edinburgh).

Between the years 138 and 162 AD, the Votadini came under Roman rule as their lands were sandwiched between Hadrian's and the Antonine Walls. The tribe became Romanised and assimilated into the emerging Scottish culture. When Agricola withdrew his legions back to Hadrian's Wall, the Votadini became friendly caretakers of the abandoned Roman buffer zone, a role they continued to hold until the Roman withdrawal from Britain in the early fifth century.

In March 2020, archaeologists working with Historic Environment Scotland began excavating a site overlooking the Firth of Forth at the top of Arthur's Seat, in Holyrood Park, Edinburgh, and uncovered the walls of a prehistoric hill-fort believed to have been constructed by the Votadini tribe around 3000 years ago.

The fifth-century Welsh hero, Brittonic warlord and king of Gwynedd, Cunnedda (or 'Cunedag') was born among the Votadini. According to the *Historia Brittonum*, (attributed to the monk Nennius), Cunedda came from Manaw Gododdin, in the modern-day Clackmannanshire region of Scotland, and his forebears led the Votadini and other Romano-British forces against Pictish and Irish incursions south of Hadrian's Wall.

Chapter Eleven

The Welsh Tribes

Five years after the arrival of the Romans on the southern shores of Britain in 43 AD, the Roman Governor of Britannia, Publius Ostorius Scapula, led the legions into the lands that today we call Wales. Writing at that time, the Roman historian Tacitus recorded how the Romans had defeated a tribe that he referred to as the Decangos.

Wales was populated by five Celtic tribes at that time: the Deceangli in the north-east, the Ordovices in the north-west, the Demetae in the south-west, the Silures in the south-east, and the Cornovii in the central border land. These tribes would have had no sense of nationhood as such, but would have operated at a purely tribal level; consequently there was no concerted or combined effort to resist and the Romans were able to conquer each tribe in turn. Being nearest to the Roman headquarters at *Deva Vitrix* (Chester), the Deceangi settlements in North Wales were the first to feel the weight of Roman military force, as it advanced into their territory from across the River Dee. It would take another twenty-five years to subdue the rest of Wales, though it was never more than a partial conquest and its people were never fully Romanised.

The Romans established a network of more than forty auxiliary forts throughout Wales, several on the Clwydian Range and Llantysilio Mountain. There were others at Abergavenny, Brecon, Cardhill, Castle Collen near Llandridnod Wells, Llanio, Loughor, Monmouth, Neath, Caernarfon and Usk. The main Roman administrative centres were at *Isca Augusta* (Caerleon), which garrisoned some 5,500 men, and at *Segontium* (Caernarfon). As the tribes were pacified and gradually began to accept Roman rule, the Romans became more of an occupation force than conquerors, and numbers of troops were gradually withdrawn to fight under the command of Agricola against the northern British and Caledonian tribes.

However, persistent Deceangli raids across the border into the Midlands led to Roman couter-attacks in North Wales. The Romans soon realised that the British tribes needed to be isolated so that they could deal with each one individually. To this end they established several forts around Gloucester and Usk, which formed much of the Decleagli frontier with the Silures to the south.

The Welsh landscape constituted a major obstacle to Roman foot soldiers. Its steep hills and dense wooded valleys were difficult arenas for the type of staged battles and formation fighting for which they had been trained. On the other hand,

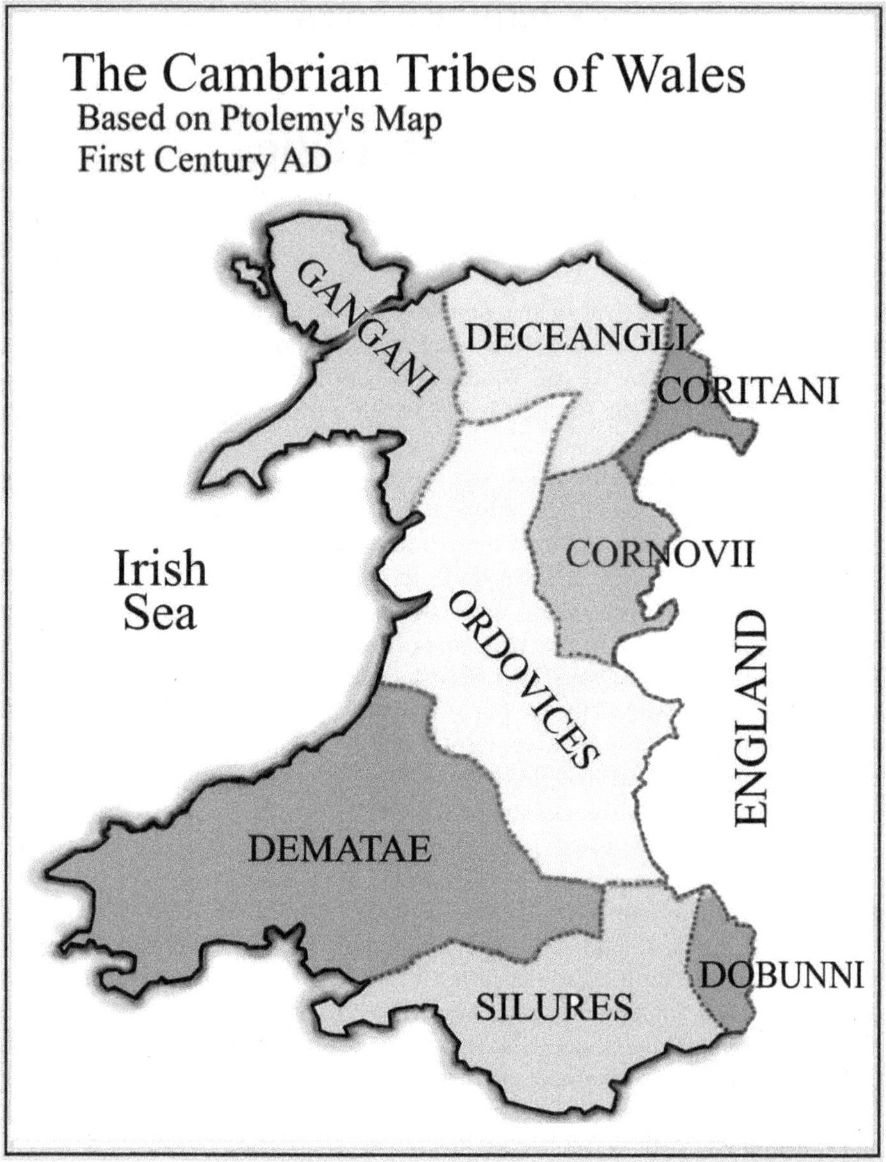

the Celtic tribes were extremely adept at guerrilla warfare, and could appear out of nowhere, stage rapid attacks and disappear back into the hills and woods. The main resistance to the Romans in Wales was led by Caractacus (known in Welsh as 'Caradoc'). He was a warrior leader and prince of the Catuvellauni tribe of Essex and headed a confederation of tribes against the Roman advance. After a crushing defeat at the River Medway in Kent, he and many of his warriors had fled to seek sanctuary in Wales.

Anglesey posed a particular problem for the Roman invaders. First, separated from the mainland by the Menai Strait, it was an island, and that made it difficult to access. But it was the island's status as the most important centre of the Druids that presented the Romans with a major impediment in their plan to dominate the whole island of Britannia.

The Druids were a powerful and culturally unifying factor among the Celtic tribes, and presided over a religious practice to which all the Celtic tribes appeared to subscribe. Anglesey, ('Mona' as the Romans called it, and 'Ynys Môn' in Welsh), had also become a refuge to which Celtic warriors fled to avoid capture. It also possessed plentiful copper supplies, which had been mined on Parys Mountain for centuries, and the Romans were keen to get their hands on that valuable commodity.

The first attempt at the island's invasion was in 60 AD, by Gaius Suetonius Paulinus. Tacitus recorded the beginning of Suetonius' assault: 'He therefore prepared to attack the island of Mona which had a powerful population and was a refuge for fugitives.' To make the crossing, Suetonius had flat-bottomed barges built to cross the Strait. Once ashore, despite being met with stiff resistance, his army was victorious. Tacitus described the battle that ensued and the way fierce tribesmen and screaming women warriors, egged on by Druids, fought fearlessly to defend their island, before becoming overwhelmed by the better equipped and trained Roman infantry.

The Druids were massacred, their altars and groves were destroyed and a Roman occupation force was installed across the whole island. It remained there for the next sixteen years, before Suetonius was recalled to *Londinium* (London) to face hostile tribal revolts led by Queen Boudicca of the Iceni in southern England.

In 77 AD, a second invasion of the island was made by Agricola, now the Roman Governor of Britannia, in response to the massacre of Roman cavalrymen by warriors of the Ordovices tribe. This marked the end of all Welsh tribal resistance. Following Agricola's successful campaign, the Romans continued to rule Anglesey for the next three centuries, and only finally left sometime around the year 383 AD. Just over twenty years later, they finally withdrew completely from Britannia and the rule of the Roman Republic had come to an end in the British Isles.

It had taken the Romans more than thirty years to subdue the Welsh tribes.

THE TRIBES

Deceangli

The Deceangli tribe, (sometimes known as 'Deceangi', 'Deceanglos', 'Decangi'), were a Celtic hill-fort-dwelling people who lived in the north coastal region of Wales. Their territory corresponded to the present-day regions of north-east Clwyd, northern Gwynedd and the historic counties of Flintshire, Denbighshire and part of

Cheshire. The region of their tribelands was known in the Early Middle Ages by its Welsh name 'Tegeingl', after the tribe.

Their name is thought to be derived from two Latin elements: 'decem', meaning 'ten', and 'angulus', signifying an angle or corner. Hence, according to this hypothesis, in its entirety the name literally means 'ten angles', a reference to a confederation of ten sub-tribes or districts. An alternative interpretation has been put forward suggesting that the prefix 'dece' is a Romanised word similar to the Welsh word 'tege', meaning 'fair' or 'beautiful'. In this latter case the tribal name may be taken to mean 'the Fair Angles' or 'the Beautiful Angles'. However, it should be borne in mind that most Celtic tribal names were ascribed to them by the Romans, and we know very little of what they might have actually called themselves before the Roman era.

Following the arrival of Roman legions in their territory under the command of Scapula in 47 AD, the Deceangli appear to have offered little resistance. However, Scapula was forced to withdraw his troops to support other Roman legions that faced a rebellious Brigantes tribe in northern England. Later, in 78 AD their territory was placed under Roman rule after a military campaign led by Julius Agricola. Their major tribal settlement at *Canovivm* (present-day Caerhun in the Conwy Valley) was created a *Roman Civitas Decangorum* and the site of an auxiliary fort, which was garrisoned until 96 AD. They had established a series of five hill-fort settlements along the entire length of the Clwydian Range, at Foel Fenlli, Moel y Gaer, Moel Arthur, Penycloddiau and Moel y Gaer in the eastern part of their territory.

Demetae

The Demetae tribe held territory that roughly corresponds to the present-day county of Dyfed in south-west Wales, which included the county of Pembrokeshire, the western half of Carmarthenshire, and about two-thirds of Ceredigion. Improbably, it has been suggested that the tribal name may be derived from the deity Demotos, whose name translates as 'the god of mead (drunkenness)'. Following the subjugation of the Demetae, in 75 AD the Romans established a fort called *Moridunum Demetarum* (present-day Carmarthen), which became the Romanised capital of the tribe. However, due to their location on the extreme south-west of Wales, the Romans made few incursions into their territory, and as such their presence tended to be restricted to their eastern borderlands.

The Demetae posed little real threat to Rome and unlike the neighbouring Silures tribe, they made a peaceful accommodation with their Roman conquerors. As a result, they were the only Welsh tribe whose tribal name remained intact throughout Roman rule. Most of its neighbours had either been slaughtered or taken away into slavery and their names were virtually expunged from historical record thereafter.

Several archaeological excavations have revealed large Roman villas in Demetae territory, indicating the degree to which the Demetae had become

Romanised and how at ease the Romans were in their territory The Castell Henllys Iron Age hill-fort, possibly the most studied Celtic hill-fort sites in Great Britain, was established by the Demetae tribe, and is regarded as an important archaeological site, having been extensively excavated since 1980. It is thought to have housed around 130 people.

Gangani

The Gangani were a minor warlike tribe whose territory was on the Lleyn (or 'Llyn') Peninsula at the extreme north-west of Wales. Ptolemy called the peninsula, *Ganganorum Promontorium,* which translates as 'headland (or promontory) of the Gangani'. They established several stone-built hill-forts on the peninsula, including one at Tre'r Cieri, said to be one of the finest Iron Age forts of its kind in Britain.

One interpretation of the tribal name Gangani suggests it might mean 'geese people', while another cites the Welsh word 'cainc', meaning 'branch', as more likely. There is a suggestion the Gangani broke away to become a branch of the Deceangli tribe, but compelling as this suggestion might be, it remains unverified. It has been proposed that sometime in the first century BC some of the Gangani tribe may have landed in the Lleyn Peninsula and forcibly driven out the Deceangli or the Ordovices tribe from the area.

Sometime before 80 AD, the Romans established an infantry garrison fort for 960 soldiers at Pen Llystyn, on the road between Tomen y Mur and *Segontium* (Caernarfon). The fort was purposely burnt to the ground and abandoned in 90 AD. Ptolemy also wrote of a Gangani tribe in Ireland, and given the many migrations that occurred before the Roman era, the two may have been related. It has been suggested that the Gangani were virtually destroyed by the Romans in 390 AD and that a surviving number fled to the region around the River Shannon in Ireland.

Octapitai

Apart from the fact that the Octapitai tribe had established an Iron Age Celtic hill-fort on St David's Head, a distinctive promontory in Pembrokeshire called Clawdd y Milwyr ('the Warrior's Dyke'), little else is known about them.

Ordovices

The Ordovices were a dominant Celtic tribe that held extensive territories in mid-Wales during the Iron Age and by the time of the Roman invasion they had taken control of Ynys Môns (the island of Anglesey). They tended to live in hill-forts, predominantly along the Deva Valley, which included those at Castell Dinas Bran,

Moel y Gaer in Llantisilio, Caer Drwyn and Caer Euni. Another was established at Craig Rhiwarth in the Tanat Valley. They were probably responsible for the construction of the multivallate hill-fort known in Welsh as 'Caer Ogyrfan' (in English, 'Old Oswestry') in the Welsh Marches. It was never overtaken by the Romans, but seems to have been abandoned shortly after their arrival in Britain in the first century. Their territory covered much of present-day south Gwynedd and south Clwyd, and included parts of western Shropshire, Herefordshire and Worcestershire in England. Their tribal name is based on Brittonic Celtic words and has been interpreted as meaning 'highly (or fighting) braves'.

Together with the Silures, the Ordovices joined the rebellion against Roman advances under the leadership of Caractacus, who took refuge in the land of the Ordovices, where he organised the resistance against the Roman General Ostorius Scapula, before he was finally defeated by the Twentieth Legion at the Battle of Caer Caradoc in 50 AD. Following another uprising, in 77 AD the Legatus Legion XX, (the Twentieth Legion) under the command of Agricola finally defeated the Ordovices, virtually annihilating the tribe. The remaining survivors were subdugated and incorporated with their lands into the Roman province of Britannia.

Segontiaci

The Segontiaci tribe, (also possibly known as 'Segonti', 'Segontii' or 'Seguntienses'), are thought to have been a sub-sect of the Ordovices. In about 77 AD, Agricola had the auxiliary Roman fort of *Segontium* built in their territory, beside the River Seiont, in Caernarfon, North Wales. The name of the city of Caernarfon is derived from 'Caer yn ar Fon', which translates as 'the fort opposite Môna'. The fort was intended to reinforce Roman control of the Menai Strait, and was garrisoned by the *Cohors I Sunicorum*, (the First Cohort of Sunici), which was made up of about 500 Belgae and an equal number of Germani soldiers. The name 'Segontium' is derived from the Brittonic word elements 'seg-ontio', which taken together mean 'strong place', and the Segontiaci were therefore 'people of the strong place'. The fort was occupied until the end of the fourth century AD, and was probably the last to be abandoned in North Wales.

Together with the Ancalites, the Bibroci and the Cenimagi, the Segontiaci may have been one of the four tribes of Kent who were mentioned by Julius Caesar. The Kentish Segontiaci were one of the five tribes who surrendered to Caesar and revealed the whereabouts of Cassivellaunus's hideout near Devil's Dyke in Sussex.

Silures

The Silures were an Iron Age tribe of southern Wales. Tacitus called them 'a naturally fierce people', and thought they came from Spain because their skin was dark and they had black curly hair. Their tribal name is often interpreted as 'offspring of kin', based on the Celtic word element 'silo', meaning 'seed' or 'offspring'. However, an alternative suggestion is that the name means 'people of the rocks', based on the mountainous topography of their territory. Their main town and tribal capital was known to the Romans as *Venta Silurum*, (later, 'Gwent' and even later as 'Caerwent'). It was located between Caerleon in Wales and Gloucester in England, and its name means 'market town of the Silures'.

Following the subjugation of the Iceni and the Brigantes tribes, in 47 AD, the new Roman Governor of Britain, Ostorius Scapula, turned his attention to the Silures tribe, bringing the *Legio XX Valeria* (the Twentieth Valerian Legion) from Colchester to the legionary fort at Kingsholme near Gloucester. Tacitus wrote that '…neither severity nor clemency converted the Silures tribe, which continued the struggle and had to be repressed by the establishment of a legionary camp'.

The Silures continued to wage such an effective guerilla-type campaign against the Romans that Scapula became obsessed with their destruction and is recorded to have remarked that the Silures 'either needed to be exterminated or transported to Gaul'. In fact, Scapula died before their subjugation, and according to Tacitus, it took three later governors, (Aulus Didius Gallus, Quintus Veranius and Suetonius Paulinus), before they finally succumbed to the overwhelming force of Rome under the governorship of Sextus Julius Frontinus in 76 AD.

Between 74 and 80 AD, Frontinus established a garrison fortress at *Isca Silurum* (Caerleon) where he stationed 5,500 heavily armed infantry of the *Legio II Augusta* (the Second Augustan Legion), located beside the River Usk so that provisions and reinforcements could be brought in by ships. Of the known eighty-five stone inscriptions found during excavations of the site, one bears the Latin text: 'From the Tenth Cohort, the centurion of Flavius Julinus (built this).'

Their territory encompassed most of present-day Glamorgan and contained several hill-fort settlements, including two at Garn Gogh on the border with Demetae territory, from which, following their eventual subjugation, they were evacuated and their strongholds disassembled. A similar fate awaited the hill-fort at Lodge Hill, which overlooked the River Usk north of Caerleon. The Pen y Crug hill-fort was reconstructed with stone defences by the Romans after the Silures had been expelled, and it became the flourishing Romano-British settlement of 'Brecon Gaer'. In due course, the Silures were Romanised and eventually became a self-governing community within the Roman Empire. In a historical sense, the Silures had posed the biggest threat to the Roman conquest of Wales.

Chapter Twelve

The Irish Tribes

No one is quite sure whether the Celts arrived in Ireland as an invasion or migrated a group at a time, (what Professor Barry Cunliffe called 'small-scale intrusions'), to be gradually assimilated into an already well-established indigenous Bronze Age culture. What is certain is that when the Celts first arrived on Irish soil in about 500 BC, they brought iron, a stronger, more durable metal, which gave them a powerful advantage, and in time the proliferation of the Celtic language, religious beliefs, artwork and ironwork was sufficient to make them the dominant culture. The discovery of a number of La Tène-style decorated artefacts, including items of horse tack, pins, brooches and trumpets, raises questions as to the origin of these early migrants. Debates continue as to whether these items were imported through trade, or manufactured in Ireland, which may therefore provide a direct link back to the very origins of Celtic culture.

In common with most Celtic peoples, the Irish tribes were never unified in any political sense and were frequently at war with each other. Despite their differences they shared a common ancestry, and shared cultural traits as well as dialects of the same language. Writing in the second century AD, the historian Ptolemy called the people of Ireland 'Iverni' or 'Ierne', and the Romans called the land 'Hibernia' after them. According to ancient texts, it was the Iverni tribe who first crossed into Britain, and were followed later by the Belgae from Gaul and the Lagin from Brittany. Later commentators referred to 'Eire Innis', meaning the 'western island', to distinguish it from mainland Britain, which they called 'Alba', meaning 'white', probably on account of the white cliffs of southern England. Eire Innis was eventually shortened to 'Erin', the forerunner of the Irish name for Ireland, 'Eireann'.

But the Celts were not the first to arrive in Ireland. According to archaeological finds in the 1970s, a Mesolithic people had arrived and settled around Mount Sandel in Coleraine, (reckoned to be the oldest site ever found in Ireland), sometime between 9000 and 6500 BC. However, evidence exists for an even earlier prehistoric human presence in Ireland during the Palaeolithic era, as early as 31000 BC. At that time, the Artic snows had not yet melted, oceans were lower and a land bridge existed between Ireland and mainland Britain; it was by this route that the earliest hunter-gatherer migrants came. By 4000 BC, they had begun to clear fields, cultivated cereal crops and created pasture for domestic animals like cows and pigs. Within the next few centuries they built field systems and burial tombs in settlements surrounding an ever-enlarging agricultural landscape.

These were the Neolithic people of the so-called New Stone Age who constructed large megalithic sites, with dolmens, stone circles and henges, as well as passage tombs like Newgrange in County Meath, dated around 3200 BC. There were similar tombs in Knowth, Dowth and Loughcrew, among many others. Bronze and copper smelting were brought to Ireland around 2400 BC with the arrival of the Bell Beaker people, so named on account of their distinctive bell-shaped pottery.

The Arrival of the Celts

It was the dawn of the Iron Age from around 500 BC that saw the arrival of the first people we might reasonable identify as Celtic. These Iron Age people brought with them a new and immensely strong metal culture, a new religion and a new language, which was an early form of an Insular Goidelic language that emerged as primitive Irish Gaelic.

Their arrival was not a peaceful matter, they were warlike and intent on conquest, subduing, driving out and assimilating the resident population to establish their own Celtic culture. They also left behind a rich legacy of artefacts, which included hordes of sophisticated iron weaponry as well as gold jewellery and ornaments. In ancient times, all Irish descendants of the Ebudeans, Ivernians, Picts or Fir Bolg shared the common name of 'Gaedhil' or 'Gall-Goídil', which literally means 'foreigner Gaels'; to others they were all known as 'Scotti'.

Despite popular belief, it was actually the Roman St Palladius, from Poitiers in Gaul, who first brought Christianity to Irish shores, having been sent by Pope Celestine, the first bishop of the Scots, as a missionary monk in 430 AD, two years earlier than St Patrick, who went on to become Ireland's patron saint. Patrick converted thousands of pagan native Celts by preaching the gospel and it was St Dichu who donated a large barn, which was converted into Patrick's first church at Sabhall in County Down.

The Roman Era

The Romans thought Ireland was not worth the taking. In his epic work *The Iliad*, Homer described Ireland as 'a land of fog and gloom – beyond it the Sea of Death'. Strabo placed Ireland geographically to the north of Britain, at the very limit of the known world at that time, and stated that it was 'barely habitable on account of the cold'. He continued by saying that the Irish '...eat human flesh and that the sexes live in promiscuous intercourse, without paying attention even to ties of blood'.

Pomponius Mela, one of the early Roman geographers, wrote in 43 AD that the severity of the Irish climate hindered the fruits of the earth from coming to maturity, although the herbage was so luxuriant that cattle could only be allowed to graze for a short part of the day, lest they should 'over-eat themselves'.

Agricola boasted that if he chose he could take the whole island with one single legion and a few auxiliaries, but after the long protracted fight to conquer Britain, especially Caledonia (Scotland), the Romans thought trade with Ireland would be a better option than open warfare. Consequently, while many Roman artefacts have been unearthed in Ireland, they were almost certainly the result of trade with Rome, rather than domestic manufacture. Roman coins bearing the likenesses of the Emperor Magnentius (AD 350–353) and Constantine the Great (AD 306–337) have been found at Dunsink and Malahide, and a large hoard of Roman coins have been discovered at Cuskinny Marsh in County Cork.

There was a real if small Roman presence in Ireland. Evidence for the existence of a minor Roman station at Drumanagh, a few miles north of Dublin, has been established, but the general consensus is that Agricola established this fortlet to safeguard visiting Roman traders and there was never any suggestion of military conquest. That said, a few dissenting voices do maintain that Agricola's presence on Irish soil was intended as a prelude to a full invasion, and that it was only called off when Roman troops were needed to deal with troubles in Scotland.

The Roman historian Tacitus had little to say about Ireland, but called Hibernia 'the Land of Winter', though he was in favour of its conquest. Others described it as a land 'luxuriant in grasses'. Even Ptolemy, who in the second century drew the first map of Irish tribes, only mentioned each of them briefly. Among the Irish tribes he named the Vennicni, Rhobogdi, Erdini, Magnatae, Autini, Gangani, Vellabori, Darini, Voluntii, Eblani, Cauci, Menapii, Coriondi and Brigantes, and beyond identifying them by name and indicating where he thought their territorial tribelands were he had little else to add.

Problematically, the fact that Ireland was never Romanised meant that there were no reliable Roman or Greek commentators like Caesar, Strabo or Livy to record its history. Whereas mainland Britain, (and England in particular), was subject to battles with the Roman legions, with skirmishes, treaties, subjugation and betrayals being almost commonplace, apart from a few inter-tribal wars and territorial squabbles, Ireland's history was comparatively peaceful. As a result, much of Ireland's so-called 'history' is enhanced legend and mythology, often written many years or even centuries after the event.

Consequently, much of what is taken to be Irish history is often impossible to disentangle from traditional folklore and manufactured events. Further, the Christianisation of Ireland in the fourth century meant that most records were written by religious clerics and inevitably tended to concentrate on matters of faith rather than factual history. As a result, many of the sources that do exist include lists of the High Kings and early clans of Ireland, (both real and imagined). These were based on documents like *The Annals of Ulster, The Book of Invasions, The Roll of the Kings* and *The Annals of the Four Masters.* Such sources were written decades or even centuries after the events that they recorded, some as late as the nineteenth century; consequently, their contents should be taken with a large degree of scepticism.

Celtic Tribes of Hibernia (Ireland)
Distribution of Territories according to Ptolemy
First Century BC
North Atlantic Ocean
VENICNII
ROBOGDII
VOLUNTII
DARINI
NAGNATAE
EBLANI
AUTEINI
Irish Sea
CAUCI
GANGANI
MANAPII
BRIGANTES
CORIONDI
VELABORI
USDIAE
IVERNI
Celtic Sea

Historians divide Irish history into four distinct cycles: the Mythology Cycle, the Ulster Cycle, the Fenian Cycle and the King's Cycle. This was done in an attempt to disentangle the often convoluted and chaotic nature of its history. The first, the Mythical Cycle, is concerned with Irish legend and folklore before the arrival of Christianity, and includes a great deal of material about the Tuatha De Dannan. The second, the Ulster Cycle, concentrates on tales of the gods, warriors and battles in pre-Celtic Ireland. Its main emphasis was around eastern Ulster and northern Leinster, and includes elements of early Christian belief. Both areas were referred to as Ulaid. The third, the Fenian Cycle, (also known as the 'Finn Cycle' or the 'Finnian Tales'), deals with warriors and heroes, rather than gods. Finally, and fourth, the King's Cycle, (sometimes known as the Historical Cycle), deals with the medieval history of kings, bards and battles. The cycles are concerned more with storytelling than recording actual history, and hard factual information is hard to come by.

In the fourth and fifth centuries, Ireland was divided into five kingdoms, which were known as 'The Five Fifths', (in Old Irish, 'coiceda', and in Modern Irish, 'cuige'). They were Ulster, Meath, Leinster, Munster and Connacht. The High King of all Ireland ruled over them from the royal seat at Tara in County Meath, while each of the other four kingdoms had their own kings, who in turn were subject to him.

Of the five kingdoms, Ulster, (in Irish, 'Ulaidh'), was known to be the territory of Ireland's fiercest warriors, of which the group of tribes known as Ulaidh were the most powerful and notorious. Ulster is named after the tribe. In the fourth century, Ulster was split into three separate kingdoms: Oriel, or Airgialla in central Ulster, Aileach in western Ulster, and the smaller kingdom of Ulaid in eastern Ulster. The six present-day Ulster counties are Antrim, Down, Armagh, Londonderry, Tyrone and Fermanagh.

The name 'Meath' (in Irish, 'Midhe') means 'middle of the island'. It contained the Hill of Tara, the traditional royal seat of the High Kings of Ireland, who ruled from the 'Rath na Rithe' ring-fort, known as the 'Ring-fort of the Kings'. It was reputedly founded by Tuathal Teachmhar, a legendary conqueror of Ireland in the first century AD. Tara was an important political and spiritual meeting place for ancient tribes. It was here that the High Kings met annually with the other kings for a week of celebrations and to settle inter-tribal disputes.

Leinster, (in Irish, 'Laigin'), being in the east of Ireland and possessing an extensive coastline, was an important centre for foreign trade. Its name derives from Laigin, one of the powerful tribes that ruled the region. The tribes of Leinster were united by Hugony the Great (in Irish, 'Ugaine Mor'), who divided the kingdom into twenty-five portions, one to each of his sons and daughters. It was in Leinster that St Palladius first arrived in Ireland in 431 AD to bring Christianity to the pagan tribes. It comprises the present-day counties of Carlow, Dublin, Kildare, Kilkenny, Offaly, Longford, Louth, Meath, Laoighis, Westmeath, Wexford and Wicklow.

Munster is made up of the counties of Clare, Cork, Kerry, Limerick, Tipperary and Waterford. It takes its name from the Celtic god Muman, with the added suffix '-ster' coming from a Norse word that means 'homestead' or 'dwelling'. Hence, 'Muman's homestead'.

The last of the five-fifths, the province of Connacht, was the place of druids, and in many ways the centre of Irish spiritualism before the coming of Christianity. It takes its name from King Conn, (known as Conn of the Hundred Battles), and translates as 'the descendants of Conn'. The province comprises the modern-day counties of Mayo, Sligo, Leitrim, Galway, and Roscommon.

THE TRIBES

Ailech

Ailech was a kingdom that from about 425 AD dominated lands that were formerly owned by the Ulaid of Northern Ireland. The three sons of Niall, High King of Ireland, (known as 'Niall of the Nine Hostages') inherited the territory on the death of their father. The descendants of Niall, known as the Ui Neill, divided the kingdom into two parts. The Northern Ui Neill, originally called 'In Fochla', simply meaning 'the North', was ruled by his two sons, Conall and Eogain.

The Southern Ui Neill was initially ruled by Cenel Conaill and became known as the Ailech. The main Ailech royal seat and stronghold was at Grianan of Aileach, a hill-fort on Greenan Mountain on the Inishowen Peninsula of County Donegal, thought to have been built by Cenel nEogain during the sixth or seventh centuries, (although other accounts date it much later). According to some Irish sources, Grianan of Aileach was destroyed in 1101 by King Muirchertach Ua Briain of Munster, at which time the kings of Northern Ireland moved their capital to Tulochog in County Tyrone.

By the ninth century the coast of Ailech territory was repeatedly subjected to Viking raids, so that in about 866 AD, King Aed Finnliach of the Ailech defeated the Vikings at the Battle of Lough Foyle and drove them out of Ireland, virtually putting all Viking incursions to an end.

Autini

The ancient Autini tribe, (sometimes 'Auteini' or 'Auteinoi', and also known as 'Uaithni' or 'Uaithne'), held territory to the west of the River Shannon, in north-eastern County Limerick and part of County Tipperary, and were mentioned by Ptolemy in his *Geographia*. Two branches of the tribe existed: the Uaithni Cliach in Limerick, and the Uaithni Loingsigh in Tipperary. The Uaithni tribal name was eventually anglicised as 'Owney', and its two baronies in the east of Limerick city, became known as Owneybeg (Little Owney) and Owney-and-Arra. There is a suggestion that the Uaithni were actually minor tribal descendants of the Auteini of Connacht.

Bolgic

The Bolgic arrived in Ireland as part of a second wave of immigrant peoples around 500 BC and quickly grew to dominate most of Ireland's land mass. They contained four sub-groups or septs: the Uluti, who controlled most of Northern Ireland, the Darini and Robogdii, who established settlements in the north-east, the Iverni, who held territory in Munster, and the Ebdani, who settled in eastern Ireland.

The Bolgic came into conflict with the later arrival of the Laginian tribe from Brittany, when they made a bid to take over the ill-defended Bolgic territory in Connacht. A battle ensued at Moytura in Sligo when the Laginian tribe, under the leadership of their king, Cairbre, won the day and the Bolgic warriors fled to the refuge of the Aran Islands, where they built forts at Dun Aengus and Dun Conor, as well as Dun Balor on Tory Island. Dun Aengus (in Irish, 'Dun Aenghusa a n-Araind'), one of several prehistoric strongholds built by the Bolbic on Aran, was possibly begun sometime in the late Bronze Age and completed in the second century BC. It is regarded by many as one of the most remarkable in Ireland.

Brigantes

Besides being one of the largest of the British tribes, the Brigantes were also named by Ptolemy as a tribe who had settled around Wexford, Kilkenny and Waterford in the south-east of Ireland. Another tribe, possibly the ancestors of the Irish Brigantes, were the Brigantii of the Alpine Vindelici tribe identified by Strabo. Their name comes from the Celtic goddess Brigantia, where the element 'brigant' means 'high' or 'exalted', itself derived from the Brittonic word 'briga', meaning 'high'. The Brigantes tribal name may have been a reference to them as 'highlanders' or to one of their hill-fort settlements. The early Christian missionaries to Ireland co-opted Brigantia into their pantheon as St Brigid. She was the equivalent of the Roman goddess Minerva and the Greek goddess Athena.

Another group were known to have lived in Spain, and may have been the first of the tribe to migrate, first to Ireland, and then to Scotland and England, while it is thought that a breakaway group fled to Ireland to escape from the advance of Roman legions into northern England. Roman writers referred to the tribe as 'Scoto (or Scuta) Brigantes', indicating an Irish or Scottish connection. The Roman Stoic philosopher Seneca called them 'Scotogantes'. What the Brigantes of Britain, Spain and Ireland all share is a common lineage, as Celto-Scythians speaking dialects of the same language.

Cauci

The Cauci tribe, (also known as 'Chauci', 'Cauchi' and 'Chauchi'), were a Germanic tribe that originated beyond the River Rhine, between the River Ems and Elba in Germania, and were probably related to the Angles and Saxons. They migrated to Ireland, probably having been dispossessed of their territory by the Romans under Caesar and later by Germanicus.

The Cauci were among the sixteen Irish tribes listed by Ptolemy in the second century, though he placed them in County Wicklow. However, their main territory is generally thought to have been in the area of Dublin, south of the Epdani tribelands.

By the first century AD, the British and Irish Cauci tribes were known as a sea-going people to the Romans, with whom they came into conflict because of their piratical sea raids on the west coast of Wales, where they even established small communities. According to Tacitus, the Cauci were finally subdued during the reign of Tiberius (14 AD to 37 AD). By the second century, groups of Cauci served as auxiliaries in the Roman army. The Irish Cauci appeared to be become integrated with and later absorbed into the Saxon tribal confederation.

Coriondi

The Coriondi, (sometimes spelled 'Koriondi'), were an early tribal people of Ireland, referred to in Ptolemy's *Geographia* as living in southern Leinster; he believed their name was a corruption of the Celtic British Coritani (or 'Corionototae') tribe, a probable sub-tribe or sept of the Brigantes, and that they may have originally been ancestrally related and could even have been the same people. It has been argued that the Coriondi may have accompanied the Brigantes migration to Ireland, which lends a degree of authenticity to the proposition. Their tribal name is derived from the Gaulish word 'corios', which means 'army'. Enniscorthy in County Wexford may have been their main settlement and capital city. Together with the neighbouring Eblani, and Iverni, the Coriondi were important ring-fort builders, and were known for their metalworking, from which they established a flourishing trade across Europe and Britain.

Cruithni

The Cruithni, (sometimes 'Cruithnig' or 'Cruthin'), were a Pictish people who are said to have populated much of the Irish mainland in the early medieval period, before the arrival of the Celts, and were especially prolific in Ulster. That said, many scholars have thrown doubts upon the notion that the Cruithni were Picts or that they existed at all. Cruithni is the Irish name that corresponds to the Pretani. According to Nennius, these Pictish people descended from the Geloni, a people of Scythia mentioned by Herodotus. The name 'Cruithni' means 'people of the shapes or designs', a reference to their extensive use of tattooed body ornamentation. The Cruithni left no literature or archaeology so that much of what is 'known' of them comes from a pseudo-historical and oral tradition and is thereby ultimately unverifiable. Typical examples of such Irish legends are found in the *Book of Lecain,* in which Cruithne was recorded as the son of Cinge, father of the Pictish tribes of Ireland who reputedly ruled for 135 years.

Dal Riata

The history of Dal Riata, (sometimes known as 'Dalraida' or simply 'Raita'), is steeped in uncertainty and folklore. In the second century, they were identified by Ptolemy as living in modern-day County Antrim, part of a confederation of tribes that included the Cruithni and the Dal Fiatach, who were also known as the Uluti, and dominated the confederation. The name Dal Riata is derived from the legendary founder Reti or Reuda (according to Bede), of which the Old Gaelic element 'dal' signifies a portion or share. Hence their name in its entirety means 'Reti's portion or share'.

Dal Riata is said to have been founded by the legendary King Fergus Mor MacEarca, (also known as Fergus the Great). Some of the tribe's number began moving across the twelve-mile stretch of the Irish Sea into Argyl in south-western Scotland between the third and fifth centuries, and established stronghold settlements at Dunadd and Dunolly under the rule of King Erc, (or 'Eirc'), who was said to be the father of Fergus Mor. Fergus and his successors continued to rule both the Irish Dal Riata and the Scottish Dal Raita as a single kingdom until 637 AD when the two became independent kingdoms.

By the end of the fifth century the Dal Raita kingdom had extended to both sides of the North Channel of the Irish Sea and encompassed part of the present-day County Antrim and an area of the present-day county of Londonderry, east of the Bann, known as the north-eastern Liberties of Coleraine, as well as part of the Inner Hebrides and Argyll.

The name 'Argyll' translates as 'coast of the Gaels'. One of their legacies was in providing a line of kings of Scotland, among whom Mac Bethad mac Findlaich, better known as Macbeth, was numbered. The Dal Riata were early speakers of the Gaelic language. Their powerful control of large areas of north-eastern Ireland declined as a result of a series of sustained Viking incursions and raids from 794 AD.

Darini

According to the entry in Ptolemy's *Geographia,* the Darini (also known as 'Darnii', and sometimes as 'Darinoi') were one of the sixteen ancient tribes of Ireland. He placed their territory in the south of County Antrim and the north of County Down, before the rise of the Dal Riata in that area. The town of Dundrum in County

Down has been cited as the most probable location of their capital as its ancient name was *Dun Droma Dairine*, which means 'Fort of the Ridge of the Dairini'.

The tribe is said to have descended from God Daire (or 'Daire Barrach'), whose name meant 'the High One' or 'the Bright One'. Others see the Darini tribal name as being related to the Irish word 'dair', meaning 'oak', as found in the name of the city of Derry, whose Old Irish name was 'Daire', meaning 'oak grove'. In time the Irish personal name Daire came to mean 'violent' and by implication the Darini were considered a people of great violence. Ptolemy had earlier identified the present-day county of Londonderry as part of territory of the Darini. It is also the name he called the Dal Raida in his second-century map of Ireland, believing that they were Scythian or possibly Samaritan by descent.

Eoganachta

According to tradition, the Eoghachata tribe was founded by the legendary figure Connal Corc (known as Conall the Purple and as Corc mac Laire) on the Rock of Cashel, which he established as his royal seat in the fifth century. The tribe was often referred to as the Eoganacht Cashel, in reference to the limestone outcrop in Golden Vale, Tipperary, which is also known as St Patrick's Rock. Traditionally they were said to be descended from Oengus mac Nad Froich, the first Christian king of Munster, but once again the problem of disentangling historical fact from traditional myth and folklore raises its head.

What is certain, however, is that through their military prowess and political skill the tribe became the dominant dynasty in pre-Christian and Celtic-Christian Munster from the sixth to the tenth centuries, ruling the lands of the Eoganacht Aine from their fortress near Cnoc Aine (present-day Knockainy). In fact, they took their name from the Hill of Aine.

The tribal name has the Irish meaning 'people of Eoghan'. A branch of the tribe, known as the Eoganacht Chaisil, was the ruling dynasty of Munster between the fifth and tenth centuries. They took their name from Cashel in County Tipperary. The Irish word 'Eoghan' means 'born of the yew tree', and 'caiseal', which is related to the Latin 'castellum', signifies a castle or a stronghold.

Many of the kings of the Eoganachta are recorded in the *An Leabhar Muimhneach* (The Book of Munster). Their ruling power came to an end with the Norman invasion of Ireland in 1171.

Epdani

Ptolemy recorded a tribe called the 'Ebdani' and placed their main settlement called Eblana, (present-day Dublin), north of the River Liffey and south of the Boyne, somewhere around the fertile plain of Meath. Also known as 'Eblani', and according to Ptolemy, probable ancestors of the Ulaid and the Darini, they were known in Irish as the 'Ui Echach'. As to their tribal name, the 'Ep' element is thought to be a Gaulish or Brittonic pronunciation of the Irish word 'ech', meaning 'horse'. Hence, their complete name referred to them as horse riders or 'cavaliers'. Their influence reached across the Irish Sea, where settlements around Kintyre on the west coast of Scotland were established by a splinter group of the tribe, sometimes referred to as Epidii. By the end of the second century AD, the Epdani had converted to Christianity, after which their name disappears from all recorded history.

Erdini

The Erdini, (sometimes 'Erpeditani', and in Irish, 'Ernaigh'), were one of the earliest known tribes of Ireland and controlled a territory in the north-west around Donegal Bay and covered much of Leitrim and Fermanagh counties, which was anciently known as 'Breifne'. Some writers have placed the tribe in County Tyrone. According to Irish legend, the tribe were part of the Fir Bolg invasion from Greece, attested in the *Annala Ríoghachta Eireann* ('The Annals of the Four Masters'), in which they were called 'Erna Firbolg'. Ptolemy recorded a tribe just north of Loch Erne as the Erdini. There have been many variant spellings of the name through the centuries, including Ederney, Eadarnaidh, Edernagh and Ederny. Their tribal name means 'water people', and is preserved in the names of Lough Erne and the River Erne.

Fianna

The Fianna, (in Gaelic, 'Feinne'), were small warrior-hunter bands in Gaelic Ireland during the Iron Age and early Middle Ages. They were predominantly made up of high-born but landless males known as 'Fiann', who spent their days hunting or acting as mercenaries in local battles. They feature largely in the *Fenian Cycle* of Irish mythology, where they were led by Fion mac Cumhaill (also known as 'Finn mac Cool'), and often worked as bodyguards or household troops to the High Kings of Ireland. Fion is arguably one of the most famous figures in Irish folklore. What has been recorded is more tradition than reliable history.

Fir Bolg

The Fir Bolg, according to Irish myth, were said to be the fourth wave of immigrants to Ireland. They were descended from the earlier tribe of Muintir Nemid, who abandoned the land and went to resettle in different parts of Europe. Those who went to Greece became known as the Fir Bolg. Apparently, they were enslaved for 230 years by the Greeks and forced to carry bags of stone, clay and soil in various building and landscaping projects, which earned them the name 'Fir Bolg', meaning 'men of bags'. Eventually, they managed to steal Greek ships and numbering a reported 5000, they escaped from Greece and returned to Ireland, where they settled in the present-day province of Munster, under the leadership of five brothers: Slainge, Rudraige, Genann, Gann and Sengann. These brothers are said to have assembled at the Hill of Tara, an ancient ceremonial and burial site near Skryne in County Meath, where they divided Ireland up between them into five territories, which became the five provinces.

The account is described in the *Lebor Gabala Erenn*, which literally translates into English as 'The Book of the Takings of the Land of Ireland', more commonly known as 'The Book of Invasions', written in around 1050 AD. According to the book, for thirty-seven years Ireland thrived under the reigns of seven Fir Bolg kings, but when another warrior tribe, the Tuatha De Danann, arrived and demanded a portion of their land, the Fir Bolg refused and warfare broke out. The Fir Bolg were defeated at the Battle of Moytura and driven from their territory. Of course, the Fir Bolg were an actual, historical people, and probably of original Belgic descent, but the account in the *Book of Invasions* serves only as popular Celtic mythology.

Formorians

The Formorians (in Old Irish, 'Fomoire', and in Modern Irish, 'Fomhoraigh') were yet another mythical Irish race. In this instance they were semi-divine giants, traditionally said to be the earliest inhabitants of Ireland, reputedly arriving with 200 men and 600 women. According to the tradition, they conquered the first people to invade and settle in Ireland, the Partholon (or 'Parthalan'). Formorians are often described as hideous-looking and hostile monsters, thought to personify chaos and nature, and were the bitter enemies of the Tuatha De Danann and anyone else that came to conquer Ireland. In the seventeenth-century *History of Ireland* by Geoffrey Keating, the Fomorians were said to be seafaring people who were descended from Noah's son, Ham. They were first defeated in battle against the tribe of Nemed at Ros Fraechain, and again against the Fir Bolg, descendants of the Nemedians. They were finally crushed by the Tuatha De Danann and forced to retreat into the shadows of the sea and other deep dark places, from which they are said to occasionally emerge.

Gangiani

The Gangiani, (sometimes 'Gangani' or 'Ganganoi'), lived around the River Shannon estuary according to Ptolemy, and were most probably related to the tribe of the same name who occupied the Llyn Peninsula of Caernarvonshire in Wales, a region Ptolemy called 'the promontory of the Gangani'. It has been suggested that the tribal name may be derived from Genann Mac Dal of the Fir Bolg, the legendary joint High King of Ireland with his brother Gann. Others cite a relationship with the Galengani tribe, with whom they shared territory, as a possible root of the tribal name, related to 'gae', an old Irish word for a spear. Hence, 'the spearmen'. However, most explanations are speculative and no satisfactory explanation of the tribal name has yet been categorially proven.

Iverni

In the second century AD, Ptolemy placed the Iverni occupying a territory around Cork, in the south-west of Ireland and in the modern-day province of Munster. He described them as one of the most dominant tribes of the island, and placed their main city at 'Ivernis', which according to his description was at the mouth of the River Iernos, the site of present-day Castlemaine Harbour. Their Roman name was 'Ierne', which means 'the fertile land', from which we get 'Hibernia' (or 'Ibernae' in Latin), and was derived from their tribal name. They were later known as Erainn, which simply means 'people of the land'. The tribe arrived in Ireland around 500 BC and spoke a dialect known as Ivernic, a P-Celtic language sometimes referred to as 'primitive Irish'. The anglicised term 'Ivernian' frequently referred to the ancient Irish people as a whole. Also, given that the Iverni were probably the first native Irish tribe with whom foreign traders came into contact, it goes some way to explain why their tribal name emerged as the Latin name for the whole island of Ireland.

Laigin

The Laigin, or Laginians, are thought to have been the third migrant group from Normandy and north-west Gaul to arrive in Ireland sometime around 600 BC. They were a confederation of tribes that established settlements on the west coast, in the modern-day province of Connacht as well as in a substantial part of Leinster. Their tribal name was known in Latin as 'Laginae', based on the word for the kind of broad lances that their warriors carried, and the word 'Laigin' is the older form of Leinster. The tribe were mythologically referred to as the Tuatha De Danann and their main settlement was at Cnoc na Teamhrach (present-day Teamhair – the 'Hill of Tara'), which became the traditional seat of the High Kings of Ireland. Following the break-up of Roman rule and occupation in the Britannic Isles, Laigin colonists crossed the Irish Sea and settled in Anglesey, Caernarvonshire and Denbighshire in North Wales.

The Kingdom of Laigin was said to be created by Ugaine Mor, known as Hugony the Great, who united the tribes of the region and became the first king of Laigin. Following its break-up during the intrastate civil wars, the kingdom was refounded by Cathair Mor in 186 AD. The last Laigin king, Domhnall Spainneach mac Murchadha Caomhanach, lost his throne in 1603, when James I of England subjected Leinster to English rule.

Manapii

The precise relationship between the Manapii tribe of County Wicklow and the Menapii Belgic tribe of northern Gaul is uncertain, but they are likely to have been the same people. Both names derive from a common source, a proto-Celtic word 'menak' or 'manak', which is loosely translated as 'mountain people'. The original homeland of the Irish tribe was around the Rhine and the Scheldt estuaries, stretching across the modern-day Netherlands and Belgium. The name is sometimes spelled 'Manaig', 'Monaigh' or 'Monarch' in Irish, and the placename *Druim Monach* (present-day Drumanagh), which translates as 'the hill of the Manapii', is named after them. It was here that they established a coastal fortress near to Dublin, which became their chief tribal centre and in time the capital city of Ireland.They are often classified as a branch of the Fir Bolg, and later they became known as the Fir Manach, giving the name to County Fermanagh. Ptolemy placed their capital town of Manapia, probably located on the mud flats of Dublin Bay. It has been suggested that the Isle of Man might have once been known as Manapii after a sept of the tribe, though this is hotly disputed.

Milesians

According to the eleventh-century *Book of the Taking of Ireland*, the Milesians were a nomadic people who originated in Scythia, a region now known as southern Siberia, though other sources have them arriving via the Iberian Peninsula. Traditionally, they are regarded as the Gaels, the final race to settle in Ireland having first arrived around 1000 BC. Legend has it that they were descended from Milesius of Spain, whose sons took possession of Ireland a thousand years before the Christian era. According to legend, on their arrival the Milesians had to face the resident and powerful Tuatha De Danaan, whom they defeated before agreeing a pact, whereby they would take the land above ground and the Tuatha De Danann would rule the world below, known as 'the Otherworld'. Their name and the story are thought to be largely an invention of the early Christian writers, though there are some who regard the Milesian as the race who became the ancestors of the Celtic Irish people.

Nagnatae

Ptolemy's second-century *Geographia* described the Nagnatae (or 'Magnatae') as an ancient Irish tribe who lived in County Mayo on its border with Sligo, around the north of the present-day province of Connacht. They are classified as a Celtic people, and said to have founded the provincial kingdom of Connacht. Their chief town, Nagnata, was probably located on the coast or near Sligo town and may have been an earlier name for Drumcliffe in the present-day barony of Carbury. Others have suggested that Nagnata may have been located on Clew Bay in Westport. It is thought that the last element of the name, 'Connacht' (i.e. '-nacht'), is derived from the name Nagatae.

By the first century the tribe had inhabited the whole of County Mayo except for a small portion in the south, which was the territory of the Auterii tribe. The tribal name Nagnatae in Irish is 'Na-gae-taegh', meaning an abode or dwelling near or beside the sea. Similarly, 'Slioght gae' means 'settlement (or race) beside the sea' – the origin of the Sligo placename and its county name.

Nemedians

According to Irish tradition, Nemid was an adventurer from the Black Sea region of central Europe, who arrived in Ireland ahead of 1000 followers. The *Lebor Gabala Erenn*, (The Book of Invasions), tells how he employed Formians from Africa to build two royal fortresses, one in Armagh and the other in Antrim, and killed them when they had completed the task. In retaliation, the Formians went into battle and the Nemedians were subjugated and forced to pay a humiliating annual tribute. They eventually reneged and rallied to mount an assault on the heavily defended Fomorian tower of Tor Conaind on Tory Island, off Donegal. In the battle that ensued the Nemedian hero Fergus Lethderg killed the Fomorian champion Conand. However, the Nemedians were ultimately overwhelmed, Nemid died of the plague and the tribe was virtually all slaughtered. Only thirty of their warriors survived, some fleeing to Greece while others fled north to join the Tuatha De Danann.

Priteni

The Priteni ('Pretanoi' or 'Pritani') are believed to have been one and the same tribe as the Cruithne, and were said to be the first Celtic or Pictish people to inhabit the British Islands, arriving between 700 BC and 500 BC. It is pretty well established that the Priteni were the first Celtic tribe to reach Ireland, where they settled in the modern-day provinces of Ulster and Leinster. They spoke a form of the P-Celtic language, and in the north of Scotland were known to the Romans as 'Picti' (the painted people), largely as a result of their custom of extensive body painting and tattooing.

The Greek geographer and astronomer Pytheas of Massalia described Great Britain and Ireland in around 320 BC as the 'Islands of Prettanike', with their peoples called the Priteni or Pretani. Other Greek writers described Britain and Ireland as the 'Pritenic Islands'. Over time these became the 'Britannic' or 'British Islands', while its people were collectively known to the Romans as 'Britanni'.

According to some sources the Priteni were actually an indigenous race who were descended from an earlier Neolithic population, but some consider that they could have been a mixture of both indigenous and migratory peoples.

Robogdii

The Robogdii, (sometimes 'Rhobogdioi'), were identified in the second century by Ptolemy as one of the sixteen Irish tribes. The Robogdii are generally thought to have held territory in the Fair Head promontory near Ballycastle in County Antrim, on the north-east corner of Ireland. This explains why Ptolemy called their land *Promontorium Robogdium* (the headland of the Robogdii). The small town of Robogh in Ulster is said to have been named after them. Its Irish name is 'Rath Bhoth', which means 'ringfort of the huts', and it has been argued that their name may have been a corruption of Redodii, possibly a sept or early form of the Dal Riata who went on later to colonise Scotland. However, the town's precise location is disputed by some, and it has been suggested that Robogh is actually the town of Raphoe in County Donegal, not in Antrim as was previously thought. The Robogdii tribal name is Celtic and translates as 'the breakers' or 'batterers', related to the Gaulish word 'borgio', which means 'destroyer'. Along with the Uluti, Darini, Iverni and Ebdani, they arrived as one of four Bolgic tribes in Ireland around 500 BC.

Scotti

Scotti, ('Scottii' or 'Scotae'), was the Latin name that the Romans initially gave to the Gaelic tribes of Ireland, but it later became attached to the Gaels in northern Britain and specifically to Scotland in the third century AD. The Roman term meant 'pirates' or 'bandits', a reference to the frequent attacks by Irish Scotti tribes on fourth-century Roman Britain. The name 'Scotia' denoted Ireland, but by the late third-century it had been replaced by 'Hibernia' in Roman texts, and the term 'Scoti Brittaniae' was applied to those Gaelic tribes of the Dal Riata who had migrated to Scotland.

An entry in the *Annals of Tighernach*, supposedly written around 500 AD, reads: 'Fergus Mor mac Erc, with the nation of Dal Riada, took (or held) part of Britain.' Later chronicles refer to Erc as a Scottish king who '...had twelve sons, (and) six of them took possession of Alba'. Alba, of course, is the early name for Scotland. In around 400 AD, following Roman control of Britain, certain Dal Riata tribes began migrations to the Scottish coast and established settlements in Argyl, while others went further south and settled in Cornwall and south Wales.

By 490 AD, sufficient numbers of Scotti had migrated from Ireland for them to move the seat of Dal Riata to Scotland. These migrant Scotti tribes eventually settled most of Western Scotland, thereby driving the Picts to the east. Despite many open conflicts between the two peoples, the Scotti and the Picts were eventually united under the rule of Cinaed mac Ailp'n (better known as Kenneth mcAlpine) in 844 AD. The land of the combined Scotti and Pictish people eventually became Scotland. Thereby, Scottish Gaelic is a Celtic language that evolved from the Old Irish language.

Tuatha De Danann

The Tuatha De Danann (whose name means 'people or tribe of the goddess Danu') were known earlier as 'Tuath De', meaning 'tribe of the gods'. According to legend, they were a pre-Celtic supernatural race, masters of the 'Otherworld', practitioners of magical arts and formidable adversaries of the Fir Bolg. Irish legend has it that they were descended from Nemed, leader of the Nemedians, who had arrived as an earlier wave of migrants to Ireland. On their arrival they reputedly demanded half of the land of the Fir Bolg, which led to the Battle of Magh Tuireadh, in which the Tuatha De Dannan were victorious.

According to the *Lebor Gabala Erenn* (the Book of Invasions of Ireland), written by Christian monks around 1150, they were an Israelite people, the lost tribe of Dan, who came in flying ships hidden among dark clouds and landed on Sliabh an Iarainn (the Iron Mountain) in County Leitrim. Other less spectacular accounts have them arriving more conventionally in sailing ships.

The Tuatha De Danann fought the Formorians in the second Battle of Magh Tuireadh in which their leader, King Nuada, was killed by Balor's poisonous eye. Then, Lugh slew Balor by smashing his eye using a slingshot, and took Nuada's place as king of the Tuatha De Danann. They went on to fight a third battle against the Milesians and were defeated at Tailtiu (present-day Teltown) in County Meath. Ireland was then divided into two regions, with the Milesians taking the lands above ground, while the Tuathha De Danann were cast below ground, into the Otherworld. As masters of that place they are often associated with death and with ancient passage tombs. Here they are said to have withered away to become little people, often likened to elves or to the Hidden Faerie Folk.

Uí Bairrche

The Uí Bairrche, whose original home was in Wexford, had territory that extended into Leinster, which they ruled until the fifth century AD. They were a Laigan tribe that were said to be related to the Brigantes tribe of northern Britain. Their tribal name means 'the strong or brave battlers'. They claimed to be the descendants of Daire Barrach (or 'Barraigh'), son of Cathair Mor, who was High King of Ireland in the second century. Some consider them one of the Fir Bolg tribes of Leinster. The tribe were especially devotees of Christianity and many of the Ui Bairrche became celebrated clerics, missionaries and saints in their time.

There are many recorded instances of the Uí Bairrche's piety. For example, Fiacc of Slebte (present-day Sletty in County Laois), the first bishop of Leinster and member of the Uí Bairrche, was appointed by St Patrick himself. Sometime during the late sixth century, King Cormac mac Diarmata of the Uí Bairrche abdicated his kingship to become a monk at the monastery of Bangor. Much later, King Olafr Cuarán of Dublin retired to the monastery of Iona. The Uí Bairrche were defeated in a struggle for control of Leinster territory with their cousins, the Uí Cheinnselaig, and were eventually expelled from their lands, which were given to the Deisi Muman tribe of Munster. Most of the Uí Bairrche moved south to resettle on the coast of Wexford.

Ulaid

Ulaid, (sometimes 'Ulaidh', or in Latin, 'Ulidia'), was a Gaelic over-kingdom of confederated tribal groups that ruled north-eastern Ireland from the fifth century, and would eventually give the name to the province of Ulster. Their capital was at Emain Macha, or Navan Fort, near the present-day city of Armagh. Traditionally, the city was founded by and named after the goddess Macha sometime between the seventh and fifth centuries BC. She was associated with war and horses.

Historically, Ulaid would also become the name given to all Irish people. The Dal Fiatach was the ruling dynasty, and the title 'Ri Ulad' was given to the over-king of the Ulaid, and occasionally, the title 'Ri in Choicid' was applied, meaning 'King of the Fifth', indicating that their kingdom covered one-fifth of the Irish land mass. Their territorial control was recorded in the *Ulster Cycle* as being east of the River Bann, west of the River Boyne and the River Dowes in the south.

In 1003, most of the ruling class of the Ulaid were slain in battle with the Ailech and in 1005, the Ulaid surrendered to Brian Boru, who was king of Munster from 978 to 1014. The Ulaid kingdom lasted in one form or another right up to the twelfth century when in 1177 the Norman knight, John de Courcy, became the Earl of Ulster and established his headquarters at Downpatrick.

Usdiae

The Usdiae tribe, (also known as 'Udiae'or 'Uodiae' and sometimes as 'Vodii'), were one of the early Gaelic peoples of the territory known as Osraige, which was later anglicised to become Ossory. This medieval kingdom comprised most of modern-day County Kilkenny and the western part of County Laois. The Usidae were one of the seventeen Pretani tribes that Ptolemy included in his second-century map of Ireland. Their name is thought to mean 'those most beyond' or 'the furthest', indicating their location on the most westerly point of Europe's peninsulas.

Uterni

Also known as 'Outernoi', 'Uterini' or 'Uternoi', the Uterni were a Gaelic Irish tribe who had extensive territories in Munster and around western Cork, a region then known as 'Desmond'. Later commentators asserted that the Uterni were the same people as the Iverni, and saw them as migrants from Iberia (modern-day Spain and Portugal). According to Ptolemy, their chief city was Uverni, situated on the sea-coast, and called 'Insovenach' by the native people.

Velabri

According to Ptolemy's designation, the Velabri were also known as 'Ouellaboroi' or 'Vellibori' and lived on the Iveragh Peninsula in what was to become County Kerry. The early seventeenth-century *Camden's Britannia* asserted that the tribe had originated in Galicia in northern Spain. The fifth-century Christian theologian Paulus Orosius commentated that '…the Scena and the two tribes of the Velabri and Luceni are placed in the south-western part of the island, which faces Spain'. The 'Scena' he referred to was the modern-day River Shannon, whose Old Irish name is 'Sinann' or 'Sinna' and Ptolemy called the 'Senu'.

Orosius clearly saw an obvious migratory sea crossing link between north-west Spain and south-east Ireland, despite his inaccuracy regarding their geographical location and his underestimation of the distance between. Their tribal name derives from the word element 'vel', meaning 'the mouth', and 'abet', signifying a river. Hence, 'at the mouth of a river', alluding to their settlement's location near the mouth of Castlemaine River on Dingle Bay. It has been suggested that the Velibori may have been a sept or sub-group of the Belgic Eibhearni tribe.

Vennicnii

The name of the Vennicnii people translates simply as 'the people' or 'the family'. Ptolemy mentioned their location on a headland on the north coast of Ireland, which he called *Promontorium Vennicnium*, subsequently identified as either Horn Head, near Dunfanaghy, some thirty miles north-west of Derry city, or Fanad Head, lying between Lough Swilly and Mulroy Bay on the north coast of County Donegal. It is possible that they were the same people or a branch of the Venicones who migrated to Ireland from Fife in Scotland.

Volunti

Ptolemy's Voluntii were probably the same group that were known in Irish as the Ulaid, and were one of the earliest known Celtic tribes of Northern Ireland. Their capital city was probably in Navan Fort (Eamhain Mhacha), County Armagh. (See: 'Ulaid'.)

Wenniknioi

The obscure Wenniknioi tribe, (also known as the 'Vennicnii', 'Ouenniknioi' or 'Wennikni'), occupied land on what was known as the Wenniknion Peninsula (thought to be Main Head) at the mouth of the River Widwa (the River Foyle), on the most northerly point of mainland Ireland.

Chapter Thirteen

The Germanic Tribes

Precisely who were Celts and who were Germans is a debate that has spanned the centuries, and the distinction has not always been clear-cut. Many of the earliest classical writers did not differentiate between Celtic and Germanic peoples. The traditional view is that sometime around 1000 BC Germanic tribes migrated southwards from southern Scandinavia and the North Sea coastal area, particularly from the Jutland Peninsula of Denmark, to settle around the lower Danube, the Rhine and in Transylvania, as well as other parts of Western Europe.

The earliest known definition of a German culture was by Poseidonus, a Greek geographer and historian, who maintained that Celts and Germans both belonged to the Indo-European language group, and that they were descended from the same source. But it was not until the first century BC that the Romans began to distinguish precisely what differences there were between the people they called 'Germani' and 'Celtae'.

It was Julius Caesar who called them Germani, after his first meeting with some of their tribes in 51 BC. Following that meeting, he commented: 'The customs of the Germani differ widely from those of the Gauls, for neither have they Druids to preside over religious services, nor do they give much attention to sacrifices.' He saw them as inherently warlike and a possible future threat to the stability of the Roman Republic. According to him, their territorial tribelands lay in the region between the Rhine, the Danube and the Black Sea, a region he named 'Germania', with the Rhine marking the limit of the Roman Empire. According to his definition, those on the western side of the river he called Gauls, who were an integral part of the Empire, while those whose territories lay on the eastern side were Germani, and at least for the time being, not part of it.

The Greek geographer Ptolemy called the Germanic tribes Teutones (or 'Teutonoaroi'), after the dominant tribe of that name, and placed them living in 'Germania'. The name 'Teuton', which was originally applied solely to a Celtic tribe in northern Europe, soon became synonymous with the name of a Germanic people as a whole, as many tribes amalgamated, probably by intermarriage with the original Celts.

Tacitus had a dim view of the German tribes. In his essay *Origin, Location, Manners, and Inhabitants of Germany*, published in 98 AD, he wrote: 'When not engaged in war they pass much of their time in the chase, and still more in idleness, giving themselves up to sleep and feasting. The bravest and most warlike do no work; they give over the management of the household, of the home and of the land to the women, the old men, and the weakest members of the family in times of peace, while they themselves remain in the most sluggish inactivity.' He had an equally poor view of German territory, calling it '...a hideous blood-curdling place, full of dark woods and swamplands'. The name 'Germani' translates as 'men of the forest', a term that eminently described the nature of their heavily wooded territories at that time.

Having originally migrated south from Scandinavia, Germanic tribes eventually began to carve out tribelands between the Rhine and the Pripet Marshes of modern-day Belarus. It was here that they gradually began to establish permanent settlements and powerful kingdoms whose formation would eventually threaten Rome itself, as Caesar had feared they might. He was quick to realise that this *status quo* was a fragile accommodation that might break at any time. His fears would turn out to be well-founded.

The first confrontation between the Romans and the Germani occurred in 114 BC when Cimbri and Teutones tribes from Jutland crossed the Rhine and invaded Roman Empire lands in southern Gaul and northern Italy. These two tribes were perceived by Rome as posing a significant threat to their security and it was clear that preparations were needed to wage war against such interloping tribes. But the threat was far more wide-ranging than Rome had anticipated. In 105 BC, at the Battle of Arausio (near present-day Orange in southern France), the Cimbri led by Boiorix and the Teutones commanded by Teutobod killed more than 100,000 Romans soldiers, and several legions were completely annihilated. The subjugation of the Germanic tribes would be a long and protracted war of attrition. The very future of Rome was at stake.

In the year 9 BC the Romans sought to expand their empire further and moved their frontier eastward from the River Rhine to the Elbe, well into Germani territory. The Germans immediately retaliated and led by the tribal leader, a warlord called Arminius, they inflicted a resounding defeat on the Roman army, virtually destroying three legions under the command of Publius Quinctilius Varo (or 'Varus') in the Teutoburg Forest, forcing the Romans back across the Rhine.

The Roman General Germanicus made a brief foray back into German territory under orders from the Emperor Tiberius, ostensibly to reclaim the lost eagles of the fallen legions, and exacted revenge on a few tribes, but withdrew with little to show for the effort. Thereafter, Tiberius, who had sanctioned the invasion, gave up all hope of conquering Germania and instead stationed eight legions along the frontier, fearing a German invasion.

In 117 AD, the Emperor Hadrian, intent on securing the Empire against future Germanic incursions, began work on building defensive earthworks, known as 'limes', along the border. The work was completed by his successor, the Emperor Antoninus, in 138 AD.

The tribal system of the Germani operated without formal government. Instead, gatherings of warriors regularly met to decide issues, whether for peace or for war. During times of war, temporary war chiefs, what the Romans called the 'Dux Bellorum' (meaning 'leader of battles' or 'war duke'), were elected on the basis of their leadership qualities and fighting prowess, and at the end of the conflict they would relinquish the post. The main tribes of Western Germania included the Marcomanni, Alemanni, Franks, Angles and Saxons. The tribes of Eastern Germania north of the Danube included the Vandals, Gepids, Ostrogoths and the Visigoths.

THE TRIBES

Adrabaecampi

The only known record of this tribe was by Ptolemy in the second century AD, when he identified them as the 'Adrabaikampoi'. According to him they were a Germanic tribe living on the north bank of the Danube and south of the Gabreta Forest (covering parts of the present-day Czech Republic and Bavaria in Germany), but given the integration of many people of the region during these times, there is some debate as to whether they were in fact a misidentified Celtic tribe. He placed their territory south of the Quadi tribeland, west of the Baemi and with the Sudini and Marcomanni to their north.

Aduatuci

The Aduatuci tribe, (sometimes 'Atuatuci'), were defined as Germans by Caesar, but they should more properly be called Celto (or Gallic) Germans, living as they did among the Belgic tribes of Gallia Belgica (modern-day Belgium). They are thought to have descended from the Cimbri and Teutones tribes. Their territory was on both sides of the River Meuse, midway between Limburg and Namur, and their chief town and capital (oppidum) was at Aduatuca (present-day Thuin). They sent troops to assist the 60,000 fighting men of the Nervii tribe in their fight against the six Romans legions commanded by Julius Caesar at the Battle of the River Sabis in northern France. However, when they discovered that the Nervii had already been defeated before they could reach Sabis, the Aduatuci returned to their homeland.

When Caesar learned that the Aduatuci had planned to join the Nervii, he gave chase, and in 57 BC, he entered their territory and laid siege to their stronghold at Aduatuca. The city fell, some 4000 Aduatuci warriors were slain and the remaining population, which according to Caesar's much exaggerated figure numbered around 53,000 men, women and children, were sold into slavery.

Despite their defeat, Caesar's account of the Aduatuci warriors was full of praise. In Book Two of his *Commentarii de Bello Gallico* (Commentaries on the Gallic Wars), he wrote: 'The enemy showed enormous courage even though their hopes of survival were almost gone; when their front lines had fallen, those behind stepped forward onto the bodies and fought from there. They too were brought down and the corpses piled up, but the survivors moved up and, as if from the top of a mound, kept on hurling their spears, intercepting our javelins and flinging them back at us.'

Notwithstanding the complete rout of the Aduatuci, a number, reckoned to be just 600, mainly women and older men, managed to escape and joined the Germanic Tungri tribe. The Aduatuci completely disappear from all historical record thereafter.

Aelvaeones

This tribe was also known as 'Helveconae' by Tacitus, as 'Aelvaones' and 'Hilleviones' by Ptolemy in the second century, and as 'Helvaeonae', 'Helvecones' and 'Ailouaiones' elsewhere. They were identified as a Germanic tribe by Tacitus in his *Germania*, and a sub-tribe of the powerful Lugii confederation, thereby living in the Silesia region of modern-day Poland, although, in the first century AD, Pliny the Elder had identified them as Hilleviones and located their settlements in southern Sweden. According to the account in his *Naturalis Historia* they occupied an island called Scatinavia, which is reckoned to be a reference to the Scandinavian Peninsula. There is some debate that they may have been either Celtic or Germanised Celts, but nothing conclusive can be determined.

Alemanni

The first recorded mention of the Alemanni was by Cassius Dio in 213 AD, when he located this confederation of Germanic tribes, which included the Hermunduri, Sedusii Bucinobantes and the Semnones, living in the region of the Upper Rhine River. The Alemanni (sometimes spelled 'Alamanni', and also known as the 'Almans') had settlements in the Upper Rhine area of modern-day south-western Germany, northern Switzerland and the French region of Alsace. The Benedictine monk Walafrid Strabo, writing in the ninth century, wrote that '…only foreigners call them Alemanni, they call themselves Suebi'.

They were a Germanic tribe, possibly a splinter group of the Suebi confederation, with whom their tribal name is virtually interchangeable. Their name derives from the Germanic 'alle mannen', which translates as 'all men' or 'united men'. It survives today in several European languages: as 'Allemagne' in French, 'Almanya' in Turkish, 'Alemania' in Spanish, and 'Alemanha' in Portuguese.

One of the earliest written records of the tribe was by Cassius Dio in 213 AD when he wrote of the defeat of the Alemanni by the *Legio Secundus Traiana* (the Second Trajan Legion) during the campaigns of Caracalla. The Roman victory earned the legion the name 'Germanica' and Caracalla the honorary name 'Alemannicus'.

The tribal confederation made a series of incursions: first, across the Rhine into Italy, where they were driven back by the Emperor Claudius II who defeated them at the Battle of Benacus, and then into Gaul, from where they were repelled by Aurelian. Thereafter they continued to make aggressive migrations into Gaul, where they were a permanent threat to Roman security right up to the third century.

Alemanni tribes, led by King Chnodomar, were defeated at the Battle of Strasbourg by the Emperor Julian in 357 AD, when Chnodomarius surrendered to the Romans and was taken back to Rome. In the year 496 AD the Alemanni were conquered by the Franks under King Clovis at the Battle of Tolbiac, and were subsumed into the Frankish Empire. By the seventh century they had become Christianised.

Ambrones

The Ambrones tribe, (also known as 'Obrones'), were a Celto-Germanic people who are thought to have originated north of the Frisian Islands in Jutland, and migrated south-eastwards sometime before 100 BC. They were mentioned by Plutarch as a tribe of Denmark. In 102 BC they formed an alliance with the Cimbri, Teutones, Tigurini and Toygeni tribes, and invaded northern Italy. These unprovoked territorial invasions, uncontrolled pillaging and attacks on lands within the Roman Empire brought matters to a head when they came face to face with the Roman army, estimated to number up to 80,000 men, led by Consul General Gaius Marius during the Battle at Aquae Sextiae (Aix-en-Provence).

Plutarch recorded the nature of the Ambrones warriors on the battlefield, remarking upon their rhythmic jumping, the clashing of weapons and shields and the loud screaming and chanting of their tribal name – all designed to strike fear into their opponents. In the event, these strategies proved ineffective and both the Teutones and the Ambrones were soundly defeated. A large number of their surviving warriors were taken prisoner to serve as gladiators in Rome. Many took part in the revolt of slaves under Spartacus during what became known as the Third Servile War, sometimes known as the 'War of Spartacus'. Roman records show that some 300 Ambrones women committed mass suicide rather than be captured or thrown into slavery.

Anartes

The Anartes, ('Anarti' or 'Anartoi'), may have been a Celtic tribe that had a settlement along the Danube, in the region of Dacia, (part of Romania and Slovakia), before they were subjugated and assimilated by the Germanic Dacians. They had refused to assist the Romans earlier in their war with the Marcomanni in 172 AD and as a punishment the Emperor Marcus Aurelius ordered the whole tribe to be deported to the Roman province of Pannonia Inferior, a region that included parts of western Hungary, eastern Austria, Serbia, Croatia and Slovenia at that time. As a result of this forced migration, the Celtic Anartes found themselves in Germani territory, having settled at a place called *Vicus Anartorum* on the north bank of the Tibiscus (the River Tisza) in northern Transylvania, where they became subjects of the Dacian tribes.

Angrivarii

The Angrivarii tribe, were also known as Angarii, Aggeri, Aggerimenses, Angerienses, Angri and Angeri. Apart from passing mentions by Tacitus and Ptolemy, little is known about them, except that their settlement was at Engern, located where the Visurgis (the River Weser) joins the River Aller in the Lower Saxony region of north-west Germany. They participated in the Battle of Teutoburg in 9 AD where a confederation of Germanic tribes massacred three elite Roman legions. Later, in a move to finally subdue the German tribes, a new assault was made to quell the Angrivarii by the Roman army under Germanicus, the son of Tiberius Caesar. However, the tribe surrendered unconditionally, and made a peaceful accommodation with Rome. Eventually, now seen as an ally, the tribe sent warriors as elite auxiliary troops to support the Roman army at the time of Augustus. Tacitus recorded that in the late first century AD, together with the Chamavi, they drove out the Bructeri, virtually exterminating the tribe, before establishing settlements in the former Bructeri territory. Their tribal name can be broken into two elements, 'angri' and 'varii', which taken together mean 'the men of Engern'.

Arabiates

The Arabiates were a tribe living around the River Danube in western Hungary and eastern Austria, an area that became the Roman province of Pannonia. They took their tribal name from the Arabo (the River Raba). Their main settlement was probably at modern-day Velem near Guns (Koszeg) in Hungary, and for a time, their territory was part of the confederation that dominated much of Austria and Slovenia.

Bastarnae

The Bastarnae people originated around the River Vistula region of Poland, and according to Strabo they comprised three sub-groups or smaller tribes: the Atmoni, Peucini and Sidoni. Like many tribes on the eastern side of the River Rhine and

Lower Danube, they may have had Celtic or Belgic roots and by the Roman era that had clearly emerged as of Celto-Germanic ethnicity. That said, most scholars believe that the Bastarnae were essentially Germanic in their language and culture. Classical authors including Tacitus, Pliny, Ptolemy and others located their territory in the Northern Carpathian region, corresponding to the Republic of Moldova and western part of southern Ukraine. Their tribal name was based on the proto-Celtic word 'basedo', meaning 'boar'. Hence, their name means 'boar people'.

Late in the second century BC, warriors of the tribe served as mercenaries of King Perseus of Macedonia in his war with Rome. Consequently, as allies of Perseus, hostile relations emerged between them and the Romans. Inevitably, they came into direct conflict in the first century BC, when together with the Dacians and Sarmatians, they resisted Roman expansion into Moesia, their territory on the southern bank of the Danube.

The tribe was ultimately subdued by the Roman General Marcus Licinius Crassus in 29 BC. However, their continued raids and incursions into Balkan provinces of the Roman Empire rekindled hostilities and in the year 280 AD 100,000 Bastarnae people were finally forcibly moved across the Danube into Thrace, and the Emperor Diocletian had the remainder resettled later in Pannonia.

Batavi

The Batavi, (or 'Batavii'), were said by Tacitus to be part of the Chatti tribe who had settled in the modern-day region of southern Netherlands and northern Belgium. Their territory was known to the Romans as 'Batavia', and became the ancient name for the Netherlands. They were initially subjugated by Rome in 12 AD and became a *gens foederata* (an 'allied people'), and supplied many troops to the Roman army as well as forming most of the Emperor's personal bodyguard. Some of the tribe's warriors also saw action in the Roman seaborne assault on Anglesey (Ynys Môn) in a bid to destroy the Druids.

Under the Batavian chieftain, Gaius Julius Civilis, (who was intent on avenging his brother Paulus's execution for treason against Nero), together with other disgruntled German tribes who had joined the insurgent Batavians, they mounted a revolt against Roman rule in 69 AD. Julius Civilis, also known as Gaius or Claudius, was the son of a high-born Batavian family and served for a time in the Roman army. However, seriously disaffected, he turned on Rome and swore an oath that he would dye his hair red and let it grow until such time as he had annihilated the Roman legions. Civilis also made attempts to co-opt the eight Bavarian cohorts of the Roman army to join in the rebellion.

Tacitus quotes Civilis's rousing speech to his troops before battle: '...the alliance (with Rome) is no longer observed on the old terms', he reputedly said, '...and we are treated as chattels'. Despite the rhetoric, the rebellious tribes were soon defeated and Civilis was taken to Rome in chains. Finally pardoned and freed, Civilis returned home and headed another rebellion, defeating at least two Roman legions. The whole of central Gaul rose in support of his rebellion before being defeated at *Augusta Treverorum* (modern-day Trèves) by the *Legio X Gemina* (the Tenth Gemini Legion), and surrendered to their commander, Quintus Petillius Cerialis.

Apparently, Civilis resumed friendly relations with Rome, but his fate remains unknown and nothing is heard of him thereafter. A limestone monument to Civilis was erected in the Tervuren Park in Belgium in 1822.

Bavarii

Also known as 'Bavarians' or 'Baiuvarii', the Bavarii were a confederation of tribes that had established settlements in south-east Germany and Austria sometime between 488 and 520 BC. It is thought they were a polyethnic mixture of both Celtic and German tribes and may have descended from the Celtic Boii people before settling in Bavaria and intermingling with the local Germanic population.

Their territory included the Roman provinces of Raetia and Noricum, which eventually became Bavaria. Their tribal name in the ancient German language was 'baio-warioz', of which the first element relates to the Boii tribe, while the entire name translates as 'men of Bohemia'. Bohemia, in present-day Czechia (formerly the Czech Republic), is thought to have been their original homeland, before they migrated to Bavaria in southern Germany in the first century AD. It is also thought that the Rugians (or 'Rugii'), who seem to have disappeared from history, may possibly have become renamed as Bavarii, or at least subsumed into the Bavarii Confederation. Bavarii territory was eventually overrun by the Quadi and Marcomanni tribes. Finally, in the sixth century, their former territory was overtaken by the Franks and in 788 AD it was incorporated into Charlemagne's Frankish Empire.

Belgites

The Belgites were a Celtic tribe that according to Pliny migrated to Illyria, in what became the Roman province of Pannonia. He made a passing reference to a town called Belgida, which may have been a Belgites settlement, but its exact location is unknown.

Breuci

The Breuci were an Illyrian tribe of the Balkans, in the Roman province of Pannonia, having migrated to live along the Lower Sava River sometime in the third or fourth century BC. As one of the strongest tribes in southern Pannonia, they offered strong resistance to the Roman invasion, taking part in the revolt against Tiberius from 6 to 9 AD, led by their chieftain, Bato (or 'Baton'). They were eventually subdued around 10 AD, and many of their people were sold into slavery, while the remainder became Roman citizens.

Following their subjugation, numbers of Breuci warriors joined the Roman army as auxiliaries and a 500-strong infantry regiment formed the *Cohors Quartae Breucorum Antoninianae* (the Fourth Breuci Cohort, known as 'Antonine's Own'), and in the early third century AD they were posted to Ebchester, near Newcastle-upon-Tyne in northern Britain, in support of Hadrian's Wall. The city of Brcko in Bosnia is named after the tribe.

Bructeri

The Bructeri, ('Bructerians'or 'Bructri'), were a small Germanic tribe whose territory lay around the Amasia (the River Ems) in the North Rhine-Westphalia region of modern-day Germany in the first century AD. According to Tacitus, they were a warlike tribe, who were known to have killed some 60,000 warriors of the Chamavi tribe in an inter-tribal battle. He is quoted as saying: 'I pray that the foreign tribes may retain, if not a hatred of us (the Romans), at least a hatred for each other, and fortune can bestow on us no better gift than discord among our foes.' The Bructeri also took part in the revolt against the Roman General Varus in the year 9 AD, and were active participants, together with the Cherusci, Chauci, Chatti, Marsi and Sicambri tribes under the command of Arminius in the Battle of Teutoburg Forest, where they reputedly captured the eagle of the Nineteenth Roman legion (the *Legio XIX*), one of three lost in that battle.

According to Strabo's account in his *Geographia*, the Bructeri were defeated by Drusus at a battle on the Ems in 12 BC. The survivors moved to resettle south of the Lupia (the River Lippe). The lost eagle was finally recovered in 15 AD by Senator Germanicus Lucius Stertinius, former proconsul in Hispania Ulterior. Stertinius exacted vicious and vengeful retribution on the Bructeri, destroying and pillaging all the villages in their territorial tribelands, destroying their farmland and slaughtering their livestock. A number of their people were transported back to Rome to face death in the Colosseum, while others were driven from their lands.

One of the Bructeri women, a so-called wise woman, priestess and seer called Velleda, became a venerated figure, and was elevated to the rank of a deity among many Germanic tribes. It is generally thought that she was captured by the Romans.

During the early medieval period, between 150 and 400 AD, the Bructeri virtually disappeared from recorded history. It is thought that some were absorbed into the Frankish Empire, while others fled to Britain and established settlements in East Anglia.

Buri

The Buri were a small Germanic tribe, probably a sub-tribe of the Suebi confederation, whose territory was around the source of the River Oder in the Carpathian region of Poland. Ethnically they were likely to have been an intermixture of Germanic and Celtic people, who were probably originally Celtic in origin, but were taken over by Germanic warriors sometime around 100 AD. Ptolemy thought that the Buri were part of the Lugii confederation, with whom they were known to have close ties. Later, around 166 AD, the Buri joined the Marcomanni confederation in attacks on the Roman Empire, which immediately set in motion decades of war with the Roman armies of Emperor Marcus Aurelius. Finally, the Buri made a peaceful settlement with Rome, which earned them disfavour with the other Germanic tribes, and after such prolonged warfare, the tribe were virtually destitute, having lost most of their fighting men.

Around 409 AD, a group of the Buri, together with some of the Suebi tribes, migrated south to settle in modern-day Spain, in an area known as *Terras de Bouro* (Lands of the Buri), while the remainder are thought to have joined the Bavarii tribe.

Cadusii

Strabo described the Cadusii, (also known as 'Cadusians'), as a nomadic warlike tribe who were constantly at war with their neighbours and who lived in the mountains, fought chiefly on foot and were highly skilled javelin throwers. Their territory was in the mountainous district of Media Atropatene (modern-day Iran and Azerbaijan), on the south-west shores of the Caspian Sea.

Caerosi

Also sometimes called the 'Caeresi' or 'Caeroesi', the Caerosi were a Gallic-Germanic tribe of the Roman province of Gallia Belgica. They lived in present-day central Belgium, south of the River Meuse and the west of the Rhine during the first century AD. Their territory was close to Luxembourg, possibly in the Eiffel region or the Ardennes, and their main centre and capital was in Orchimont (Vresse-sur-Semois) near the Franco-Belgian border. Julius Caesar identified the Caerosi as a tribe of the Belgae confederacy, a Celto-Germanic people who had originated in Germany. In his *Germania*, Tacitus names the Caerosi as one of four tribes, whose population had 'a strong Celtic element'; the others being the Condrusi, the Eubrones and the Paemani. He called the tribe 'Caeracates'.

Chasuarii

The Chasuarii tribe, (also known as 'Chattuarii', 'Chatwari' and sometimes as 'Attoarii'), were a small and relatively obscure tribe who held territory to the east of the Lower Rhine, and during the first century AD were probably one of the Suebi confederation. Later, by the fourth century, they moved to live between the Rhine and the Mosa (the River Meuse, or in Dutch, 'Maas'), and had become part of the Frankish Empire. The name Chasuarii is thought to mean 'people who live on the River Hase', a tributary to the River Ems.

Chatti

The Chatti (also known as 'Catti', 'Chatthi' and 'Cattai') were a powerful Germanic tribe whose territory encompassed the Weser and the Main rivers in the Hesse and southern Saxony regions of modern-day Germany. In their fight against the Roman occupation of their lands, the Chatti joined an alliance of tribes that under the leadership of the Cherusci chieftain Arminius fought and defeated the Romans at the Battle of Teutoburg Forest in the year 9 AD. Their tribal capital was at a place known as Mattium; its precise location is uncertain, but it is thought to have been somewhere around Fritzlar in northern Hesse.

Tacitus commented that the Chatti differed from the other Germanic tribes in the strictness of their infantry's discipline, where he said their main strength lay, and described typical Chatti warriors as having '...hardy frames, close-knit limbs, fierce countenances and particularly vigorous courage'.

The Chatti fought the Romans for most of the first century AD, and in 15 AD Germanicus entered their territory ahead of four legions amounting to 10,000 auxiliaries in pursuit of Arminius. Failing to catch the warlord, he burned Mattium to the ground. Arminius was eventually assassinated by some of his own men in 21 AD. Undeterred by constant setbacks, in 50 AD the Chatti were again at war with Rome, but defeated by Publius Pompoius Secundus.

In the year 70 AD they participated in the rebellion of Civilis, in which they were defeated by forces led by the Emperor Domitian in 83 AD and forced to sue for peace. However, still aggressive and warlike, they constantly raided Roman lands and were in perpetual inter-tribal conflict with their neighbouring enemy, the Cherusci tribe. These constant disturbances of the *Pax Romana* (the Roman peace) saw Rome move to permanently end Chatti dominance of the region and their ultimate subjugation was accomplished by Emperor Marcus Aurelius in 169 AD, after which nothing more is heard of the tribe. It has been suggested by some that a section of the Chatti were incorporated into the Frankish Kingdom of Clovis in the early sixth century.

Chauci

By the second century AD the Chauci tribe, (also known as 'Cauci', 'Chauken' and 'Caulci'), were settled in north-west Germany between the River Rhine and the Elbe, having expelled the formerly resident Ampsivarii tribe. The Romans referred to the Chauci living between the Weser and Elbe as the 'Greater Chauci', and those living between the Ems and Weser as the 'Lesser Chauci'.

The tribe was known for their coastal settlements, which consisted of artificial mounds called 'terpen', built well above the high-tide level. Pliny described the Chauci of these coastal settlements as '...living on a barren coast in small or huts on hilltops, or on mounds of turf'. The coastal location of this section of the Chauci tribe earned them a reputation as pirates, with recorded incidents of their raiding coastal settlements throughout Roman Belgica in 41 AD, as well as others in the English Channel as late as 175 AD.

Ironically, Tacitus regarded them as a peaceful people, describing the way '...without ambition, without lawless violence, they live peaceful and secluded, never provoking a war or injuring others by rapine and robbery'. He was evidently describing the group of Chauci who were settled inland. Despite his assertion, it is thought that the Chauci joined the German tribal revolt in 9 AD that culminated in the Battle of Teutoburg Forest.

By around 58 AD they had evidently been pacified. Some of the tribe had become Romanised and provided auxiliaries to the Roman army for at least the next 200 years. This meant that for some time there were Chauci men fighting on both sides of the conflict with Rome, with the remaining tribe continuing an aggressive anti-Roman posture. In the third century, most of the Chauci people had merged with the Saxons.

Cherusci

The Cherusci were a loose confederation of Germanic tribes that lived between the Weser and Elbe rivers in land south of their enemy, the Chatti tribe. Their first encounter with Rome occurred in 53 BC, when the army of Julius Caesar entered their territory as part of his invasion of Germania. Later, in 9 AD, led by their chieftain and warlord, Arminius, the Cherusci, together with many other disaffected German tribes, were responsible for the destruction of three Roman legions commanded by Varus at the Battle of Teutoburg Forest. Following that battle, the tribe were subjugated by the Roman Governor of the Rhine region, Nero Drusus. However, they continued to offer resistance to Roman domination and joined the neighbouring Langobards and Semnones in the Suebi confederation, whose territory was on the other side of the Hartz Mountains.

The Roman General Germanicus made several unsuccessful moves to subjugate them, but as all attempts had failed, Rome decided to leave the Cherusci to their own devices for the time being, and a sort of uneasy stand-off was established. The peace only held until 16 AD, when the tribe joined Arminius' rebellion in battle at the Angrivarian Wall. They were roundly defeated and finally subjugated, after which Germanicus was awarded a triumphal entry into Rome. His victory was recorded by Tacitus in his *Annals* in 17 AD: 'Germanicus Caesar celebrated his triumph over the Cherusci, Chatti, and Angrivarii, and the other tribes which extend as far as the Elbe.'

In 47 AD, a delegation of the Cherusci leaders travelled to Rome with a request to grant them their own ruler, and they were given Italicus, a nephew of Arminius, who was appointed as a puppet king, living much of his remaining life as a hostage in Rome.

Despite coming to terms with Rome, in 100 AD Tacitus recorded that the Cherusci were in conflict with the Chatti again, but with their manpower and resources so depleted after prolonged war with the Roman legions, they were subjugated by the Chatti. By the third century AD, the Cherusci were absorbed into a confederation of Saxon and Frankish alliances. Little more is known of them afterwards.

Cimbri

The Cimbri originated on the Jutland Peninsula of Denmark, but due to a rapidly expanding population, in the late second century BC large numbers sought new lands southwards and trespassed into the territory of the Roman Empire. Together with the Teutones, which Plutarch numbered around 300,000 people, their migration led them into the Balkans. From here they entered Gaul and crossed the Alps into Italy and the Pyrenees into Spain, where they came face to face with the Roman legions. In 113 BC the sheer weight and number of Cimbri warriors overwhelmed and defeated the army of Consul Gnaeus Papirius Carbo at the Battle of Noreia in the eastern Alps. Carbo later committed suicide in disgrace.

In 109 BC, after being refused permission to settle in the territory, Rome responded by sending another army to engage them, this time commanded by Consul Marcus Junius Silanus. Despite the force and strength of his Roman legions, the Cimbri overpowered and defeated them at an unknown location somewhere in southern Gaul.

Rome could not accept such a humiliating defeat and on his return to Rome Silanus was put on trial for his military failure. However, he was finally acquitted. There followed a succession of Cimbri victories against Rome, including the defeat of Gnaeus Mallius Maximus and Quintus Servilius Caepio, whose armies were virtually annihilated in 105 BC at the Battle of Arausio, (modern-day Orange in southern France). Roman losses reportedly numbered almost 80,000 legionaries and a further 40,000 auxiliary troops in that battle – 120,000 in all.

In Spain, the newly arrived Cimbri faction fought the resident Celtiberian tribes but were gradually repelled and were pushed back into Gaul, where they moved north as far as the River Seine. Here, the Belgic tribes also mounted stiff resistance to these new migrants. Later, the Cimbri army were joined by warriors of the Teutones and elements of the Helvetii tribes and together they crossed the Alps into northern Italy, where in 101 BC they confronted a Roman army commanded by Quintus Lutatius Catulus on the Raudine Plain near Vercellae. A ferocious battle ensued, in which the Cimbri King Boiorix was killed and his army was massacred. The so-called Cimbri Wars (113–101 BC) brought an end to their incursions in Gaul, but in the process they had tested the might of Rome, and threatened to destabilise the very foundations of the Republic.

There is an ongoing debate regarding Cimbri ethnicity – some maintain that they were Germanic, while others insist that they were Celts. Tacitus, Plutarch and Strabo all declared that they were Germans, while others, including the Roman author Julius Florus, insisted that the Cimbri were of Celtic descent. Certainly, during their long migrations they gathered different peoples and languages to their number, and would have evolved into a Germanic-Celtic tribal coalition.

Condrusi

The Condrusi were a Germanic tribe based lived north-west of the Ardennes, midway between the rivers Liège and the Namur in Belgium, in a region now called Condroz, which was named after them. The Romans called them 'Germani on this side of the Rhine'. In the mid-first century BC, the Condrusi, Eburones, Caeroesi and the Paemani were an alliance of Belgic tribes mentioned by Caesar as client tribes of the larger Treveri people and described by him as part of the 'Germani Cisrhenani', (that is 'Left Bank Celts'). Though they are now identified by most scholars as a German tribe, their tribal name is probably of Celtic origin, and the fact that they had settled in an otherwise Celtic region illustrates the sort of social and cross-cultural integrations that were taking place at that time.

Cotini

The Cotini (or according to Tacitus, the 'Gotini', and occasionally called 'Gutones') was a Celtic tribe that migrated north from their homeland in the region of present-day Germany sometime around the sixth century BC and settled in Silesia, an area of Poland, Slovakia and the Czech Republic. The tribe established a large settlement around the *Liptovska Mara* (the Liptov Sea region of Slovakia), and have been identified as part of the so-called Puchov culture after the Puchov-Skalka archaeological site in Slovakia. Their territory had extensive iron ore mines, which enabled them to produce high-quality weapons.

According to Cassio Dio, during the Marcomannic Wars (166 to 180 AD) the Cotini, like the Boii, were subjugated by the Marcomanni tribe, and later enslaved to work in their iron mines by the Quadi. Finally, following the final subjugation of the Celto-Germanic tribes, the Cotini were allied with Rome and later resettled between the Danube and the Drava rivers in the Roman province of Pannonia Inferior on the order of Emperor Marcus Aurelius.

Cugerni

The main city and capital of the Cugerni, (also known as 'Cuberni' and 'Guberni'), was *Cibernodorum*, which means 'marketplace of the Cugerni'; it was located near modern-day Xanten in the North Rhine-Westphalia region of Germany. Eventually they occupied a settlement near *Castra Vetera*, which became the base camp of the *Legio VI Victrix*, (the Victorious Sixth Legion) from 110 to 119 AD. The legion is best known for its participation in the war against the Cantabrians that finally brought all the Iberian Peninsula under Roman rule during the reign of Augustus.

At least some of the tribe were thought to be descended from the Sicambri (or 'Sugambri'), who many regard as their parent tribe. Sometime around 11 BC, the Cugerni crossed the Rhine from Germania into the Roman Empire lands and proved to be one of Rome's most aggressive enemies. During the Batavian revolt in 69 AD, the Cugerni joined other rebellious tribes under their leader, Julius Civilis. Later, together with the Chamavi and the Sallii tribes, the Cugerni were absorbed into the Frankish kingdom.

Dacians

The Dacians originated north of the River Danube in the Carpathian-Danube region of modern-day Romania. They were known to the Greeks as the 'Getae', or the 'Geto-Dacians', but the Romans referred to them simply as 'Daci'. Their initial language closely resembled Thracian, but over time, following several migrations, the Dacians interacted and mixed with many other different peoples, including Celts, Scythians, Slavs and Germans.

Dacia had existed as a kingdom since the early second century BC, and had been ruled by successive kings, including Oroles and Boerebista. Despite forming tribal confederations with the Scordisci and Dardani to fight Roman advances, in 101 AD, the Emperor Trajan conquered Dacia with two Roman legions – the *Legio V Macedona* (the Fifth Macedonian Legion) and the *Legio XIII Gemina* (the Thirteenth Gemini Legion). Trajan's army soon took the Dacian capital, *Sarmizegethusa,* razing all of their surrounding strongholds to the ground in the process, following which the tribe came under Roman rule.

In 129 AD the Emperor Hadrian split the region into Dacia Superior and Dacia Inferior, of which the former, the Roman province of Dacia Traiana, survived until around 271 AD, during the reign of Aurelian, when the Romans withdrew. However, south of the Danube, the province of Dacia Aureliana survived and eventually became modern-day Serbia.

The defeat of the Dacians is recorded in stone on Trajan's Column in Rome. Numbers of the tribe enlisted as auxiliaries in the Roman army and in 200 AD the First Cohort of around 1000 Dacian soldiers was stationed in Britain at Birdoswald on Hadrian's Wall in Cumbria. At the end of their service in 127 AD, they were honourably discharged and granted the title 'civis romanus' – full Roman citizenship.

Dulgubnii

The Dulgubinii, (sometimes 'Dulgibini' or 'Doulgoumnioi'), were a small Germanic tribe that lived around the River Weser in Lower Saxony, north of the Angrivarii and Chamavi tribes, during the first century AD. The tribe were first identified almost in passing by Ptolemy and by Tacitus in his work *Germania*; consequently, very little else is known about the tribe.

Elbe Germanic

In 1942, the German linguist Friedrich Maurer called these Elbe Germanic peoples 'Elbgermanen', 'Irminonic' or 'Erminonic'. As their tribal name suggests, they lived in a broad territory on either side of the River Elbe stretching as far as Bohemia and Moravia in the present-day Republic of Czechia. The word 'Irminonic' is a cultural and linguistic term derived from 'Irminones', which was how Tacitus referred to a large group of Germanic tribes in his *Germania*. They included the Semnones, Hermunduri, Quadi, Marcomanni and the Lombard tribes. Their descendants are generally regarded as having strongly influenced the development of German dialects and Standard German, elements of which are found later in Anglo-Frisian and Old Saxon languages. The Elbe-Germanic language is sometimes referred to as Old High German.

Eravisci

The Eravisci tribe, (also known as 'Aravisci'), were a small Celtic tribe who dwelt on the western side of the River Danube near the modern-day city of Buda (Budapest) in Hungary. Little is known about the tribe except that they were producers of fine jewellery and pottery, much of it in a distinctive La Tène cultural style. A large hoard of silver coinage has also been found in archaeological excavations that were carried out by Heidelberg University in 2017. The Eravisci established their capital at the city of Aquincum after they were conquered by the Romans and the city became a military base for a legion of about 6000 men from 41 to 54 BC. In 106 AD, it became a provincial capital.

Franks

The Franks were a group of tribes who invaded the Roman Empire in the fifth century AD, when they dominated the north of France, Belgium and western Germany. It is thought that they migrated from Denmark or Schleswig-Holstein through Lower Saxony in the Early Iron Age (c. 500 BC). In the third century they had settled on the eastern bank of the River Rhine, and although they operated independently of each other, they shared a common culture and German language. By the sixth century two ruling dynasties had emerged: the Merovingians and the Carolingians.

The Merovingians were united under King Clovis, whose family ruled the Franks and most of old Roman Gaul for the next 200 years. Clovis was responsible for driving the Visigoths from Gaul into the Iberian Peninsula, and following his conversion to Christianity he became the first Frankish king to be recognised by the Pope, who crowned him at Soissons. Clovis was commonly held to be the first king of France, and his kingdom, known as Francia, gave its name to the modern-day country of France.

The Merovingian dynasty came to an end when King Pepin the Younger (also known as 'Pepin the Short'), at just 15 years of age, supported by a group of nobles, took power and established the new Carolingian dynasty, which would rule from 751 to 843 AD. Of this dynasty, its most famous ruler was Charlemagne, who was crowned Holy Roman Emperor by the Pope on Christmas Day 800 AD. Charlemagne was called the 'Father of Europe' and his Frankish kingdom laid the foundations of western society and established a culture that became known as the 'Carolingian Renaissance'.

Frisians

The Frisians, (also known as the 'Frisii' and sometimes as 'Frissones'), were a Germanic tribe that lived in Friesland, a coastal area between the River Ems and the Rhine, in the northern Netherlands. Traces of Frisian settlements have been found dating back to the Bronze Age (around 700 BC), which makes them some of the oldest surviving tribes of Europe. In 12 BC, Frisia was conquered by the Roman General Nero Claudius Drusus. However, despite their subjugation, they seem to have maintained peaceful relations under Roman rule for the next forty years. Then, in 29 AD, they rebelled against punitive taxes that were imposed by a new administrator by the name of Collybiscus Olennius.

They held out against retaliatory Roman attacks by Lucius Apronius, who had been sent to suppress the uprising. Apronius failed and the Frisians were thereafter left to their own independent business, until 47 AD, when General Gnaeus Domitius Corbulo was appointed governor of Lower Germany. He sailed up the Rhine with a large army and defeated the Frisian resistance, but was prevented from imposing a sustained occupation when ordered back to Rome by the Emperor Claudius, freeing Frisian lowland territory from all Roman interest. The Frisians later received a brief mention by Tacitus, who recorded their participation in the Batavian Revolt of 69 AD.

The Frisians were a major power and sea traders in the coastal region, and it was predictable that sooner or later Frisian migrants would eventually cross the North Sea intent on establishing new settlements. Together with the Saxons (and possibly the Angles) in the fifth and sixth centuries, they landed on the southern coast of Britain, and brought with them a language that even today remains very closely linked to modern English.

In the eighth century, Friesland became part of the Franconian Empire, and was converted to Christianity by Wigbert, an Anglo-Saxon cleric sent by Wilfried, the Bishop of York.

Geats

The Geats, (also known as the 'Geatas' and 'Yeats'), were a Germanic tribe that lived in Götaland in southern Sweden. The city of Göteburg (in English, 'Gothenburg') was named after the tribe, and translates into English as 'fort of the Geats'. The legendary hero Beowulf was supposedly of the Geats tribe. The tribal name had several variations: as 'Gautar' in Norse, 'Gotar' in Swedish, and as 'Goths' in Latin, (although this connection is disputed by some).

In the second century AD, Ptolemy referred to them as 'Goutai' and by the sixth century they were sometimes called 'Gautigoths' and 'Ostrogoths'. Their name appears in the Swedish provinces of Vastergötland and Östergötland, (that is, the Western and Eastern lands of the Geats). The Swedes and the Geats were separate peoples, and according to some sources the Geats were conquered by the Swedes. Others maintain that the unification of the two peoples was a gradual process and took place between the sixth and ninth centuries. It was not until sometime around 1160 that papal documents record the Latin title 'Sweorum et Gothorum', that is 'King of the Swedes and the Geats', a title still borne by the Swedish monarchy.

Gepids

The Gepids were an East Germanic tribe that lived around the River Vistula and the coast of the Baltic Sea in modern-day Poland. Roman commentators sometimes referred to them as 'Gepidae', and regarded them as closely related to the Goths, with whom they migrated southwards, led by their king, Fastida, sometime around 260 AD. At that time they invaded the Roman province of Dacia and formed new settlements around the Pannonian Basin, in territory that covered Hungary, as well as parts of Czechia, Romania, Croatia and Serbia. This new territory was known for a time as 'Gepidia' and their capital city was at *Sirmium* (modern-day Sremska-Mitrovica in Serbia). In 567 AD they were attacked and subdued by Langobard and Avars invaders from the north. Most of the tribe joined the Langobard in their migration to Italy (where they became known as Lombards), and the remainder continued to live under Avar rule.

Historically, the Gepids are probably best known for the defeat of the Huns together with the Ostrogoths in the Battle of Nedao in 455 AD, which saw the death of the Hunnish leader Attila, and an end to their century-old subjugation.

By the sixth century the Gepid have disappeared from all historical record, having presumably become fully integrated with the Lombard and Avar people.

Hercuniates

During the first century BC, the Hercuniates, (also known as 'Hercuniatae'), were an obscure tribe that lived on the western side of the River Danube, near modern-day Budapest. Their tribal name suggests that they were a Celtic people, and comes from an ancient word for an oak. It is thought that the Hercuniates tribe once inhabited the Hercynian Forest, before migrating to Illyria, in what became the Roman province of Pannonia. They were described by both Pliny and Ptolemy as a wandering or nomadic tribe. Little more is known of them other than they had been subdued by Rome by the year 40 AD.

Herminones

The Herminones, (sometimes 'Irminones' or 'Hermiones'), were a Germanic group of tribes that included the Ingaevones and the Istaevones, whom Tacitus described living in central and eastern Germany. According to Pliny's *Natural History* they also included the Suebi, Hermunduri, Chatti and Cherusci tribes. Their territorial settlements were around the River Elbe and by the first century AD they had expanded into Bavaria, Swabia and Bohemia. They were allies of the Romans, a policy that afforded them some security against Rome's bitter enemy, the neighbouring Chatti tribe. The traditional ancestry of the Herminones has them descended from the god Mannus.

Istvaeones

The Istvaeones, (also known as 'Istaevones', 'Istriaones' and 'Istriones'), lived on the banks of the River Rhine in western Germany and on the Atlantic coast of the Netherlands, Belgium and northern France, at the time of the Romans. According to Tacitus, they were one of the tribes of Istaev, son of the god Mannus. Together with the Herminones and Ingvaeones they are collectively referred to as the West Germanic proto-tribe or cultural group that, according to some, would eventually develop into the Salian Franks, whose language was the precursor of Low Franconian dialects, of which modern Dutch and Flemish are prime examples.

Latovici

The Latovici tribe, (sometimes 'Latobici' or 'Latobrigi'), were a small tribe of the Balkans region that settled around the Upper Sava Valley in south-east Slovenia during the Roman period. They established cities at *Praetorium Latobicorum* (modern-day Trebnje) and *Neviodunum* (present-day Drnovo) in the former Yugoslavia. According to Julius Caesar, 14,000 Latovici joined the Helvetii in an attempt to migrate into south-west Gaul in 58 BC, but after their defeat at the Battle of Bibracte, they were ordered back across the Rhine to their homeland.

The tribe was known for its so-called 'house urns', ceramic burial receptacles shaped like houses with conical roofs, windows and door apertures. Little else is known of the tribe, but at some time after their subjugation, its warriors must have joined the Roman army as an auxiliary group, as attested by a honorific memorial to Quintus Porcius Vetustinus found in Tarragona in Spain. It reads: 'To Quintus Porcius Vetustinus, son of Quintus, of the Quirina tribe, of the Cantabri, of Iuliobriga, prefect of the first cohort of the Latobici.'

Lugii

The Lugii (sometimes 'Ligii', 'Lygii' or 'Lugians') are considered to have been a large confederation of Celtic, Germanic or Slavic tribes – nobody seems quite able to decide which. Their name was known in several variations, including Lugi, Lugiones and Lougoi, and it is thought by some that they were part of the Suebi confederation of Germanic tribes. The first record of their tribal name was by Strabo in his *Geographia*, where he suggested that they were part of a confederation of the Butones (or 'Gutones'), which included the Semnones, Sibini and Zumi tribes.

Lugii territory encompassed much of eastern Slovakia, southern Poland and western Ukraine, an area that became known as Galicia. Strabo also commented that the Lugii were ruled over by King Maroboduus of the Marcomanni tribe. It is unclear what finally became of the Lugii, but many believe they were absorbed into Slavic groups migrating into central Europe. Many scholars link them to the third-century Vandals of southern Poland.

The name 'Lugi' is also found around the Moray Firth in Scotland where it may have derived from the Pictish god Lugus (or Lugh), and not related to the Germanic Lugii tribe at all.

Marcomanni

The Marcomanni were a Germanic tribe that lived around the River Main, a tributary of the Rhine, in the first century BC. In English, their tribal name literally translates as 'markmen', but more loosely signifying 'bordermen'. Its significance is not absolutely certain, but it may have been a reference to the common border between the Celtic and Germanic tribes of the region. Both Strabo and Tacitus thought them to be a Suebian tribe, an opinion reinforced by their part in the Suebian confederation rebellion against Julius Caesar.

The Marcomanni had a fierce reputation, having destroyed *Boiohemum*, the capital of the Celtic Boii tribe in Bohemia (modern-day Czechia), after which they took over their territory. By 6 BC, their king, Maroboduus, had established a powerful kingdom and a Marcomannic confederacy, which was seen as a threat to regional stability and brought them into further conflict with Rome.

They were subdued in 19 AD, when Catualda, a young chief of the Gothones, invaded and conquered their country. King Maroboduus fled to Rome seeking protection from Tiberius, who offered him sanctuary in Italy. Maroboduus was deposed and spent the rest of his life in exile, while Catualda took his throne. There followed a period of instability when kings were overthrown or assassinated and the tribe had successive tribal rulers until 50 AD, when it was placed under Romantic-appointed puppet kings. It took a while for the Marcomanni to rise up once more to take on the Roman legions of Marcus Aurelius, in what became known as the Marcomannic Wars (167–180 AD).

The conflict began when the Marcomanni and Quadi, together with other Germanic tribes, demanded the right to expand their settlements into Roman territory. Some tribes were granted permission, but to prevent wholesale invasion, Aurelius strengthened defensive lines, including nine legions in the Danube region, four on the Rhine and another two in Dacia. These were meant to prevent barbarian tribes crossing the Alps, but the defences were ineffective and hordes of warriors overcame the defensive lines and marched into northern Italy, where they besieged several Roman townships. Major battles took place in modern-day Czechia, Austria and Hungary, and following a long drawn-out campaign, the German tribes finally surrendered to Roman superiority.

However, the peace was temporary, and the Marcomanni and Quadi rose up again in what became known as the Second Marcomannic War. The conflict was finally ended when Marcus Aurelius died in 180 AD and his son and successor, Commodus, agreed a peace treaty and withdrew the Roman legions. Under the terms of the treaty the Marcomanni and the Quadi agreed to stay clear of the Danube, to pay grain tributes and provide auxiliaries to the Roman army.

Following the gradual decline of the Roman Empire in the mid-fourth century AD, during the reign of their Queen Fritgil, the Marcomanni were converted to Christianity. Nothing more is heard of the tribe thereafter.

Marsigni

The Marsigni, (also known as 'Marsi'), were an East Germanic tribe who lived around the upper reaches of the River Elbe in Bohemia (modern-day Romania). They were part of the large Suebi confederation that in the first century AD included the Alemanni, Hermunduri, Langobards, Marcomanni, Quadi and Semnones, among others. Tacitus said that '...the Marsigni and Burii in language and dress resemble the Suebi'. Though the tribe initially had good relations with Rome, in 9 AD, their chief, Aldarich, sent 2,000 Marsigni warriors to join a large alliance of Germanic tribes, led by the Cherusci King Arminius, to fight the Romans in the decisive Battle of Teutoburg Forest.

Mattiaci

This small Germanic tribe initially occupied territory on the east bank of the River Rhine between the present-day cities of Mainz and Frankfurt in the first century BC. It is thought that they may have been a sub-group or sept of the Chatti, based on the name of the Chatti capital city of *Mattiacum* (or 'Mattium'). The earliest mention of the tribe was during the Emperor Nero Claudius Drusus's campaign to conquer Germania (12–9 BC), in which the Mattiaci, along with several other tribes, were defeated in battle. Together with the Chatti and Usipetes tribes, in 69 AD they participated in the Batavian revolt against Roman occupation and besieged the Roman legionary fort at *Mogontiacum* (modern-day Mainz).

In common with many of the Germanic tribes, the Mattiaci were eventually subdued and Romanised. Thereafter, two regiments of its warriors served in the Roman army as auxiliaries in the *Cohors II Mattiacorum Milliaria Equitata* (the Second Cohort of Mattiaci Horse Cavalry), of which two units, the Mattiaci Juniores and the Mattiaci Senioures, were recorded as 'Palatine Auxiliaries', and were listed in the fifth-century *Notitia Dignitatum*, the official administrative record of all ancient Roman civil and military posts.

Tacitus recorded that the Mattiaci were exempt from paying tribute money because of the invaluable service they gave as allies with Rome in wartime and the security their presence gave to the Gallic-German border on both the eastern and western banks of the Rhine. Mattiaci territory also found favour with the Romans on account of its hot springs, the so-called *Aquis Mattiacis*, as well as the fabrication of fine soaps to accompany bathing.

It is most probable that the tribe were eventually assimilated into the Alemanni, who later occupied their territory.

Osi

Very little is known of the mysterious Osi (or 'Osii') tribe, other than they lived in a forested mountain territory around modern-day Moravia. Some scholars believe they were a sub-group or sept of the Germanic Suebi confederation, which included the Marcomanni, the Alemanni, Angles and Quadi among others, and the debate continues as to whether they were ethnically Celtic or Dacian; some suggest that the Osi were of Germanic origin. In the face of increased incursions by aggressive Germanic tribes, the Osi migrated and resettled in the Silesian region of Poland. It is probable that, like the Cotini, following Marcus Aurelius's campaign in the Marcomanni Wars, they were forcibly moved to live in Lower Pannonia.

Quadi

By the beginning of the first century BC, the Quadi lived north of the River Main, near present-day Frankfurt, and on the eastern border of Germania, but later in that century, together with the neighbouring Marcomanni tribe, as part of the Suebi confederation, they invaded the Balkan Peninsula. These two warlike tribes were closely allied and migrated into present-day Moravia, western Slovakia and Lower Austria, displacing the Celtic peoples of the region.

They were to become a constant threat to the security of Rome and made frequent crossings into and attacks upon Roman territory. It took the full force of the Roman army to push them back into their own territory before relative equilibrium was restored to the region. However, even after peaceful settlements were agreed, the Quadi repeatedly reneged on treaties and continued to make incursive guerrilla raids on Roman settlements. Eventually, all attempts at peace failed and together with the Marcomanni, the Quadi crossed the Danube, defeated a defensive Roman army and invaded northern Italy. It was not until 178 AD that Marcus Aurelius managed to finally push the combined Quadi and Marcomanni armies back across the Danube and crush the insurrection.

Tacitus recorded that, following their initial subjugation by Rome, the Quadi, who had previously been ruled over by their own King Maroboduus and his sucessors, had puppet rulers imposed upon them. He wrote: '…then foreigners ruled over them, though the power of these rulers was dependent on that of the Roman emperors'. Disgruntled, the Quadi, together with the Marcomanni and other German tribes, rose up in rebellion yet again in what became known as the Second Marcomannic War. The Quadi defeat came in 179 AD at the Battle of Laugaricio Trencin in Slovakia, by a Roman army commanded by Marcus Valerius Maximianus.

A large part of the Quadi people was destroyed by the Huns in around 375 AD. In the fifth century AD, some of the surviving Quadi joined the Suebi and went on to conquer the Iberian Peninsula.

Rugi

The territory of the Rugi tribe, (also known as 'Rugii', 'Rogi' or 'Rugians'), was an area in modern-day Austria and north-western Poland, known in the first century AD as 'Rugiland' or 'Rogaland'. They were an East Germanic tribe who had originally migrated from Scandinavia sometime around 100 AD, and said by Tacitus to have settled around the Baltic, an area that became Pomerania. Their tribal name is thought to be derived from their place of origin, Rogaland, in south-west Norway. The name is related to the Old Norse term 'rugr', meaning 'rye', and should be taken to signify something like 'rye eaters' or 'rye growers'.

The Rugians were conquered by the Huns led by Attila in the late fourth century, and went on to invade Western Europe in 451 AD. After the death of Attila in 453 AD, following the defeat of the Huns by the Ostrogoths and the collapse of its empire, many of the Rugi tribe migrated to Bohemia, while the rest joined the Bavarii confederation and remained in Austria.

By the fifth century, the Rugi had become fully Romanised and had established a kingdom in the Roman province of Noricum, south of the Danube. By 482 AD they had adopted a heretical form of Christianity called Arianism, but by the mid-sixth century they had disappeared from all historical record.

Saxones

The Saxones, more commonly known as 'Saxons', were an alliance of Germanic tribes that became a leading tribe of the Anglo-Saxon confederation, which according to Ptolemy had settled in Holstein, north-east of the lower River Elbe, a region that became known as Saxonia. Their name is derived from the Old High German word 'sachs' ('seax' in Old English, and 'sax' in Old Norse), which refers to a kind of knife or axe, a symbol still found on the English county flags and emblems of Essex, Middlesex and Sussex.

The first known use of the name 'Saxon' was in 356 AD when the future Emperor Julian used it in a speech to the Roman General Magnus Magnentius (himself a later Roman emperor).

Around the time of the collapse of the Roman Empire in the early years of the fifth century AD, along with the Angles, Frisians and Jutes, the Saxons arrived in eastern Britannia at the invitation of Vortigern, ostensibly serving as mercenaries to protect native Britons from continual attacks by Gaels and Pictish tribes from the north.

According to contemporary accounts by chroniclers like Gildas, these German settlements on the Isle of Thanet (Kent) were initially peaceful, but after a relatively short time their takeover of southern Britain was in full flow. By the eighth century AD, Britannia had undergone an ethnic transformation and was now made up of seven Anglo-Saxon petty kingdoms.

Sciri

The Sciri, (sometimes spelled 'Scirri' or called 'Scirians'), were an East Germanic tribe who Pliny placed on the extreme frontier of Germania in what would have been present-day East Prussia, Estonia and part of Finland, a region that he called 'Eningia'. The Romans often grouped them among other tribes like the Goths, Vandals, Heruli, Rugii, Gepids and Burgundians, and referred to them as 'Gothic' peoples. Their tribal name is thought to derive from the Germanic word 'skeir', meaning 'pure', in the sense of genetically pure or 'unmixed' blood. By the third century AD, some of the Sciri had migrated to the Black Sea region in modern-day Ukraine. Later, the tribe joined a confederation of Goths, Ostrogoths and Visigoths and moved to live in the Carpathian Mountains.

They were eventually overrun by the Huns and came under their rule until the death of Attila, when they joined Ardaric of the Gepids in a revolt to overthrow the Huns at the Battle of Nedeo in 454 AD. In this conflict they freed themselves to establish their own kingdom under Edeko, (sometimes 'Ideco' or 'Edeco') in the Central Danube region. Edeko's son, Odoacer (or 'Odovakar') led the Sciri into Italy and in 476 AD took Rome to become the first barbarian self-styled king of Italy, and ruled for the next thirteen years. In 469 AD, having been forced to surrender the Italian crown, he was assassinated by Theodoric, the son of King Thiudimer of the Ostrogoths. The Sciri became allied with the Roman Empire, with many Scirian warriors serving as mercenary auxiliaries in the Roman army.

Scordisci

The Scordisci were a tribal confederation whose territory covered lands around modern-day Serbia, Croatia, Austria and Romania, and was located west of the Danubius (the River Danube). Their name suggests that they were Belgae people who had picked up elements of local culture, having subdued the original tribal occupants, the Autariatae. Opinions vary as to their true lineage, with some claiming Thracian ancestry, while others have them as Celtic or Illyrian. According to Livy, they were related to the Bastarnae.

The tribe first came into conflict with Rome in 141 BC when they successfully repulsed an attack by the Roman army, after which, together with the Maedi and Dardani tribes, the Scordisci made several attempts to invade Macedonia. In fact they managed to reach Delphi, where they raided the temple, before being driven back across the Danube by a Roman force commanded by Lucius Cornelius Scipio Asiaticus in 88 BC.

Further clashes with the legions occurred over the following decades, before they were finally subdued by Rome sometime around 15 BC, during the reign of the Emperor Tiberius. Following their subjugation, many Scordisci warriors joined the Roman army as mercenaries and were granted Roman citizenship during the reign of Trajan.

Semnones

The Semnones (or 'Sennones') were a Germanic tribe of the Suebian confederation who lived in territory between the Albis and the Viadua (the present-day rivers Elbe and Oder) in the first century AD. Tacitus described the Semnones as 'the most ancient and renowned branch of the Suebi'. Their capital city was *Calancorum*, thought to be modern-day Zgorzelec on the German-Polish border. For some unknown reason, the Semnones were also known as the 'Juthungi', a name that translates as 'the young ones'.

Sacred ritual oak groves of the Semnones have been found at Lossow near Frankfurt, which contain evidence of wholesale ritualistic human sacrifice, and some forty or so sacrificial pits have been excavated at the site, where quantities of human and animal bones, as well as large numbers of human skulls have been unearthed.

In his *Germania*, Tacitus wrote: 'At a set time all the peoples of this blood gather, in their embassies, in a wood hallowed by the auguries of their ancestors and the awe of ages. The sacrifice in public of a human victim marks the grisly opening of their savage ritual. In another way, too, reverence is paid to the grove.' He went on to describe one such grove, which he refered to as the 'Grove of the Semnones', where he said the tribe had originated. His conclusion was that the Semnones believed they actually stemmed from trees. This sort of affinity with trees, especially the oak, is commonly found in the belief systems of northern Germanic tribes.

In the third century, the Semnones migrated south and were integrated with the Alamanni. Sometime around 356 AD, together with the Alamanni, they attacked the Roman settlement of Raetia, at that time one of Rome's largest military establishments in Germania. After 178 AD, all trace of the tribe is lost, probably as a result of integration with the Alamanni, together with losing their territorial tribelands to the Huns. Later, the Alamanni were in turn conquered by the Franks.

Serdi

The Serdi were a Celtic people who, at the end of a fourth-century BC migration, established a settlement at Serdica (or 'Serdika'), present-day Sofia, the capital of Bulgaria. The Romans knew the city as *Serdnopolis* (the city of the Serdi) and it became one of the most important cities on the Balkan Peninsula. Over time the tribe became integrated with local Thracian people, the Paeonians and Dacians among them, and may have emerged as a resultant Thraco-Celtic people, while retaining much of their Celtic character and culture. They were attacked and ultimately defeated in 29 BC by Roman General Lucinius Crassus the Younger. Crassus beheaded the tribal leaders and had the hands cut off many of the Serdi warriors. Following their subjugation the Serdi were incorporated into the Roman province of Thracia, and during the reign of Emperor Trajan their capital became the primary Roman city and administrative centre of region.

Sigambri

The Sigambri tribe, (sometimes known as the 'Sicambri, 'Sugambri' or 'Sicambrians'), had originated in Scandinavia, but by the first century AD they held territory on the east bank of the River Rhine, between the Lippe and the Sieg rivers near the border with the Netherlands. On the advice of and accompanied by their Tenteri and Usipetes neighbours, they avoided direct confrontation with the advancing Roman legions of Julius Caesar by evacuating their lands and fleeing across the Rhine, carrying all of their possessions into the forests of Eburones territory. In their absence, Caesar burned all of their villages, confiscated their cattle and set fire to their cornfields. Meantime, the Sigambri plundered and pillaged much of Eburone lands and attacked the Roman settlement at Atuatuca, inflicting heavy losses on its defenders, before the arrival of Caesar, which forced them to make a tactical withdrawal and return to their own territory.

A determined Caesar was resolved to lead his army over the Rhine to strike fear into the Germanic tribes to discourage any future incursions into Gaul and to exact vengeance on the Sigambri people in particular. Together with the Chatti, the Sigambri were defeated in the Roman campaign to subdue the Germanic tribes across the Rhine by the consul Nero Claudius Drusus (known as Drusus the Elder) in 10 BC. Within two years, on the orders of Tiberius, some of the Sigambri were forcibly moved to settlements on the left side of the Rhine. By the fourth century they had become part of the Frankish confederation.

Sitones

The Sitones, (or 'Sithones'), were a small Germanic tribe, who according to Tacitus, writing in *Germania* in 97 AD, had originated somewhere in Scandinavia, probably southern Sweden or the Danish Peninsula, and had migrated to settle on the Baltic coast. He called them 'Suiones' and related them to the Swedes. His last, and nowadays politically incorrect, comments about them are that they were '...below the level of slaves because they are ruled by a woman'. He continued: 'This is the extent of their decline - not merely below freedom, but below decent slavery.' The Romans frequently described Scandinavia somewhat derogatorily as 'the Land of Women'. It was not uncommon to find other Germanic or Celtic tribes where women held the political and spiritual power and authority in tribal matters.

The Sitones tribal name is thought to mean 'settlers', and may have been ascribed to them by the resident Celtic people in the lands where they settled; it has also been suggested that they were actually Celtic, but they may have adopted the language and culture of their new territory. What little is known of the tribe is that they were part of the large and powerful Suebi confederation.

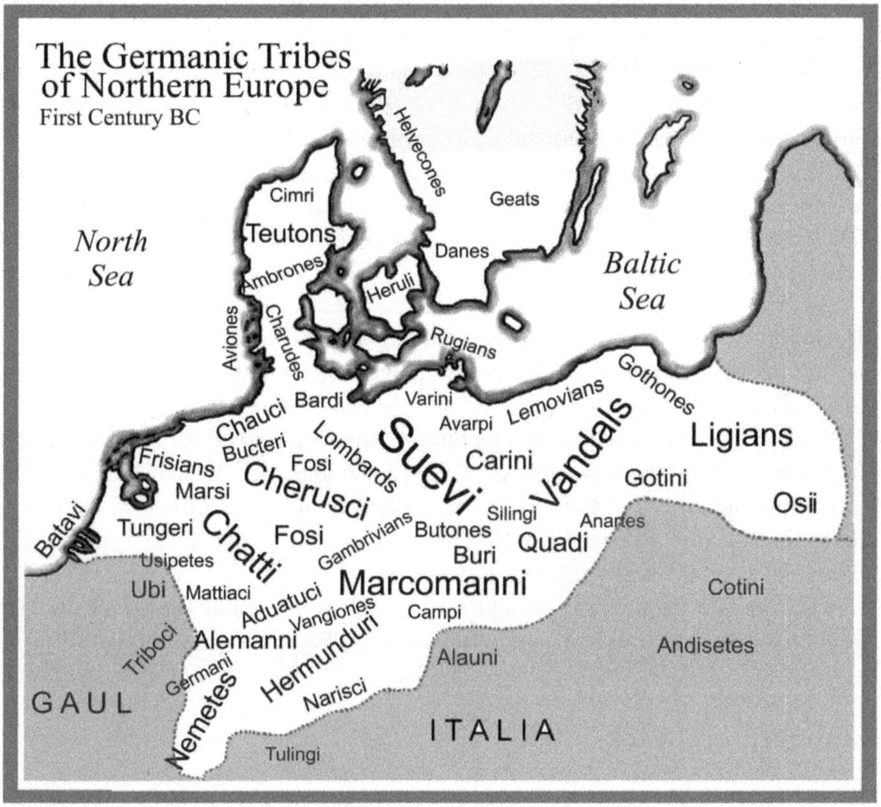

Suebi

Sometimes spelled 'Suevi', and also known as 'Suebians', the Suebi were an allied group or federation of Germanic peoples that originated in Denmark and the south-western Scandinavian Peninsula during the Bronze Age. Archaeological evidence supports the fact that the migration of the Vandals and the Suebi into the Western Roman Empire took place in 406 AD, towards the end of what became known as the Great Migration Period. The tribe gave their name to the old German Duchy of Swabia.

In his *Germania*, Tacitus included the Marcomanni, the Quadi, the Hermunduri, the Semnones and Langobardi among their number. By the first century AD they had settled around the River Elbe region in modern-day Germany and Czechia, but they were displaced by the Huns who forced them out of their territory in 409 AD, at which time some Suebi crossed the River Rhine, and overran Gaul and Hispania before settling in what became the Spanish province of Galicia, a territory they held until 585 AD.

The debate continues as to whether the Suebi were Germanic or Gaulish-Celtic, as they seemed to possess elements of both ethnicities as well as a similar social structure. However, the first mention of the Suebi by name was by Julius Caesar during his invasion of Gaul. Unlike other commentators, he regarded them as a single tribe, who had participated in the tribal rebellion of Ariovistus during the Gallic wars. Caesar reckoned the Suebi to be '…by far the largest and most warlike among the Germans'. He commented that they had driven the Usipetes and the Tencteri from their lands; these were just two of many Germanic tribes whose territory was taken in this manner.

By the mid-fifth century, led by King Rechila (sometimes 'Rechiar' or 'Rechiarius'), they returned to Gaul, pillaging as they went, before they arrived in the Iberian Peninsula and established settlements across the Roman provinces of Lusitania and Baetica.

Caesar described a particular feature of Suebian warrior hairstyles: 'Among the Suebi, even till the hair turns grey, the coarse locks are twisted back and often knotted on the crown of the head itself.' The top knot was known in German as *Suebenknoten* (the Suebian Knot). This was an important status symbol – the higher the knot, the higher the status.

The Suebian language is thought to have been the major source of the High German that emerged later in southern Germany, Austria and Switzerland.

Suiones

The Suiones, (sometimes 'Sviar' or Svear'), were first mentioned by Tacitus in 98 AD as living in Svearland (modern-day Sweden). He thought them to be possibly the same people as the Sitones, and that they had a powerful sailing fleet, and that each of their boats were driven by oarsmen on either side, and not by the use of sail. Pliny the Elder recorded that they lived on two islands, of which the most famous was 'Scatinavia' (Scandinavia); the other presumably being the Danish Peninsula.

Tencteri

The Tencteri were a small Germanic tribe who had settlements on the east bank of the Rhine in the first century AD. It has been suggested that they were related to the Usipetes tribe, and some authorities prefer to think of them as Celtic, (or Gallic), rather than a Germanic people, as in a historical sense, both tribes belonged to the Celtic La Tène culture. Both were also driven from their territorial tribelands by the Suebi in 60 or 59 BC, having withstood incursive attacks over many years, and were forced to wander as nomads around Germania for three years, searching for a new homeland. They finally reached the River Rhine, and the resident Celtic tribes fled, creating unrest and threatening instability in the eastern borderlands of the Roman Empire.

An army was quickly despatched and in 55 BC, they were attacked by eight Roman legions commanded by Julius Caesar. The outcome was a massacre of the Tencteri. In 16 BC, together with the Sicambri and Usipetes, survivors of the Tencteri massacre crossed the Rhine again and took on the Fifth Legion commanded by Senator Marcus Lollius. They defeated Lollius's army and captured the legion's standard. Badly bruised, the Roman senate settled for a peace treaty, which was agreed at the Roman settlement of *Colonia Claudia Ara Agrippinensium* (modern-day Cologne).

Many years later, following the Battle of Teutoburg Forest in 9 AD, in which a combined tribal resistance destroyed three elite Roman legions, Rome sent troops to push the barbarian tribes back across the Rhine. They advanced into Tencteri territory, threatening to annihilate the whole tribe unless they withdrew immediately. In fact, there is no evidence that the Tencteri actually took part in the battle. In the third century AD, the Tencteri were absorbed into the kingdom of the Franks.

Teutones

Both Pliny and Strabo describe the Teutones as inhabiting Jutland and central Denmark. Sometime around the late second century BC, they made a mass migration south and west to the Danube valley, where they came face-to-face with the Roman Empire. Nowadays, the word 'Teuton' is used as a portmanteau term for 'German', and 'Teutonic' is synonymous with 'Germanic'. Their name probably comes from Celtic, and they were likely to have been described by neighbouring tribes as men who lived in the forests, as in Latin the word 'Germani' means 'men of the forest'. The name 'Teuton', however, came into the early Germanic language via Celtic and means 'people of the tribe'. They were also known in Latin as 'Teutoni' and are probably best known for being allies of the Cimbri of the so-called Cimbrian War, in their resistance to Rome.

In 110 BC, together with the Cimbri, they advanced through the Roman province of Transalpine Gaul and won many victories over the Roman army. Five years later, at the Battle of Arausina, on the left bank of the River Rhône, the Teutons and Cimbri completely destroyed two Roman armies under the commands of Proconsul Quintus Servilius Cypion and Consul Gnaeus Mallius Maximus. Tacitus reported that some 80,000 Roman soldiers died in the engagement. As a result, the Romans were unable to stop the advance of the Germanic tribes from Gaul to Italy. Fortunately for Rome, the Teutones turned their attention to the Iberian Peninsula of Hispania, allowing the Roman legions to retrain and regroup to prepare for one final confrontation.

The Teutones, accompanied by warriors of the Cimbri and Ambrones tribes, were finally defeated by fifty-thousand Roman legionaries commanded by Gaius Marius at the two-day Battle of Aquae Sextiae (present-day Aix-en-Provence) in 102 BC. Unable to face such a resounding defeat, rather than being taken prisoner or sold into slavery, 300 Teutones women reportedly committed mass suicide. In a historical sense, this was the first military contact the Romans had with the Germanic tribes.

Thracians

Also known in Latin as 'Thraci', the Thracians lived in modern-day Bulgaria, Romania and Greece, as well as a large area of Anatolia. They were not one single people, but a confederation of different tribes, largely dominated by the Odrysians, who established the Odrysian kingdom in modern-day Bulgaria in the fifth century BC, with their capital city at Seuthopolis. The little we know about the ancient Thracians is largely based on Greek and Roman sources, neither of which held them in very high regard. The Greeks used the word 'Thracians' in a derogatory sense, believing them to be a wild, uncivilised and barbarian people.

In *The Iliad*, Homer described them as powerfully fierce soldiers who fought alongside Trojans against the Greeks. But their prowess as a warlike warrior people belies their skilled craftsmanship, for they were masters at producing the very highest-quality gold and silverware, including exquisite jewellery, highly decorated vessels and fine weapons. In recent years some eighty sites of Thracian treasure have been excavated in Bulgaria, having been hidden, no doubt, to safeguard against invading pillagers.

In around 514 BC, the Persian army of King Darius the Great, under the command of General Megabazus, subdued the Thracian tribes. Later, in 356 BC, King Philip II of Macedonia conquered Thrace and founded the city of Philippopolis in what became modern-day Plovdiv in Bulgaria. Despite suffering repeated incursions and conquest by Persians and Macedonians, the Thracian tribes evidently made some kind of peace to face a common enemy and joined the King Perseus of Macedon in the rebellion against the Rome in what became known as the Third Macedonian War (171–168 BC). However, Thrace was finally subjugated by the Romans in 46 AD and its people were assimilated into the Roman Empire. By the seventh century AD they had merged with various invading groups, including the Slavs, Goths and Visigoths, so that they had effectively ceased to exist as a viable people. What eventually emerged from this ethnic melting pot were the people of present-day Bulgaria.

Triboci

The Triboci, (or 'Tribocci', and sometimes 'Triboces'), were a Germanic tribe that occupied territory around present-day Strasbourg in the Alsace region of north-eastern France. In his *Gallic Wars*, Julius Caesar recorded that they were living on the west bank of the River Rhine. It is thought that they were a Celtic people who were confronted by the Mediomatrici, a migrating Germanic tribe, sometime around 10 BC, and over time became assimilated into and intermarried with that culture. The Romans named the Triboci capital city *Argentorate* or *Argentoratum* when it became a Roman military fortress in 16 AD. The city was destroyed in 69 AD, when along with other Germanic tribes the Triboci joined the rebel leader Civilis in the Batavian revolt against Rome. However, as their defeat seemed inevitable, they defected to the Roman army and helped rebuild the city so that in 80 AD it resumed its role as a legionary headquarters. Their territory remained under Roman rule well into the fifth century, when it was taken over by the Alemanni.

Ubii

The Germanic Ubii tribe held territory in the present-day North Rhine-Westphalia region of Germany, and lived on the east bank of the River Rhine at the time of Julius Caesar. According to Caesar, the Ubii became allies of Rome and assisted it in tracking down fleeing Suebian warriors, (who had been their long-term enemies), after the Battle of Vosges in 58 BC. Caesar's declared intention of attacking the German tribes was to aid the friendly Ubii tribe against Suebi oppression. A strong relationship was established in which Roman support for the Ubii eventually persuaded the Suebi to leave them in peace.

In his *Histories*, Tacitus commented on the way that some Ubii women intermarried with Roman soldiers. 'For those who came here long ago and became our comrades through marriage, and those children who came soon after, this is their homeland.'

In his *Gallic Wars*, Caesar commented the Ubii were '…a bit more cultured than those of their own race or the other Germans, and since they live on the Rhine and are visited by merchants more and they live closest to the Gauls, they are accustomed to their culture'.

The Ubii also supplied warriors to serve as auxiliaries in the Roman army, forming a substantial part of the cohort of horse guards, and were an important ally in putting down the Batavian rebellion in 70 AD. They also supported Rome in the Marcomannic Wars in 166–67 AD. According to Pliny, in 38 BC Agrippa moved the Ubii to the west of the Rhine, away from other belligerent Germanic tribes, into territory that formerly belonged to the Eburones tribe, whom the Romans had already defeated and enslaved. As ever, seeking advantage, the Romans had a hidden agenda, and this move was to create a Roman-friendly buffer zone between Roman Gaul and Germany, as well as a launching point for the planned invasion of Germani tribelands, which first occurred in 12 BC.

Their capital city, known initially to the Romans as *Oppidum Ubiorom* ('the city of the Ubii'), was renamed *Colonia Claudia Ara Agrippinensium* in 50 AD by General Marcus Vipsanius Agrippa, the son-in-law of the Emperor Augustus. It was to become the modern city of Cologne. In time the Ubii were assimilated into the Frankish kingdom.

Usipetes

The Usipetes tribe, (also known as 'Usip' and 'Usipi'), had originated in Scandinavia and accompanied by the Tencteri tribe sometime before 55 BC they migrated to the

Baltic coast. In 58 BC they occupied territory in the Laugona Valley (modern-day Lahn), a tributary of the Rhine. From here they were driven out by the dominant and warlike Suebi tribe and forced further south into the territory of the Menapii tribe, which immediately brought them into conflict with the Roman Empire. As a result, Julius Caesar set about confronting them to redress their uninvited occupation of an area of Roman Gaul. They petitioned Caesar for permission to settle, pledging themselves as allies to Rome, but he refused their request and instead ordered 5000 Roman cavalry to attack their encampment.

The confrontation that ensued saw eight Roman legions facing the Germanic warriors and the reputed slaughter of between 150,000 and 200,000 men, women and children. However, given the Roman habit of overstating their victories and playing down those of their adversaries, these numbers are almost certainly wildly exaggerated. What is certain is that the battle took place around the River Meuse near the village of Kessel in the Netherlands, where archaeologists have found large numbers of skeletal remains dumped in the river.

The outcome was disastrous for the Germans, and according to Caesar their two tribes were annihilated in the engagement. However, this was clearly untrue, as both Usipetes and Tencteri warriors are known to have participated in uprisings against Roman rule in the following decade. Also, they were almost certainly part of the confederation of rebellious tribes that defeated the Roman legions at the Battle of the Teutoburg Forest in 9 AD, as well as accompanying the Chatti and Mattiaci tribes at the siege of the Roman legionary fortress at *Mogontiacum* (modern-day Mainz) in 70 AD.

Caesar openly boasted that during that battle he had taken tribal leaders hostage and then treacherously ordered the massacre of Usipetes and Tencteri women and children during an agreed truce. His actions brought severe criticisms from certain Roman politicians, including Cato, for his violation of the ceasefire treaty he had agreed with the Germans. Caesar went on to say that what few survivors there were crossed the Rhine in boats or else they were drowned in the confusion and panic, and only a few managed to make it back to the relative security of the east.

It is thought that the remaining Usipetes moved to live alongside the Sigambri tribe, who granted them land on the northern bank of the Luppia, (the River Lippe). According to Tacitus's work *Agricola*, a detachment of Usipetes warriors served in the Roman army in Britain in 83 AD. After this date they disappear from recorded history, though there is an opinion that both the Usipetes and the Tencteri were ultimately absorbed later into the kingdom of the Franks.

Vandals

The first known record of the Vandals was in the year 77 AD, when Pliny the Elder wrote of a people he called the 'Vandilii'. Since the late eighteenth century, the name of the Germanic Vandals (or 'Vandali') has come down to us as a synonym for wilful, mindless and violent destruction, no doubt as a result of their historic sack of Rome in 455 AD. But even that attribution is overstated. Despite biased accounts from later authors, far from visiting widespread destruction on Rome, apart from raiding most of the city's wealth, they spared its citizens and very few of its buildings were burned. In fact, they were probably no more destructive than other barbarian tribes of that time and exerted the same kind of treatment and slaughter that Rome had meted out to the conquered Germanic tribes.

Rome eventually made a peace pact with the Vandals, but in 455 AD, seeing the disintegration of the Roman Empire, the Vandals reneged on the treaty and marched on Rome.

Actually, the Vandals were a group of tribes that included the Hasdingi and the Silingi, and originated in southern Sweden or the Jutland Peninsula, before numbers of their people migrated southward to the Danube Valley. As a reward for their participation as allies of Rome in the Marcomannic Wars, in 147 AD the Emperor Marcus Aurelius granted them leave to settle in Dacia. However, in the fifth century, under increasing pressure from the Huns, the Hasdingi group joined some of the Suebi and Alans tribes and moved to form settlements in Galicia in north-west Spain. Later, hearing of the rich lands in North Africa, they moved south and crossed the Gibraltar Strait. It was here, under their last king, Genseric, that they founded a kingdom that spanned the modern-day countries of Morocco and Algeria in North Africa.

They went on to capture Carthage, which became their chief city and capital. It was reported that Genseric arrived ahead of 80,000 warriors and confiscated land and property from the resident Roman citizenry who, taken by surprise at the Vandals' arrival, were unprepared for an attack. In the event they surrendered their fleet, which lay at anchor in the harbour.

It was from here that the Vandals developed a powerful navy and dominated most of the Mediterranean, intercepting and pillaging many Roman merchant ships for the best part of a century. When Genseric died in 533 AD, they were reconquered by the Roman Byzantine Empire, who took back all the North African territory that had been lost to them. Large numbers of the Vandals were sold as slaves or conscripted into the army of the Eastern Roman Empire in Constantinople, and sent to fight the Persians on the eastern front. In response to the Vandals' poor treatment of the Catholics in North Africa, Pope Leo I of the Eastern Roman Empire declared the Vandals to be heretics.

Vangiones

It is not clear whether the Vangiones (sometimes 'Vengiones', 'Vagiones' or 'Vargiones'), were a Celtic or a Belgic-Germanic tribe, despite the fact that they were a sub-group of the Suebi. Their name could be derived from the Germanic word 'wanga' or the Celtic word 'vanga', both of which suggest a wagon (as in the Old English word 'wain'), and indicating that they may have been referred to as 'wagoners' or possibly 'charioteers'.

In the first century AD their territorial tribelands were around the River Rhine at *Borbetomagus*, (present-day Worms in south-western Germany), a region that the Romans called Germania Superior. They had arrived, accompanied by the Nemetes and Triboci tribes, in around 70 BC, and established their capital and main settlement at *Argentorate*, (Strasbourg), which was a Roman military outpost that Nero Claudius Drusus had founded in 12 BC. By 90 AD it had become the permanent station of the *Legio VIII Augusta* (the Eighth Legion of Augustus).

The Vangiones joined Ariovistus in his invasion of Gaul in 58 BC, but were defeated at Belfort. Later, during the reign of Augustus, finally at peace with Rome, the tribe were integrated into the Roman Empire and given permission to settle among the Mediomatrici tribe in present-day Alsace. At this time large numbers of the tribe's warriors became auxiliary soldiers in the Roman army. For example, the First Cohort of Vangiones (the *Cohors I Vagionae*), numbering 1000 men comprising the so-called *cohors equitata* (mounted cavalry) and the *cohors milliaria*, (foot soldiers or infantry), were stationed at Chesters and Benwell forts on Hadrian's Wall. As evidence of their presence in northern Britain, an inscription found on an altar at Benwell reads: 'Sacred to the God Antenociticus: the First Cohort of Vangiones under the command of Claudius Casianus, prefect, willingly and deservedly fulfilled its vow.'

Vangiones traditional tribelands were eventually overrun by the Alemanni tribe, who assimilated them, thereafter leaving no further trace of their name in historical records.

Vindelici

The Vindelici were a mixed people of Celtic and Illyrian ancestry that occupied the Upper Bavarian Swabia plateau around Augsburg and the River Danube. Later, they moved to the east where they established Vindelicia in the Roman province of Raetia, which included part of Switzerland and southern Germany. According to Pliny, the Vindelici were made up of four sub-tribal groups: the Cosuanetes, Rucinates, Licates and Catenates. They were conquered by Tiberius and Drusus in 15 BC, and together with elements of the Raeti tribe, served as auxiliary soldiers in the Roman army, in the *Cohortes Raetorum et Vindelicorum* (the Raeti and Vindelici Cohort). Their capital and main city was named by the Romans as *Augusta Vindelicorum* (present-day Augsburg).

Volcae

The Volcae were a mixed confederation of Celtic and Germanic tribes that inhabited territories in the Bavarian region of southern Germany. Caesar recounted how in view of their expanding population and dwindling resources, certain groups of the

Volcae, (known as the Volcae Tectosages), migrated from their original territory in southern Gaul and crossed the Rhine, where they established new settlements near the Hercynian Forest of Germany. The tribe was one of several that had invaded Macedonia around 270 BC and fought the Greeks at the Battle of Thermopylae in 279 BC. Caesar recorded in his *Gallic Wars*: '…the Volcae Tectosages had seized on those parts of Germany which are the most fruitful around the Hercynian forest … and settled there.' Other groups of the Volcae Tectosages moved to Hispania and grew to dominate the entire Iberian Peninsula.

Warini

The Warini were known by several names, including by Tacitus as 'Varini', by Pliny the Elder as 'Varinnae' and Ptolemy as 'Viruni'. There were others variations, including 'Warnii', 'Werne' and 'Varni'. They were a Germanic tribe that originated in the Jutland Peninsula and southern Sweden before they migrated to settle near the Baltic Sea in the Mecklenburg region of north-eastern Germany. According to Tacitus, along with the Angles, Aviones, Eudoses, Nuitones, Reudigni and Suardones, the Warini were part of the vast Suebi confederation. Apart from this, little else is known about this obscure tribe. It is thought that the Warini may have united with the Angles in the third or fourth century AD and moved south and became known as Thuringians, a name that survives in the German state of Thuringia.

Bibliography

ALBERRO, MANUEL, *The Celticisation of the Iberian Peninsula* (CNRS Editions, 2003).

ALLEN, STEPHEN & REYNOLDS, WAYNE, *Celtic Warrior, AD 100* (Osprey Publishing, 2001).

ALLEN, STEPHEN, *Lords of Battle: Infamous Medieval Mercenaries* (Osprey Publishing, 2007).

CAESAR, JULIUS, *Commentaries on the Gallic War* (Franklin Classics, 2018).

CANESTRELLI, GIOAL, *Celtic Warfare* (Pen & Sword Military, 2022).

CHADWICK, NORA, K, *Early Brittany* (University of Wales Press, 1969).

CHURCH, ALFRED JOHN & BRODRIBB, WILLIAM JACKSON, *The Complete Works of Tacitus* (Macmillan, 1905).

CLARKE, HYDE, *Notes On the Ligurians, Aquitanians & Belgians* (Nabu Press, 2013).

COLLIS, JOHN, *The Celts: Origins, Myths & Inventions* (Tempus Publishing, 2003).

CUNLIFFE, BARRY, *Bretons and Briton*s (Oxford University Press, 2021).

CUNLIFFE, BARRY, *Exploring Celtic Origins* (Oxbow Books, 2019).

CUNLIFFE, BARRY, *The Ancient Celts* (Oxford University Press, 2018).

CURCHIN, LEONARD A, *The Romanization of Central Spain* (Routledge, 2003).

DAVIES, SIONED, (Translator), *The Mabinogion* (Oxford World's Classics, 2008).

DEFAUX, OLIVIER, *The Iberian Peninsula in Ptolemy's Geography* (Edition Topoi, 2017).

DUNLAP, JAMES E, *Tribal Boundaries in Belgic Gaul* (University of Chicago Press, 1931).

EDWARDS, H.J, *The Gallic Wars* (Harvard University Press, 1917).

FREEMAN, PHILIP, *War, Women and Druids* (Hanover Press, 2002).

FREEMAN, PHILIP, *The Philosopher and the Druids: A Journey Among the Ancient Celts* (Simon & Schuster, 2006).

GARDNER, JANE, F, *The 'Gallic Menace' in Caesar's Propaganda* (Cambridge University Press, 1983).

GASKIN, JAMES, J, *Varieties of Irish History; From Ancient and Modern Sources and Original Documents* (Hard Press, 2012).

GRAINGER, JOHN D, *The Galatians* (Pen & Sword History, 2020).

HALKON, PETER, *The Parisi: Britons and Romans in East Yorkshire* (History Press, 2013).

HANNA, W.A, *Celtic Migrations* (Pretani Press, 1985).
HARBISON, PETER, *Pre-Christian Ireland: From the First Settlers to the Early Celts* (Thames & Hudson, 1988).
HERON, DENIS, *Celtic Migrations* (Library of Alexandria, 2019).
HIGHAM, NICK, & JONES, BARRI, *The Carvetii Peoples Of Roman Britain* (Alan Sutton, 1991).
HUBERT, HENRI, (Trans: M.R.Dobie), The Greatness & Decline of the Celts, (Routledge, 2013).
JAMES, SIMON, *Exploring The World of The Celts* (Thames & Hudson, 1993).
JIMENEZ, RAMNON L, *Caesar Against The Celts* (Castle Books, 2009).
JACOBSTHAL, PAUL, *Early Celtic Art* (Oxford/Clarendon, 1969).
JONES, HORACE LEONARD, *The Geography of Strabo* (William Heinemann Ltd, 1961).
KING, JOHN, *Kingdoms of the Celts* (Blandford, 1998).
KOCH, JOHN T, *The Celtic Heroic Age* (Celtic Studies Publishers, 2003).
KULIKOWSKI, MICHAEL, *The Creation of Roman Spain* (Johns Hopkins University Press, 2004).
LEVIN, ROBIN, *In the Wake of Hannibal* (Robin E Levin, 2016).
LIVY, TITUS, (Trans: Valerie M. Warrior), *The History of Rome* (Penguin Classics, 2006).
MAIER, BERNHARD, *The Celts: A History from Earliest Times to the Present* (Edinburgh University Press, 2003).
MANCO, JEAN, *Blood of the Celts: The New Ancestral Story* (Thames & Hudson, 2015).
MCCAFFREY, CARMEL & EATON, LEO, *In Search of Ancient Ireland* (Rowman & Littlefield, 2002).
MCDEVITTE, W.A, & BOHN, W.S, (trans), *Caesar's Gallic War* (Harper & Brothers, 1869).
MILES, DAVID, *The Tribes of Britain* (Orion Publishing, 2006).
MOSS, JOHN, *Celtic Places & Placenames* (Pen & Sword History, 2022).
NEWARK, TIM, *Celtic Warriors, 400 BC-1600 AD* (Blandford Press, 1988).
OLDFATHER, C. H, (trans), *Diodorus Siculus: Library of History* (Harvard University Press, 1935).
OWEN, FRANCIS, *The Germanic People: Their Origin, Expansion, and Culture* (Literary Licensing LLC, 2011).
PAPWORTH, MARTIN, *The Search for the Durotriges* (History Press, 2011).
RANKIN, DAVID, *Celts and the Classical World* (Routledge, 1996).
REES, ALWYN & REES, BRINLEY, *Celtic Heritage: Ancient Tradition in Ireland and Wales* (Thames & Hudson, 1961).
ROBERTS, ALICE, *The Celts* (Heron Books, 2015).
ROLLER DUANE W, *The Geography of Strabo* (Cambridge University Press, 2014).
ROSS, ANNE, *Pagan Celtic Britain* (Chicago Academy Publishers, 1996).

RYLANDS, THOMAS GLAZEBROOK, *The Geography of Ptolemy Elucidated* (Hanse Books, 2020).
SCULLARD, HOWARD HAYES, *Roman Britain: Outpost of the Empire* (Thames & Hudson, 1986).
SMITH, JAMES FRANCIS, *Druids, Celts and Romans: The Founders of Europe* (CreateSpace, 2013).
STEWART, ROBERT J, *Celtic Gods, Celtic Goddesses* (Blandford, 1990).
STRZOLKA, RAINER, *The Urnfield Culture* (Independently published, 2019).
TACITUS, PUBLIUS CORNELIUS, *Agricola & Germania* (Penguin Classics, 2010).
WEBSTER, GRAHAM, *Rome Against Caratacus* (Routledge, 1993).
WILLIAMS, DEREK, *Romans and Barbarians* (St Martin's Press, 1998).
WOOD, MICHAEL, *In Search of the Dark Ages* (BBC Books, 1981).

Useful Online Resources

Early British Kingdoms – Brittany
earlybritishkingdoms.com/kingdoms/brittany.html.

BBC Ancient British History
bbc.co.uk/history/ancient/british_prehistory/iron_01.shtml

The Celtic Culture Arrives In Ireland
yourirish.com/history/ancient/iron-age/the-celts

The Celtic Tribes
englishmonarchs.co.uk/celts_6.html

Celt Site
https://www.celtsite.com/TCE/Section%20I/Tribes.htm.

The Celtic Kingdoms: The Sixth Century
doi.org/10.1017/CHOL9780521362917.011

Celtic Antecedents
americeltic.net/celtic-antecedents/

Celtic Tribes of Ireland
tartanplace.com/tartanlegend/celtictribesireland.html

The Celtic Tribal System in the Isle of Man
P.M.C. Kermode. Web Page: isle-of-man.com/manxnotebook/iomnhas/v01p477.htm

Ancient Tribe Celts – Ancestry and Origin
igenea.com/en/ancient-tribes/celts.

The Celts in the Iberian Peninsula
https://dc.uwm.edu/ekeltoi/vol6/iss1/

La Tène Culture
visual-arts-cork.com/cultural-history-of-ireland/la-tene-celtic-culture.htm

Evolution of the Celts
ruby.fgcu.edu/courses/twimberley/10580/evolve.pdf.

Livy and the Celts
academia.edu/37383001/Livy_and_the_Celts.

Livius.org
Articles on Ancient History.
https://www.livius.org/sources/content.

Pliny: Natural History
Edited by T E Page, E Capps, W H D Rouse and E H Warmington
https://ryanfb.xyz/loebolus-data/L352.pdf.

Index

List of figures, tables and maps

Figures

Tables

Maps